SNAPSHOT TIBET

A PHOTOGRAPHIC EXPLORATION

SCOTT SHAW

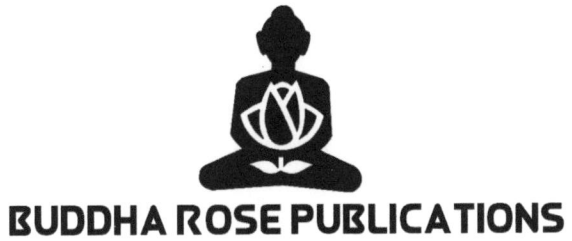

BUDDHA ROSE PUBLICATIONS

Snapshot Tibet:
A Photographic Exploration
Copyright © 1986 & 2017
By Scott Shaw
All Rights Reserved

No part of this book may be reproduced in any manner without the expressed written permission of the publisher or the photographer.

First Edition 2017

ISBN: 1-877792-97-7
ISBN 13: 978-1-877792-97-7

Printed in the United States of America

10 9 8 7 6 5 4 3 2 1

SNAPSHOT
TIBET

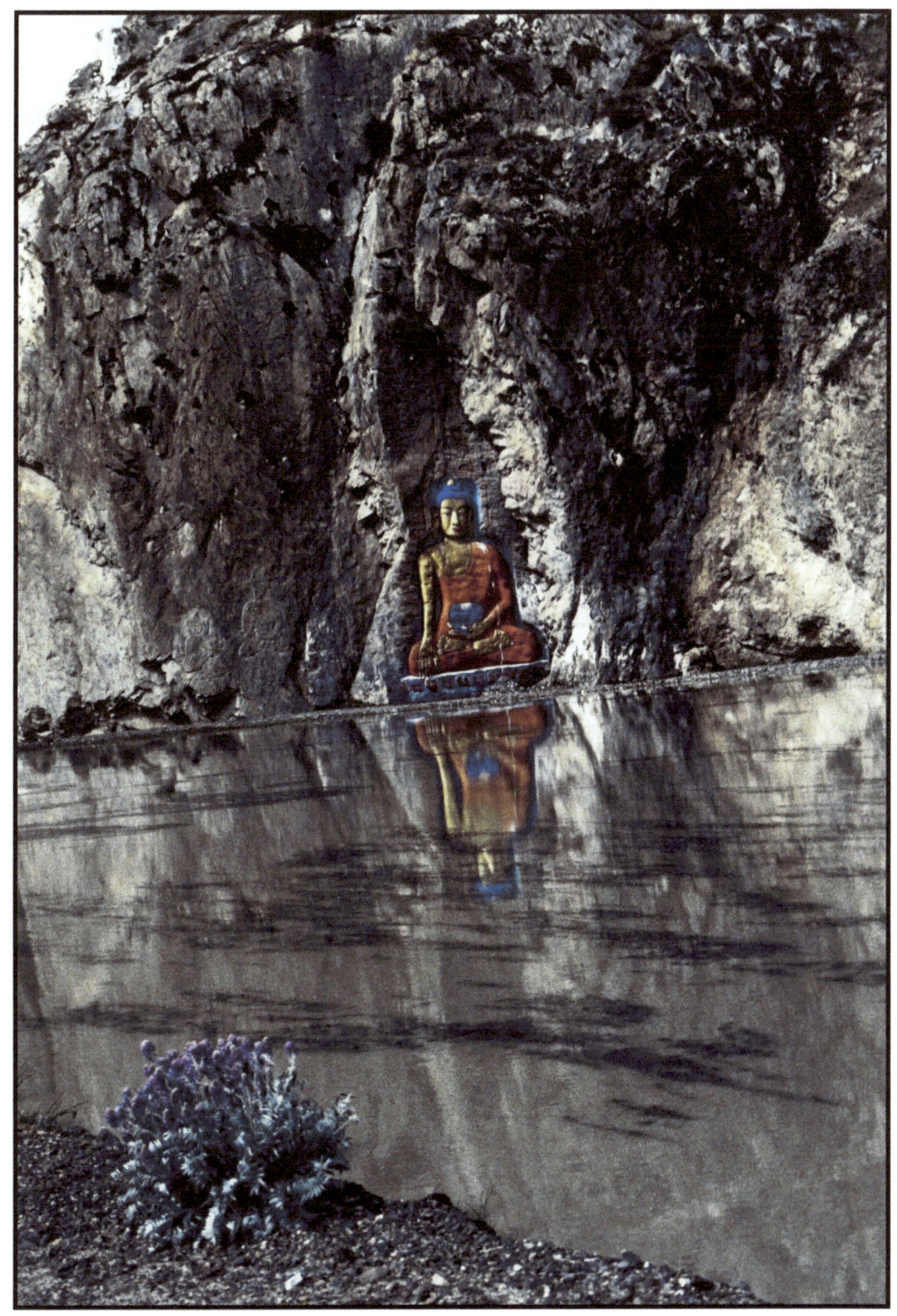

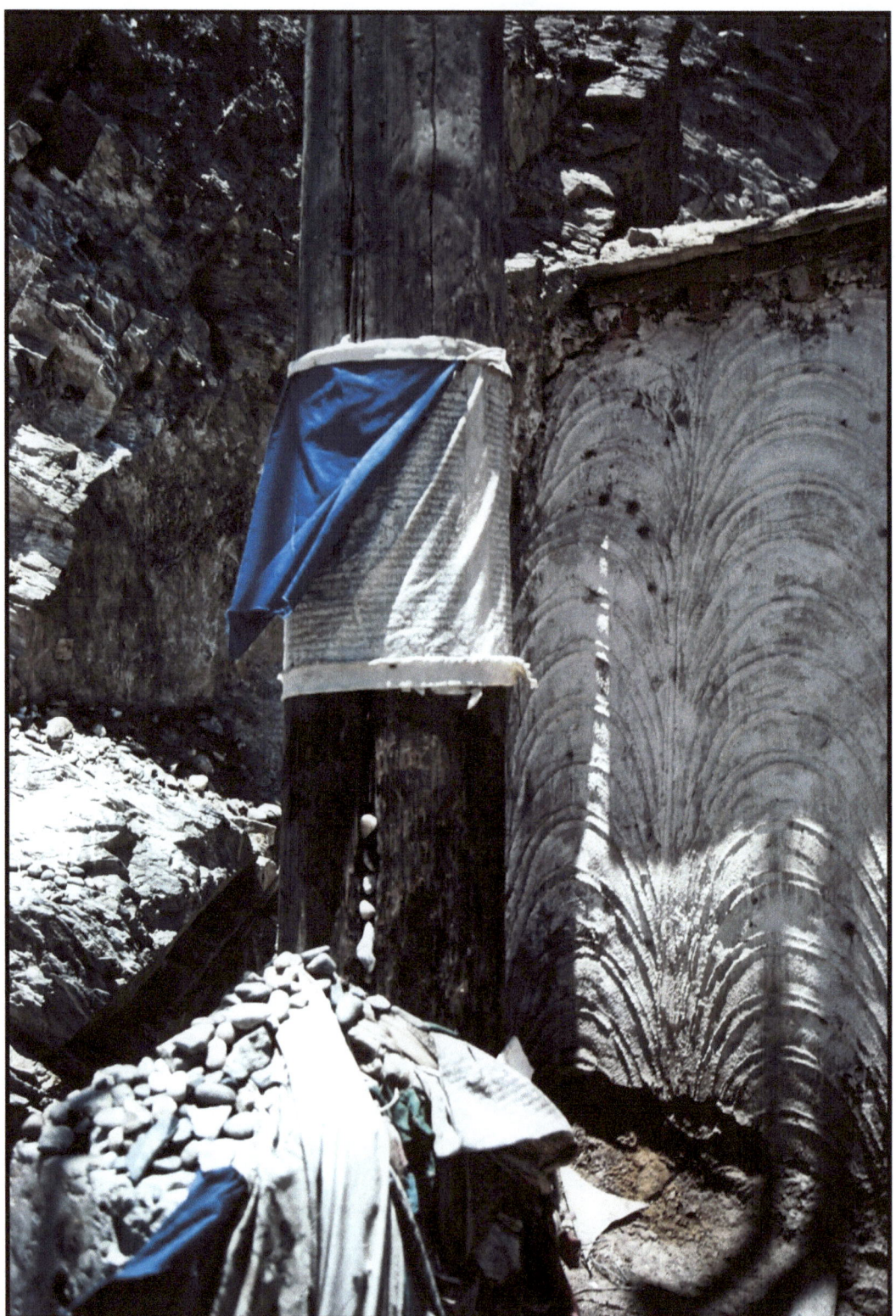

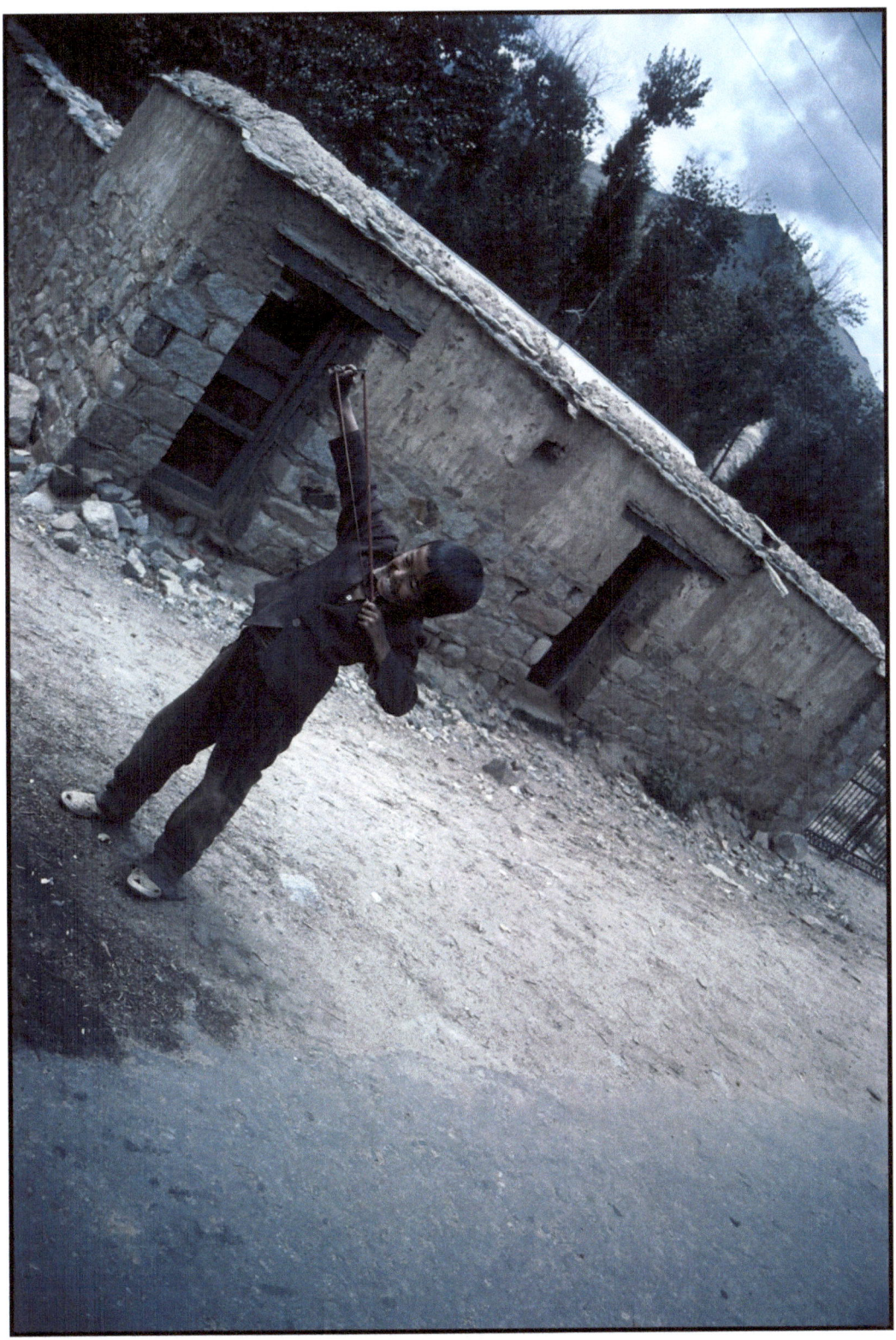

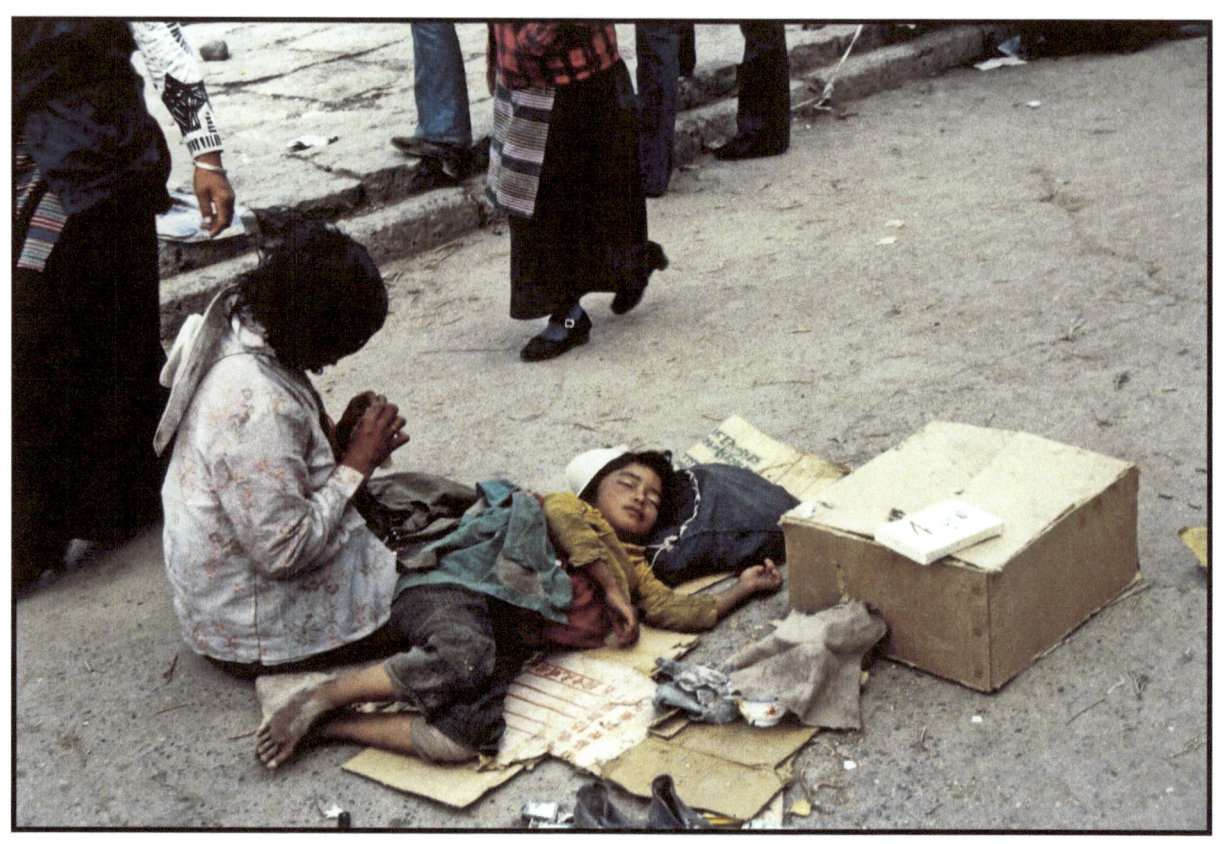

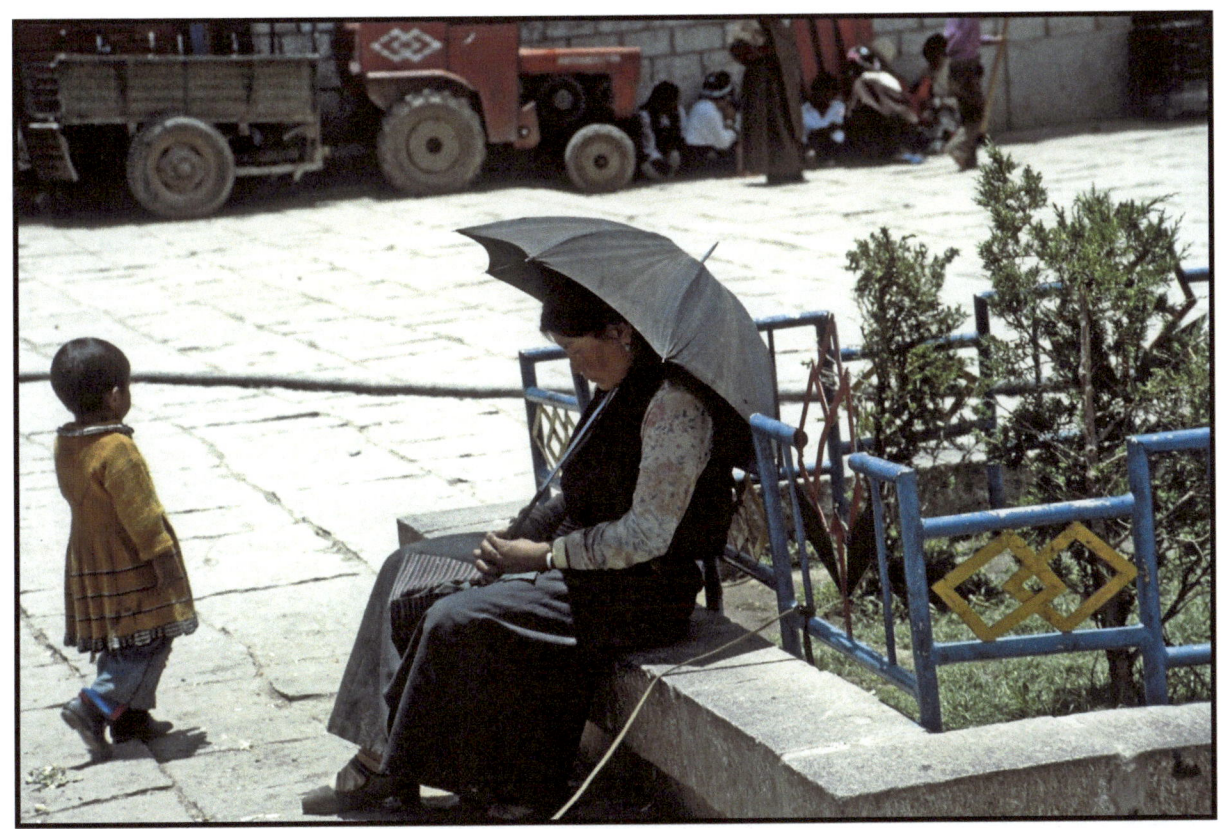

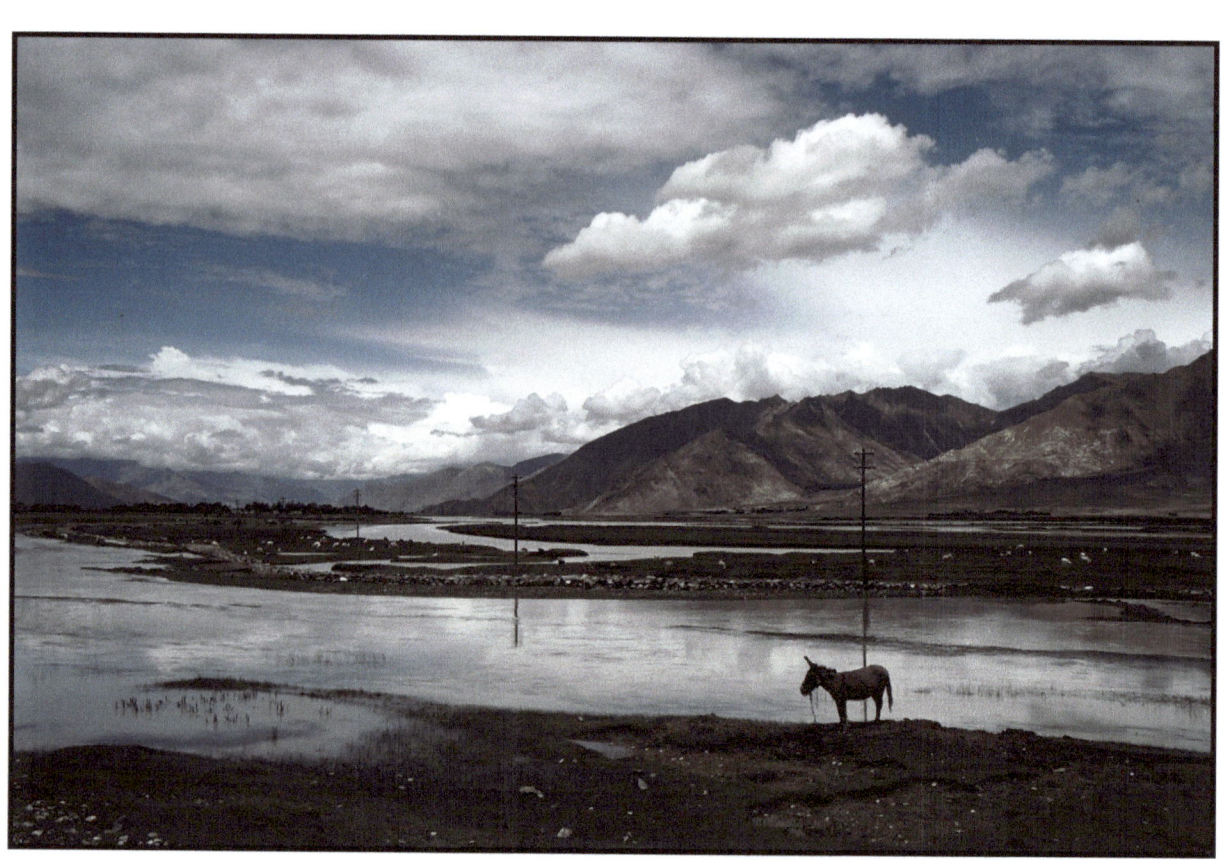

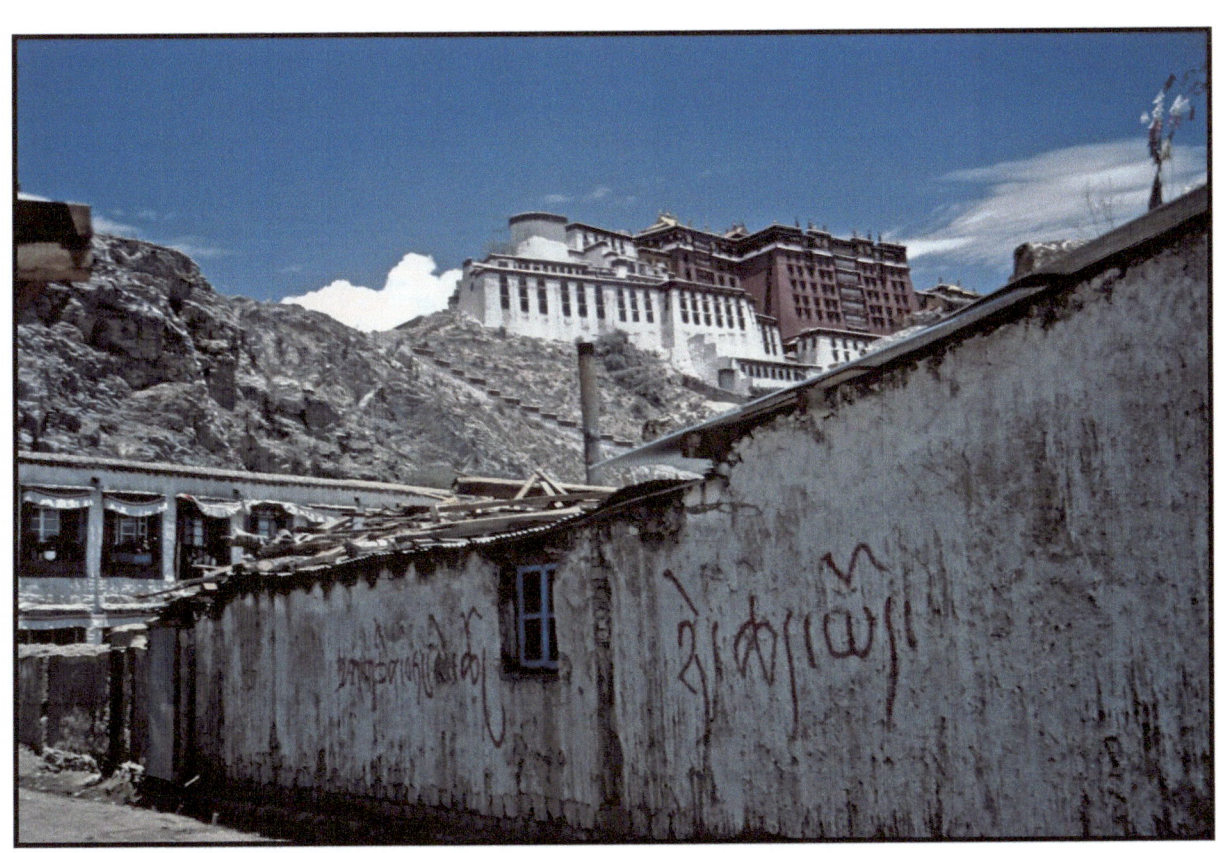

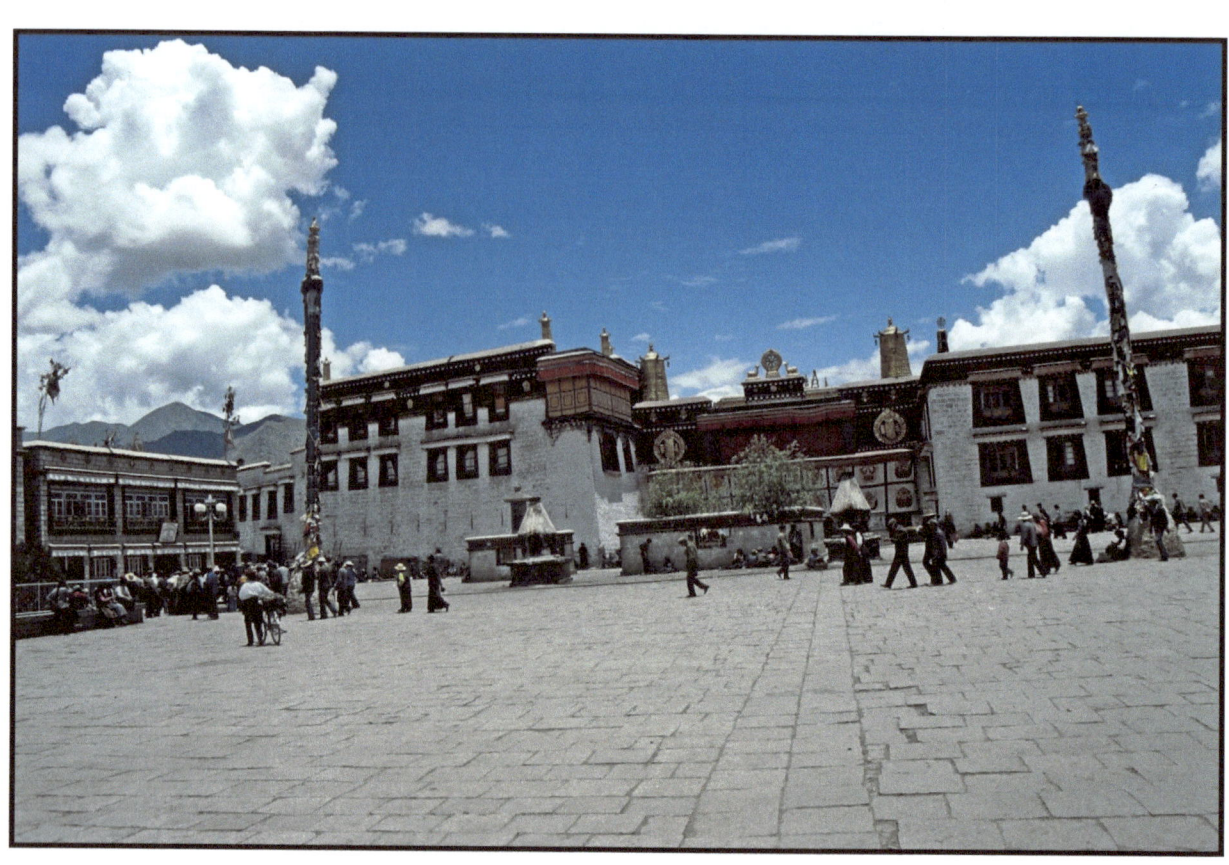

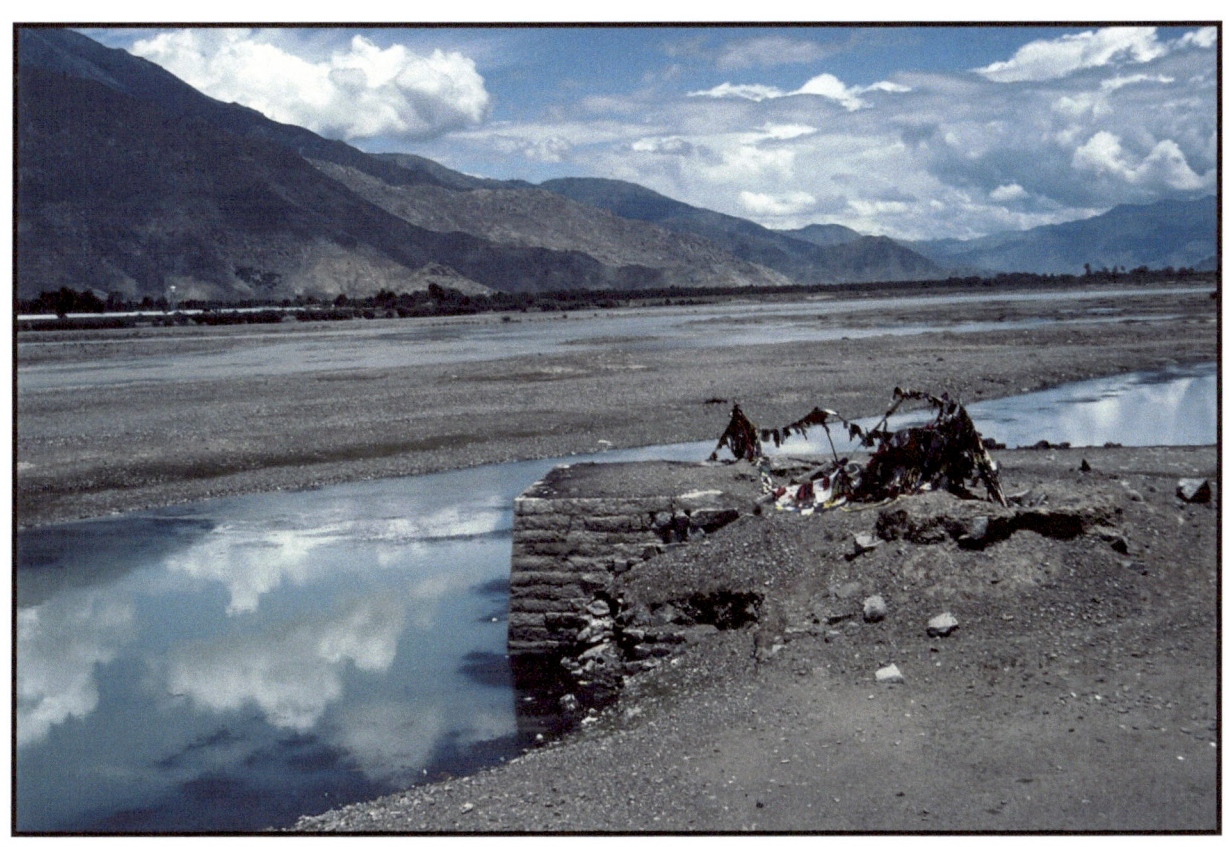

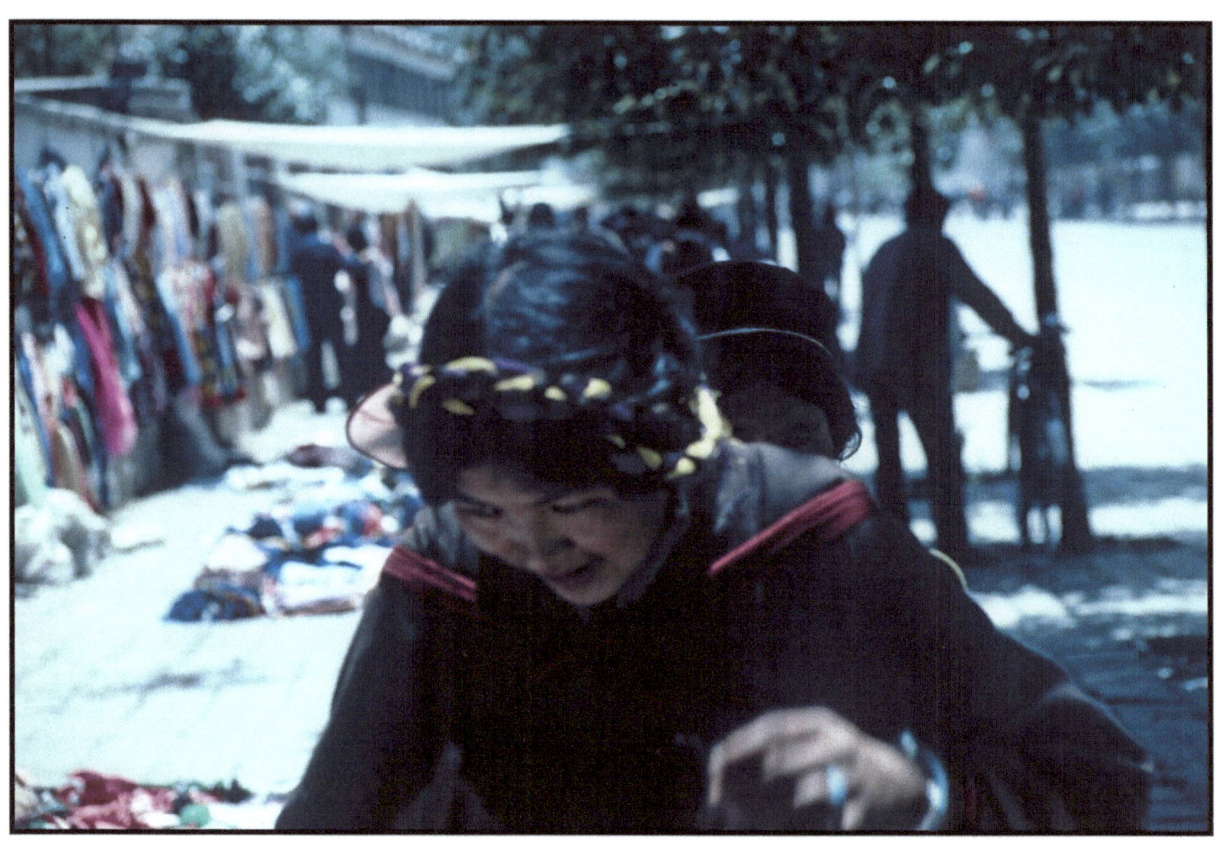

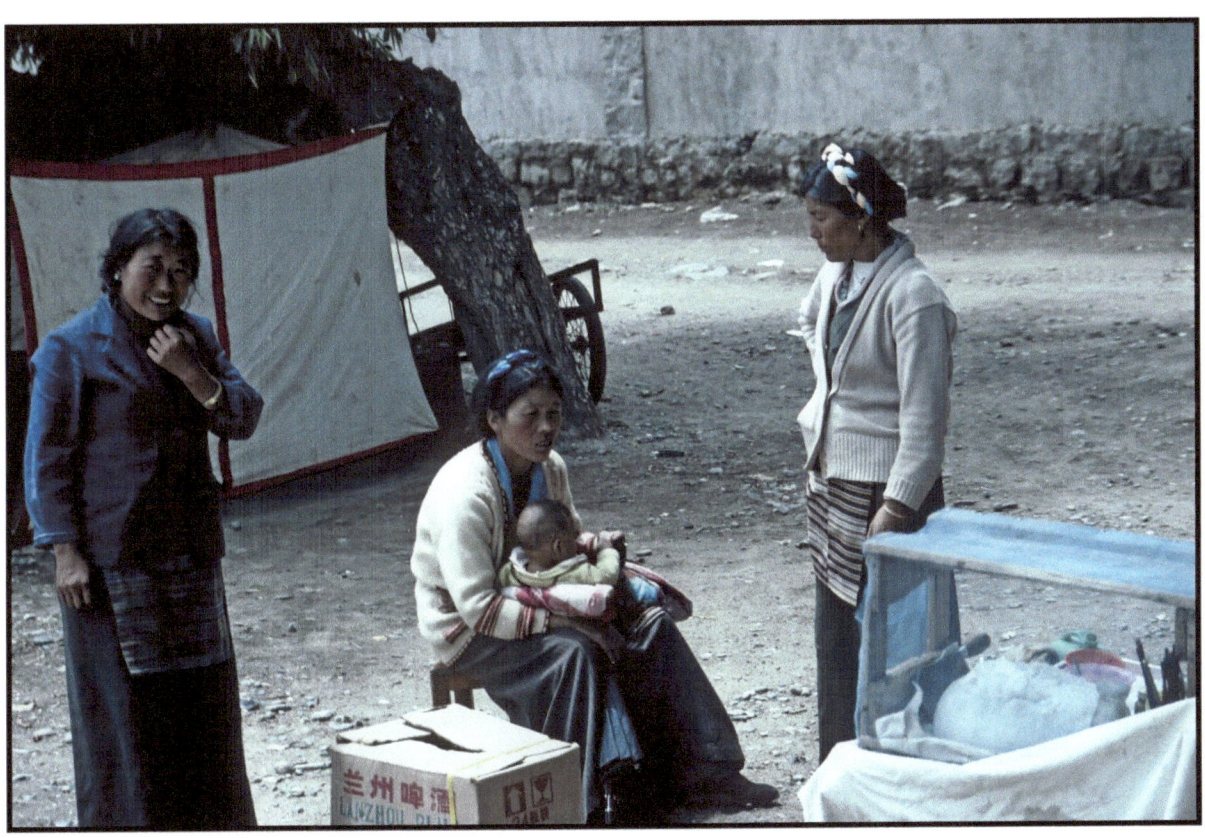

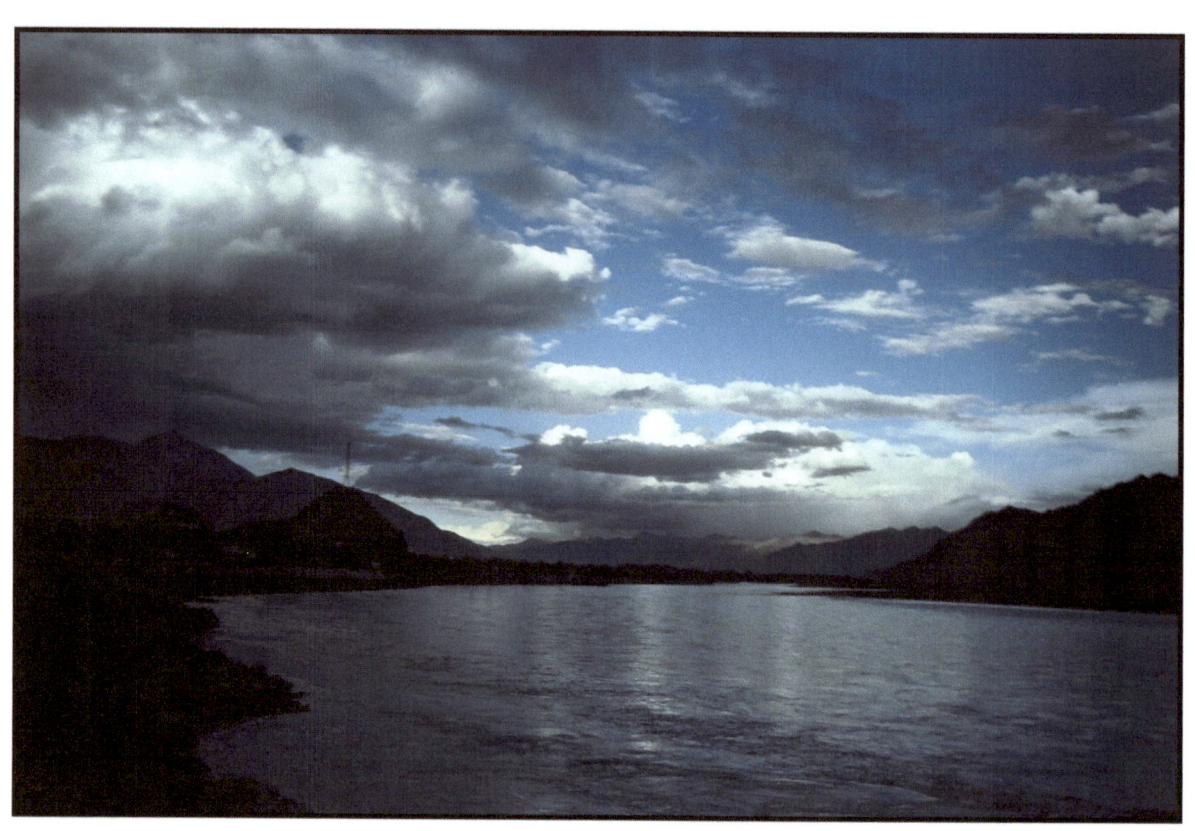

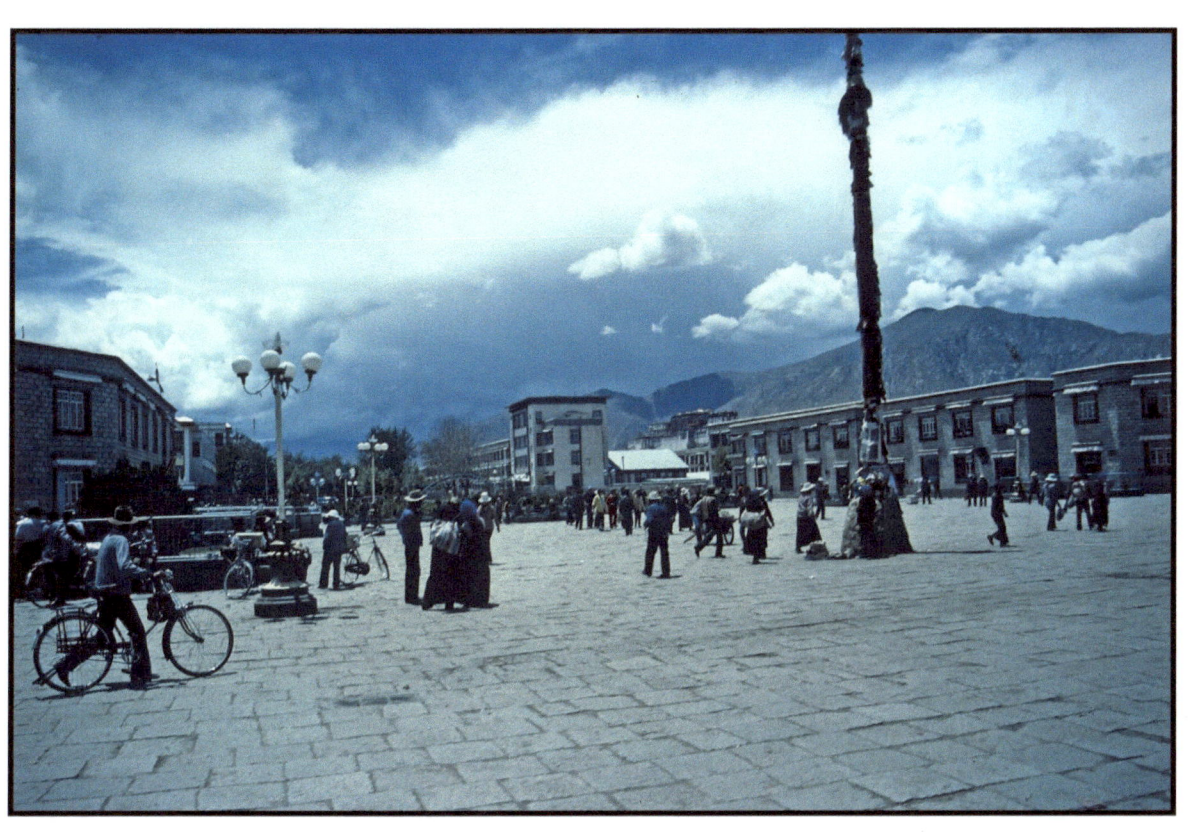

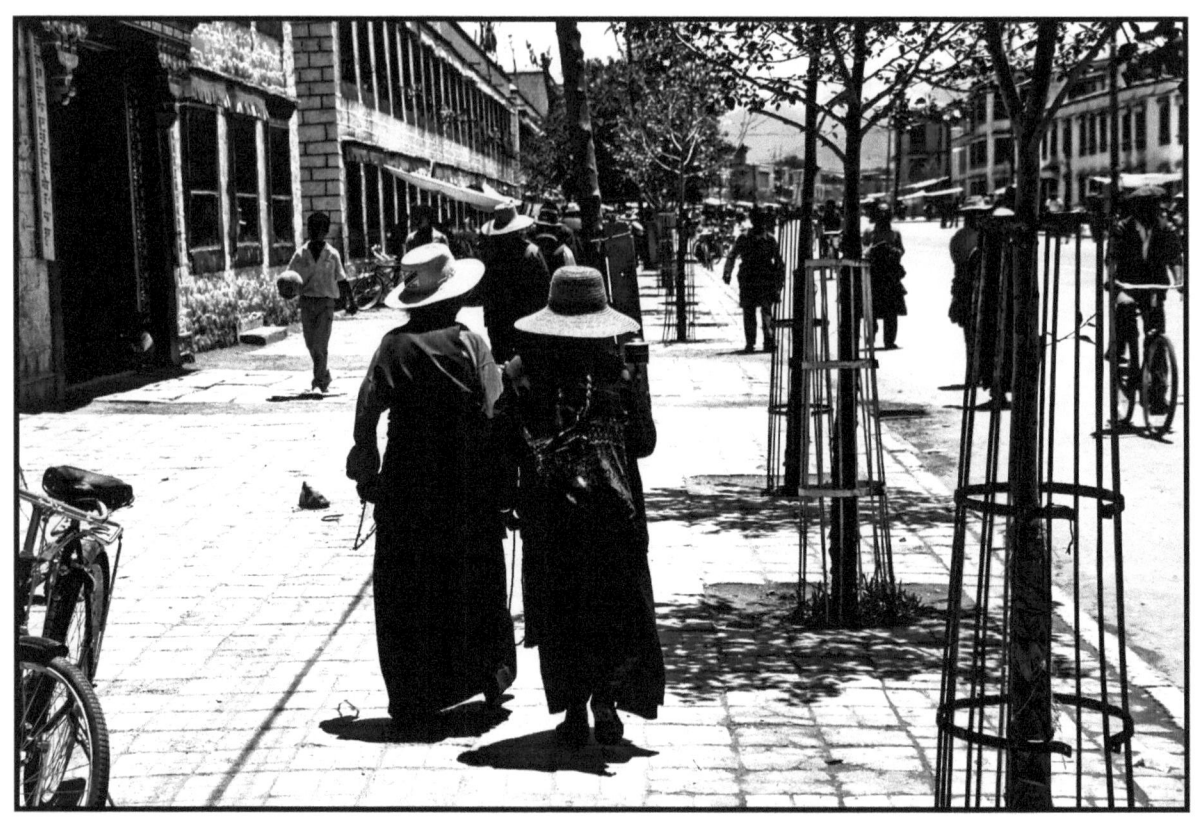

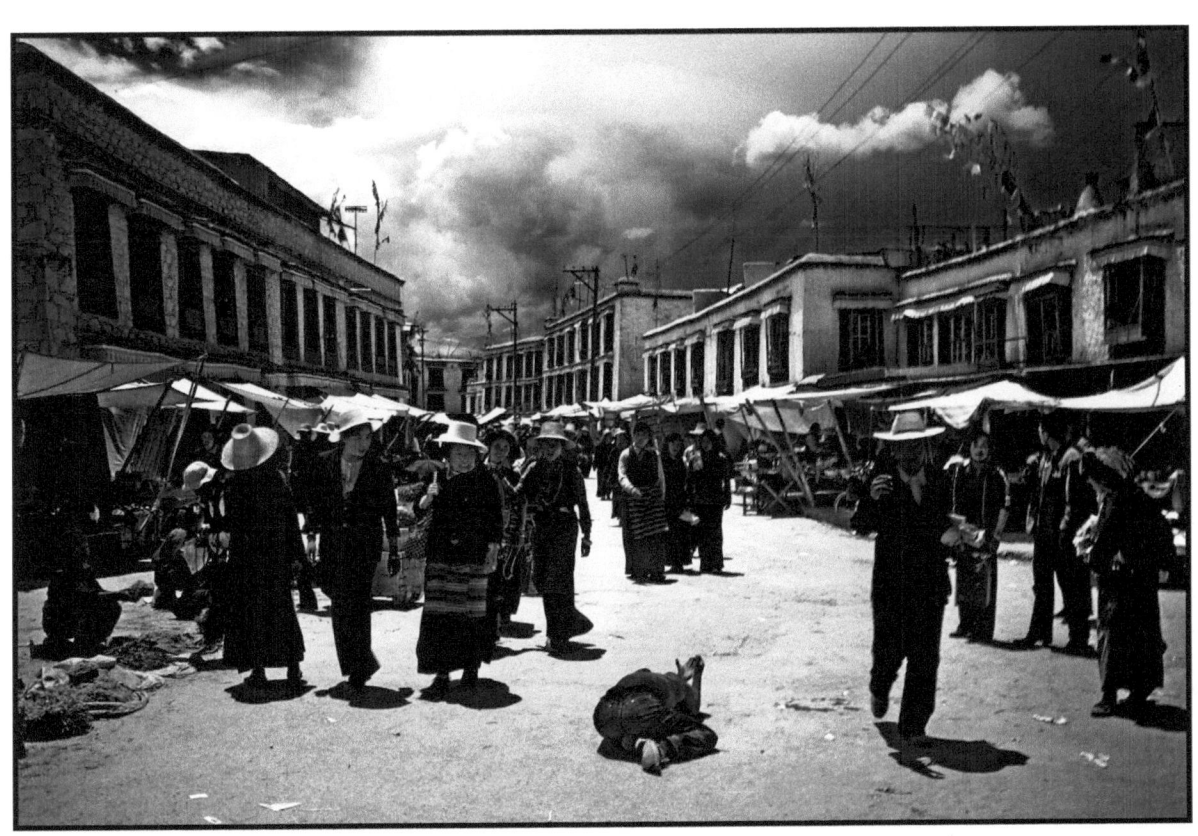

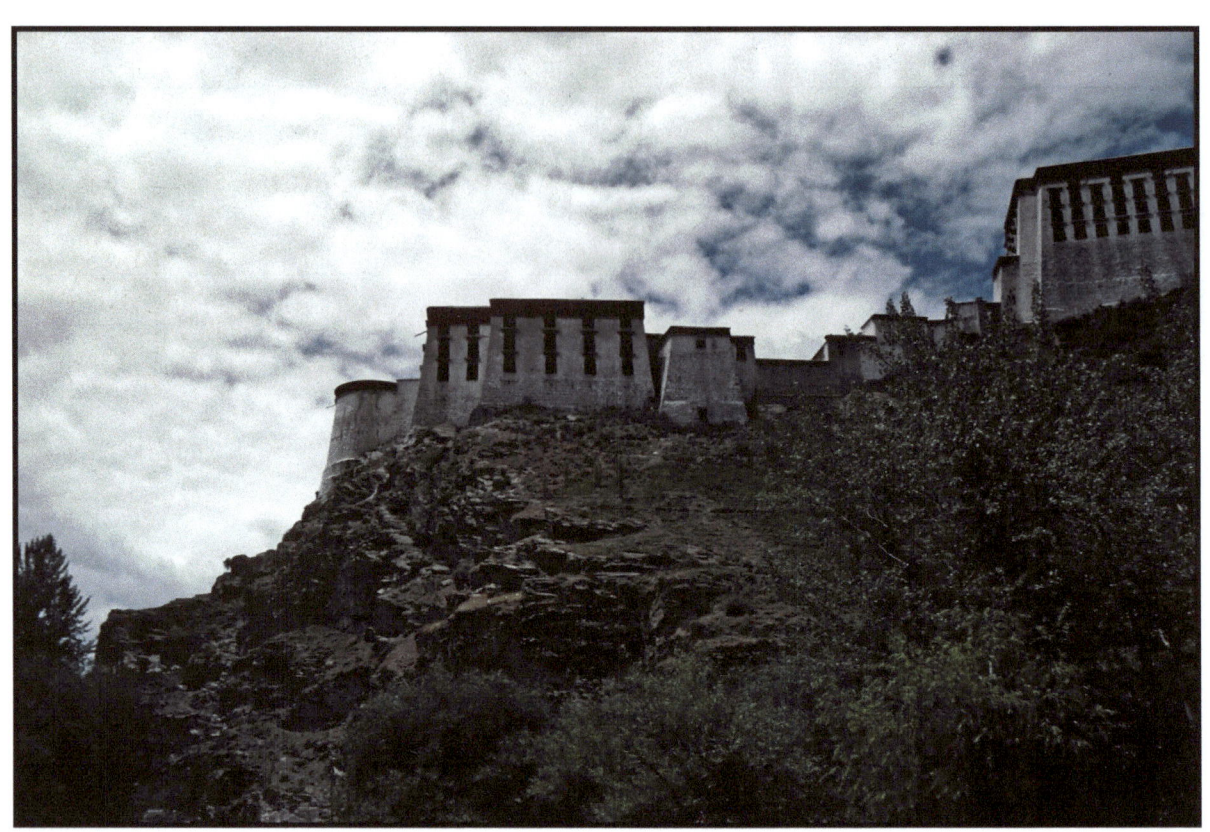

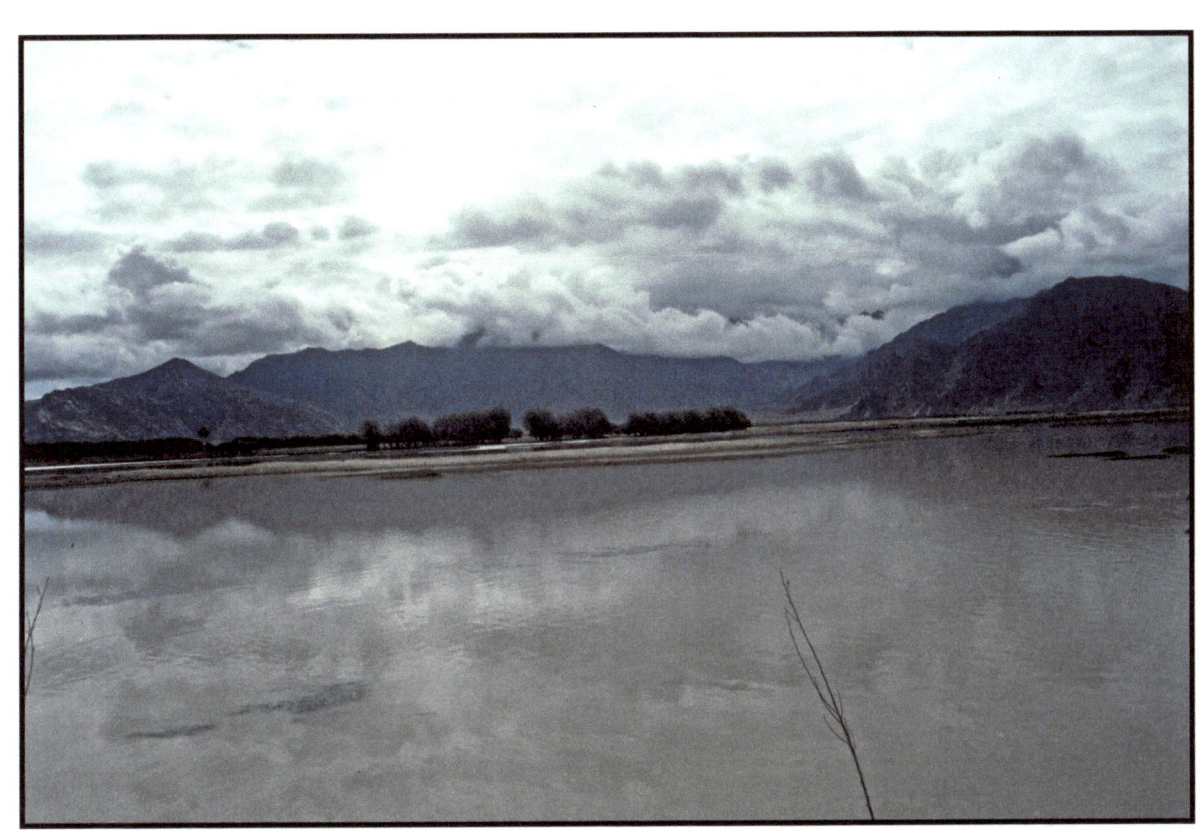

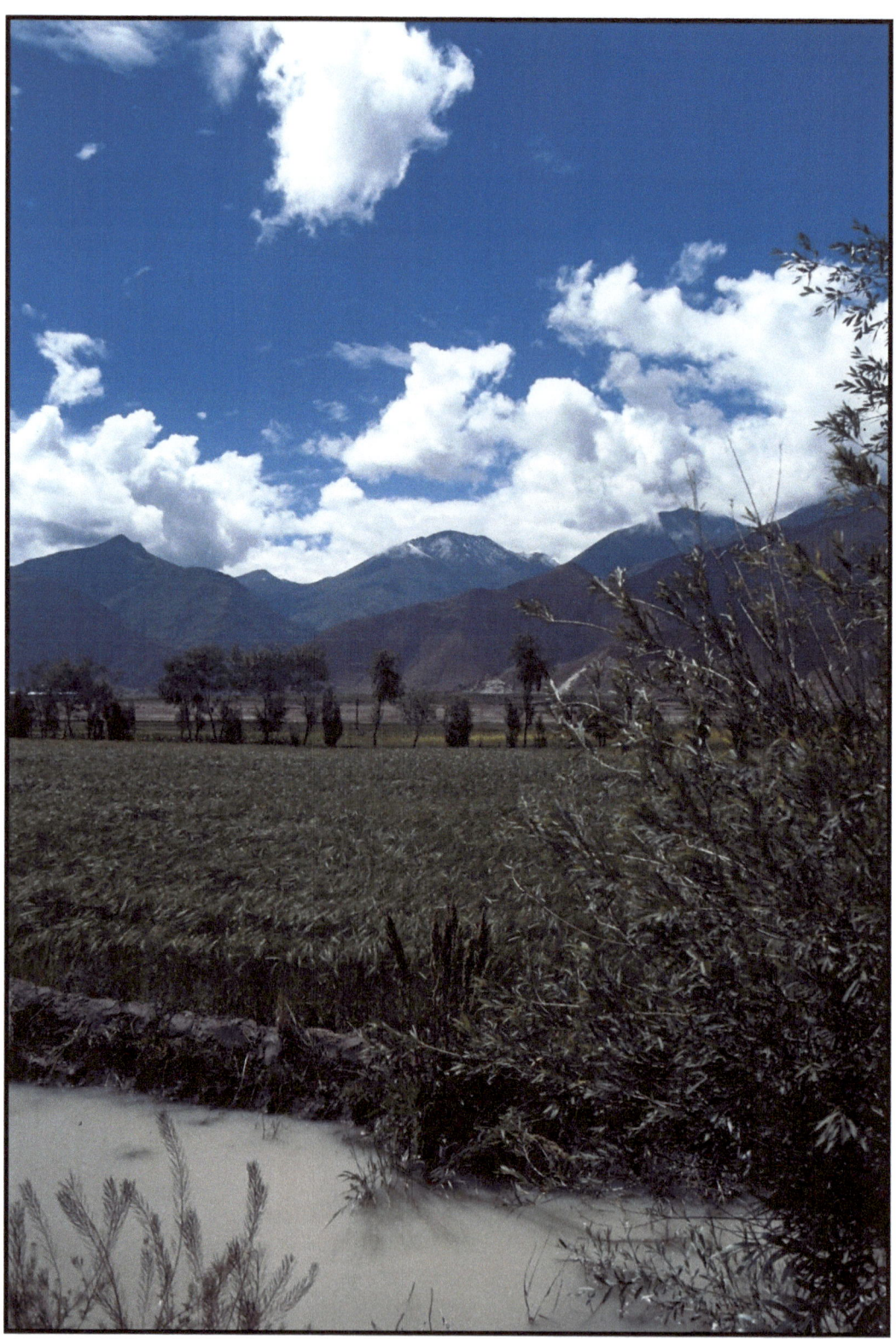

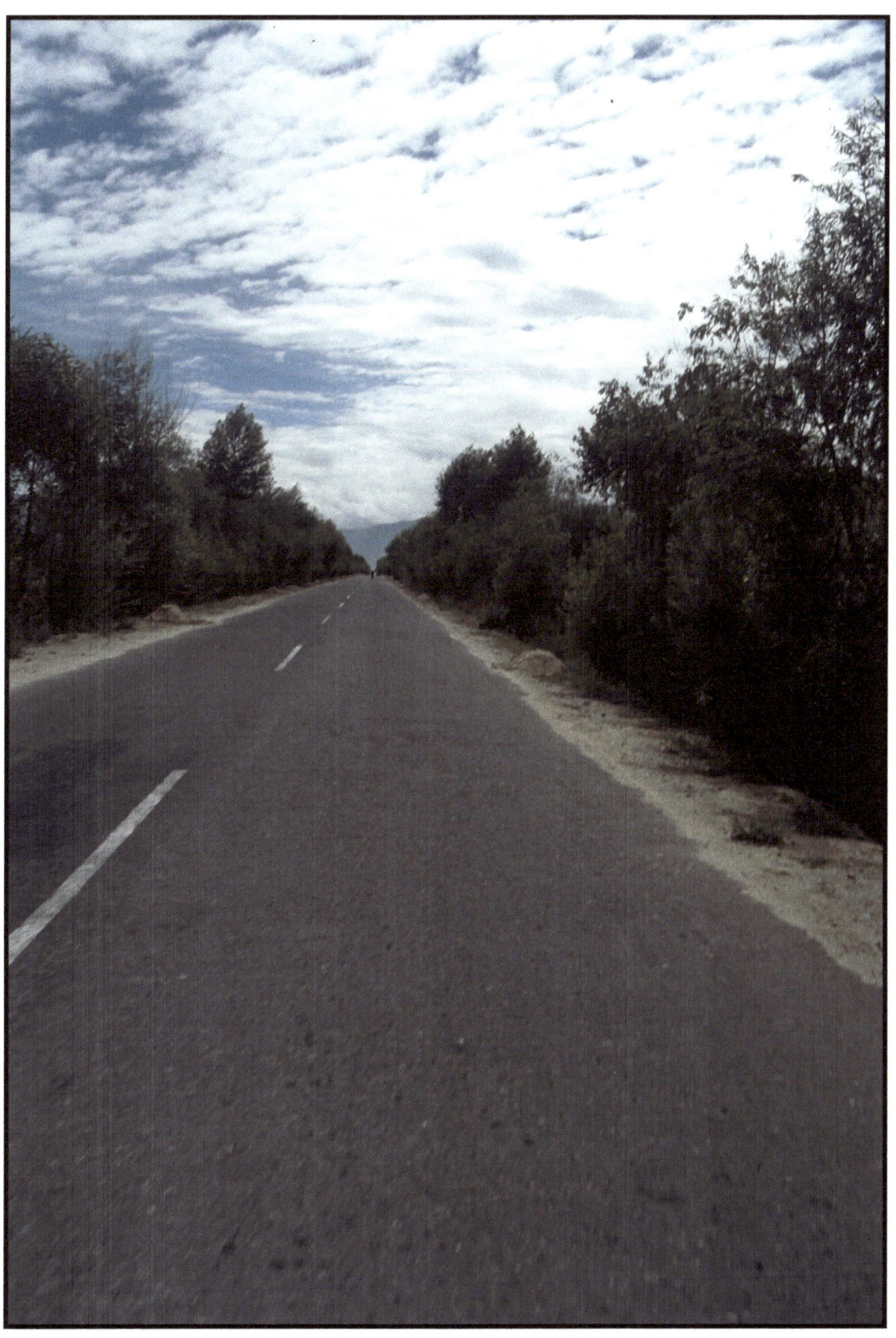

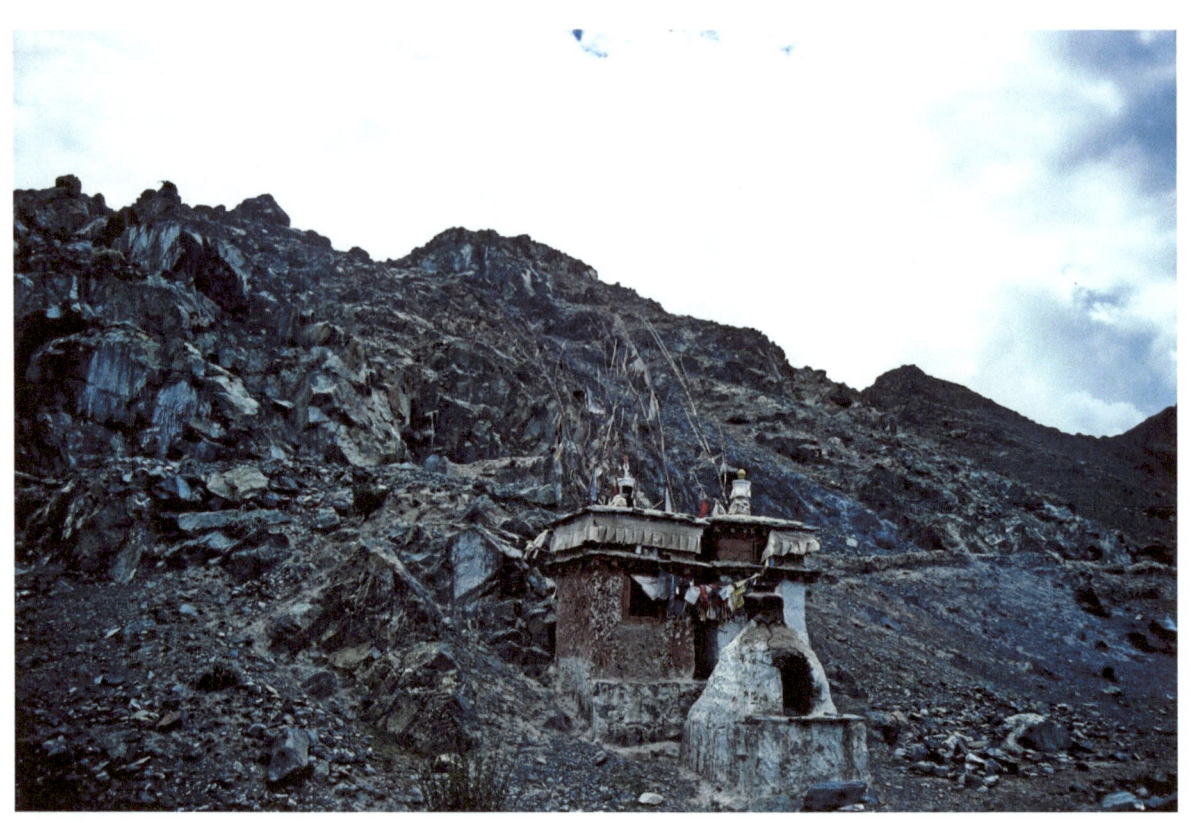

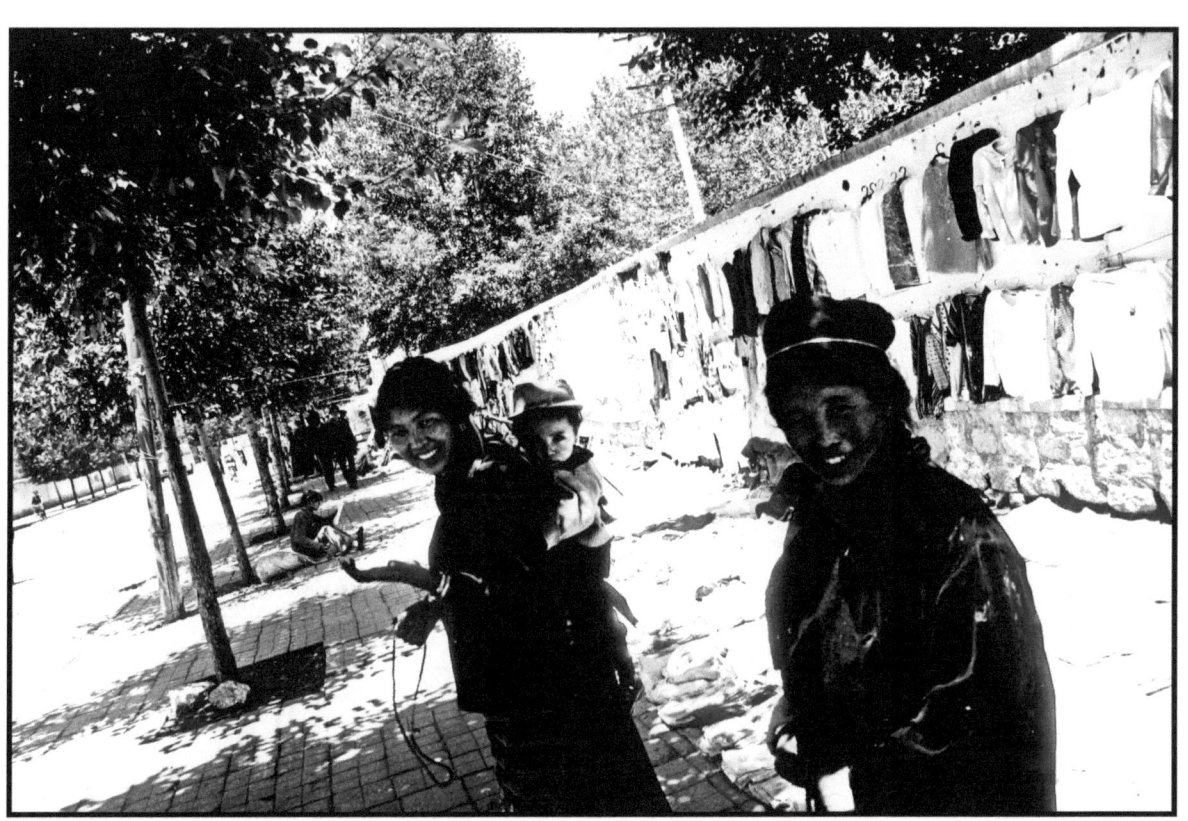

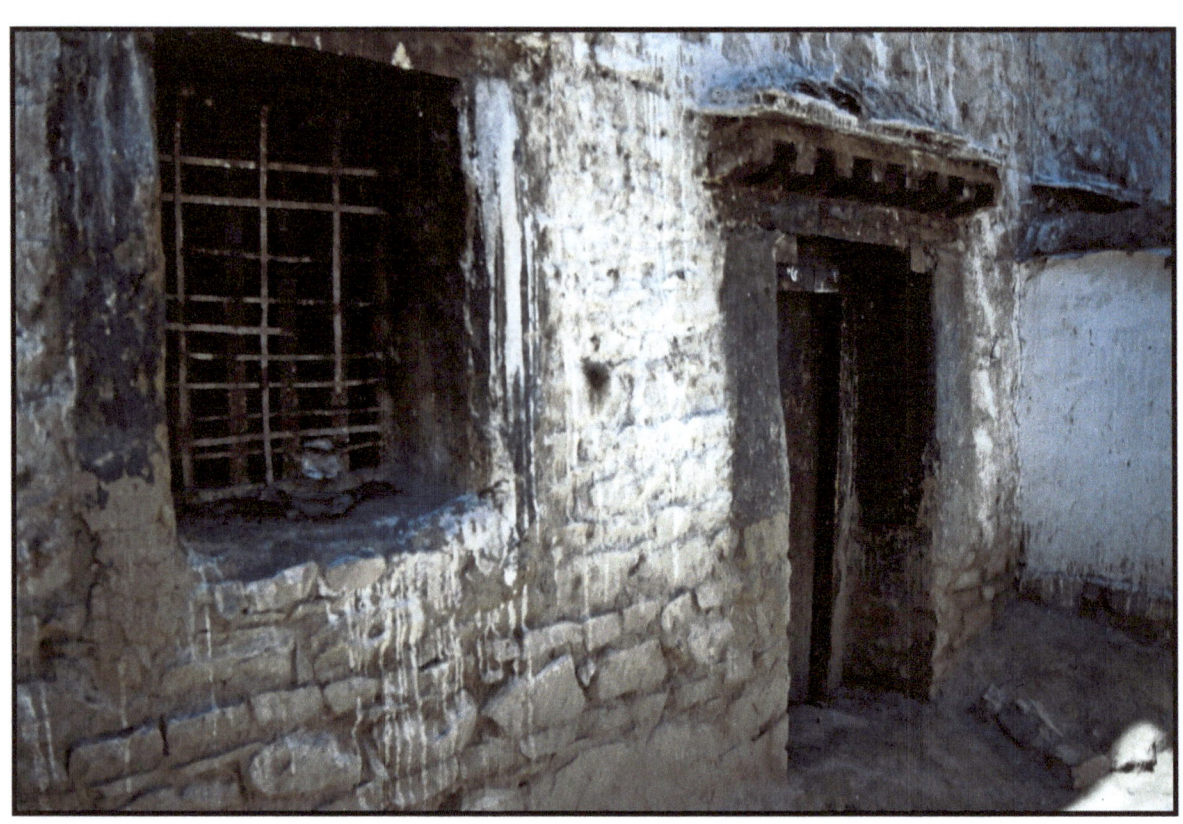

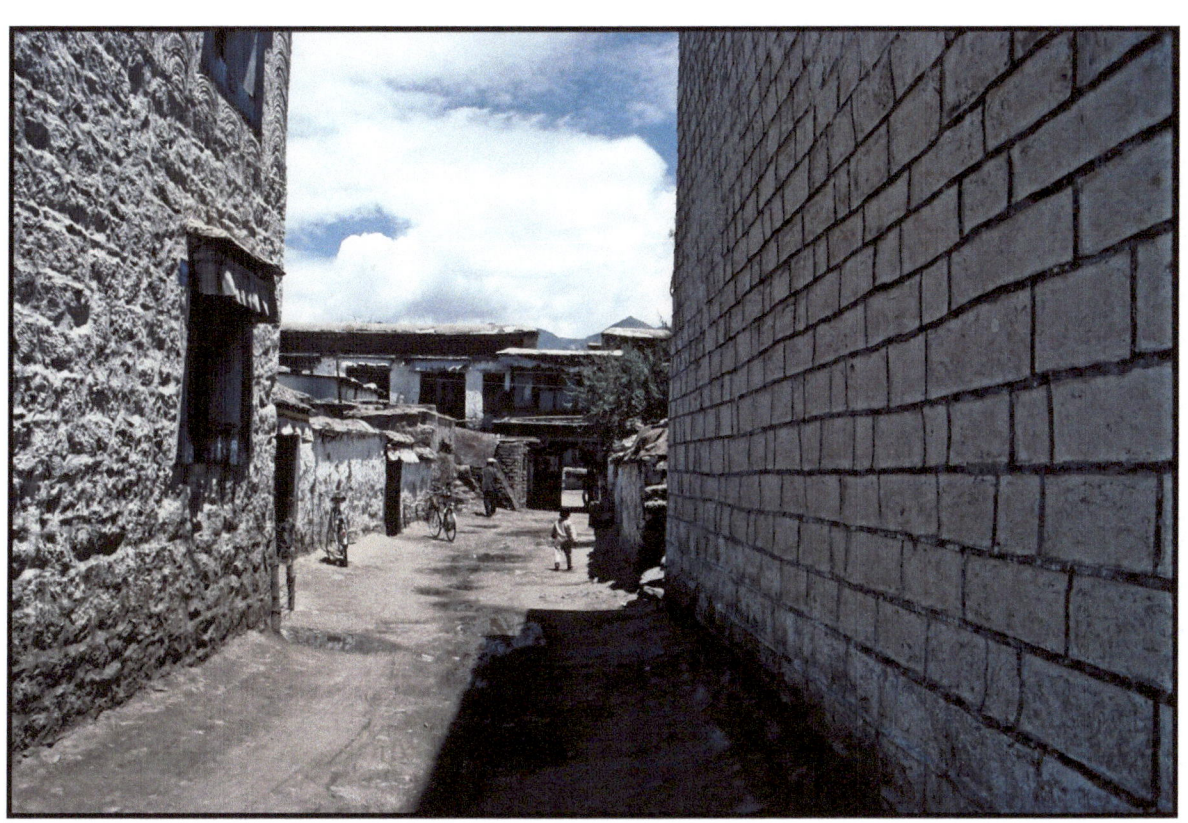

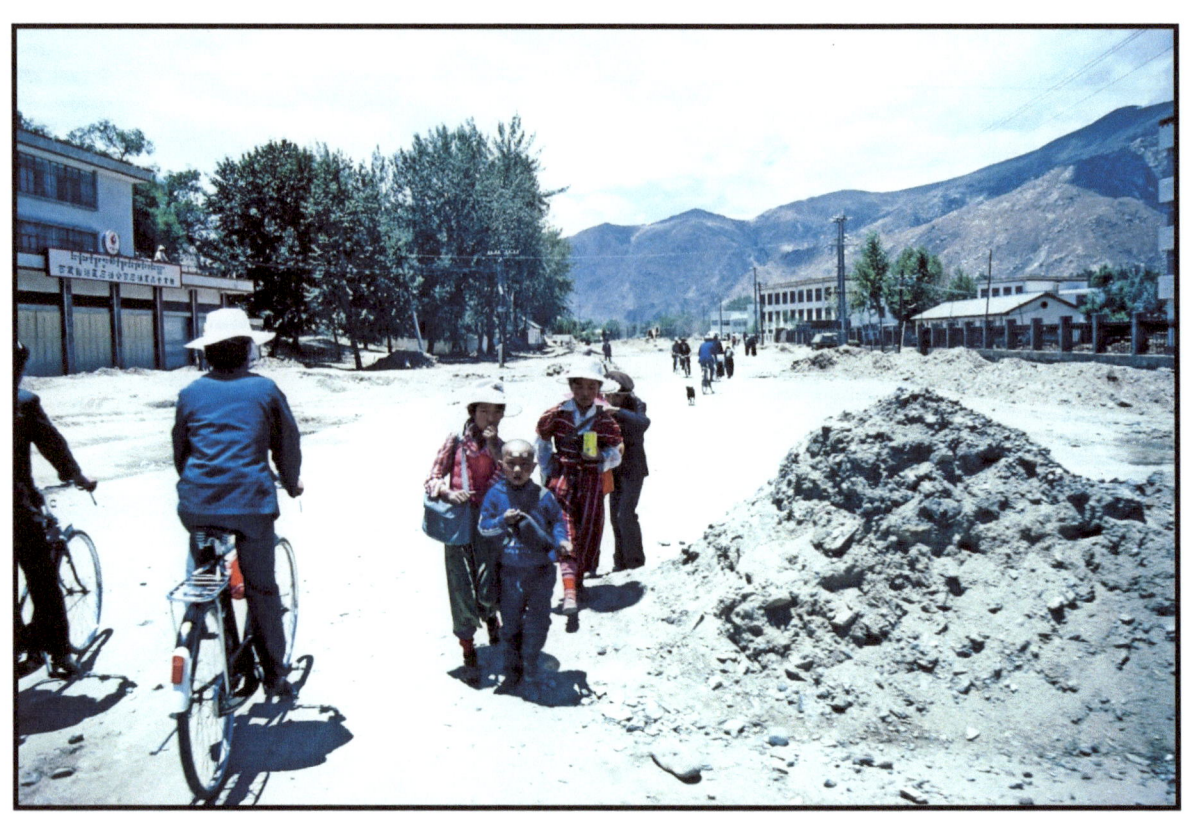

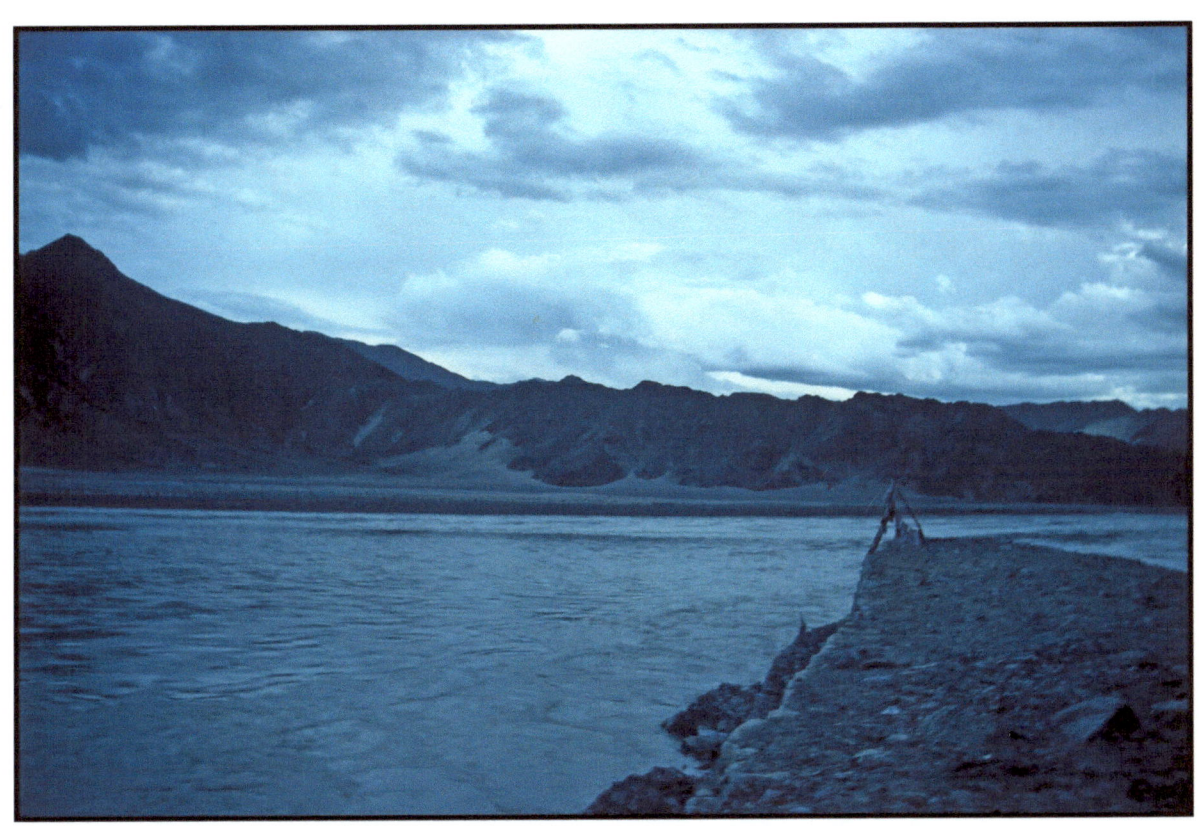

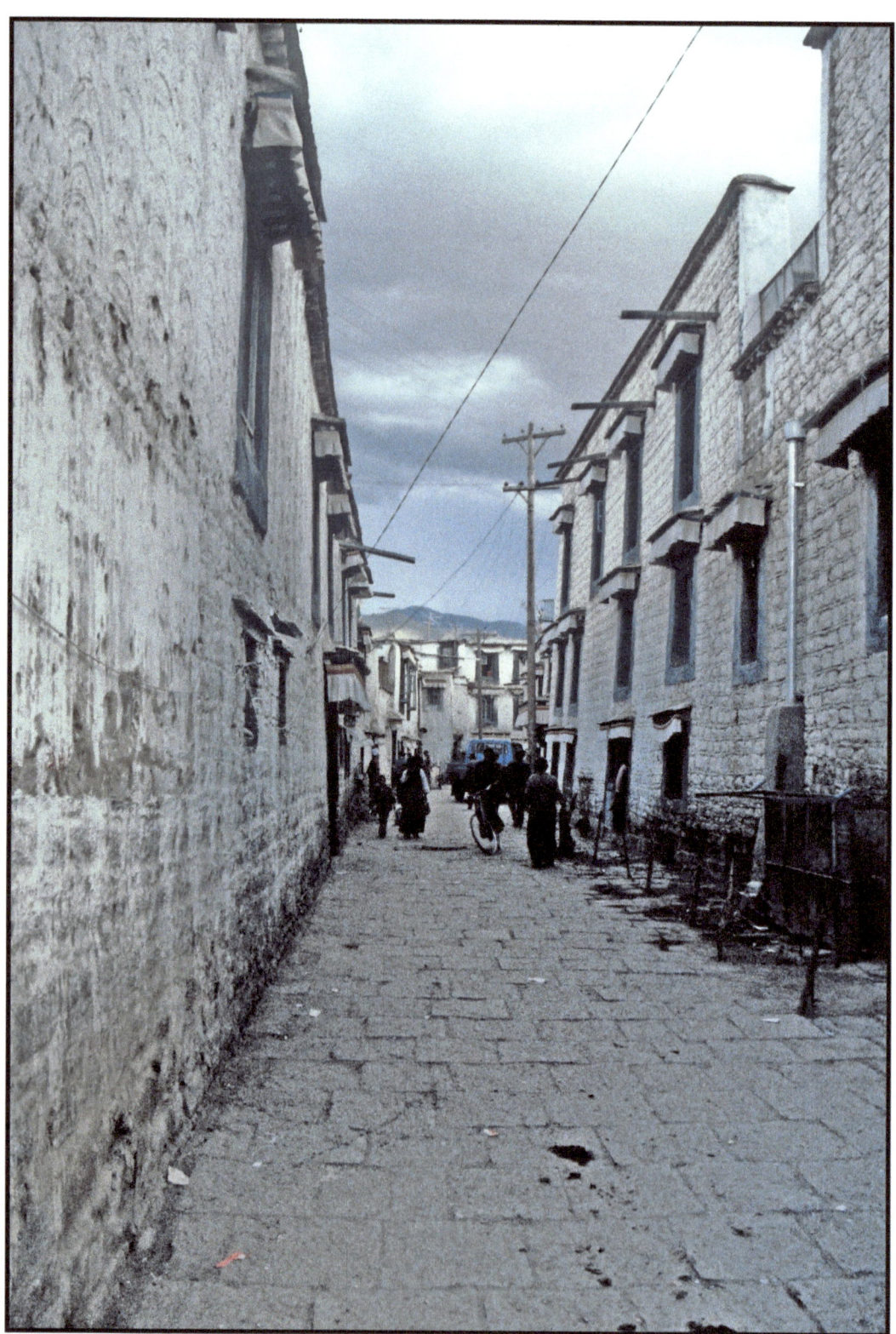

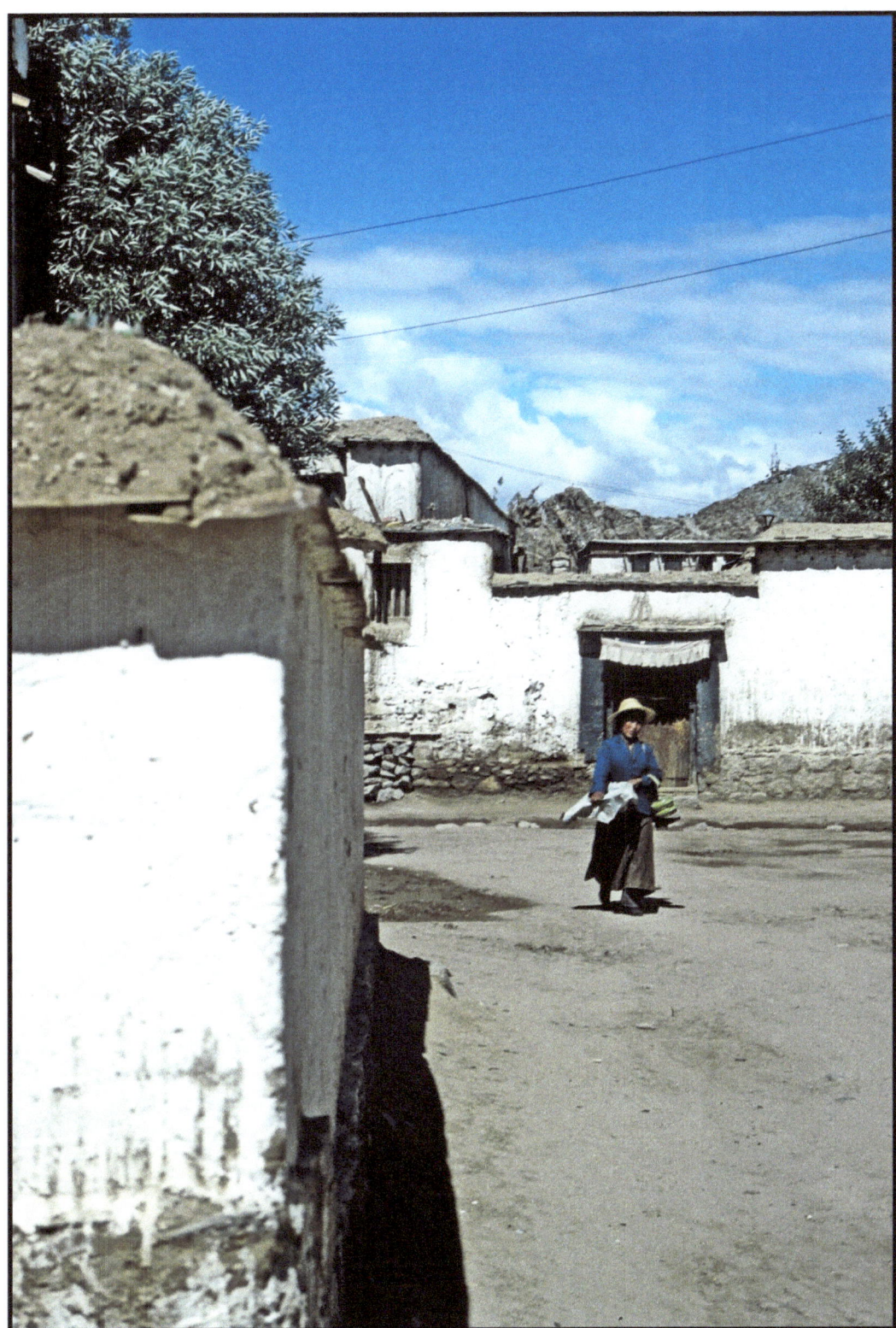

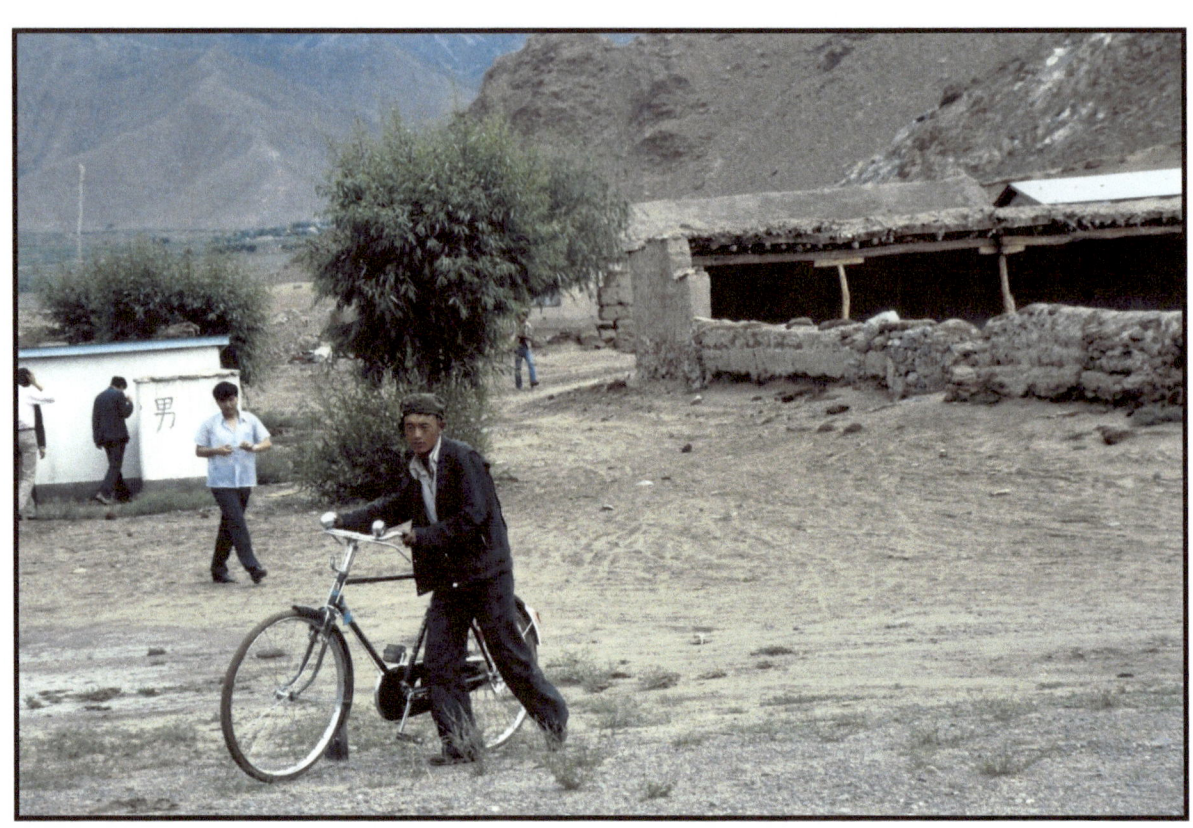

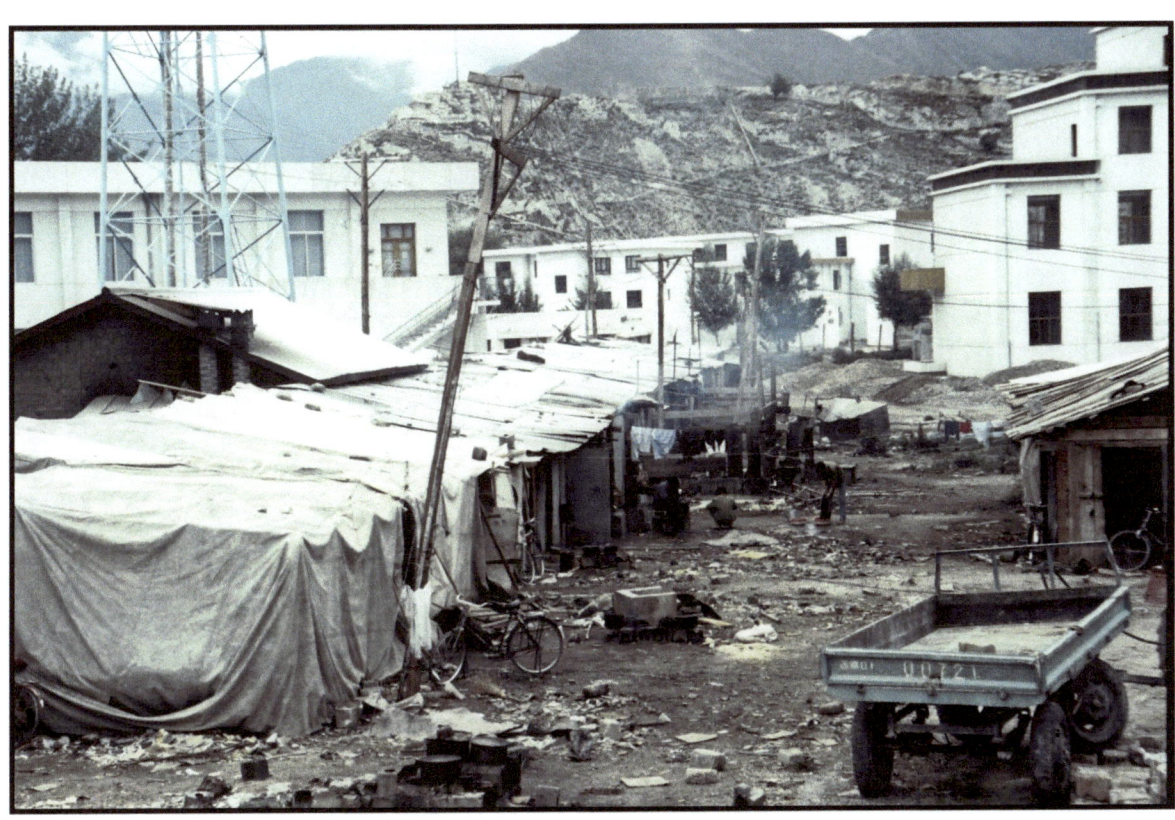

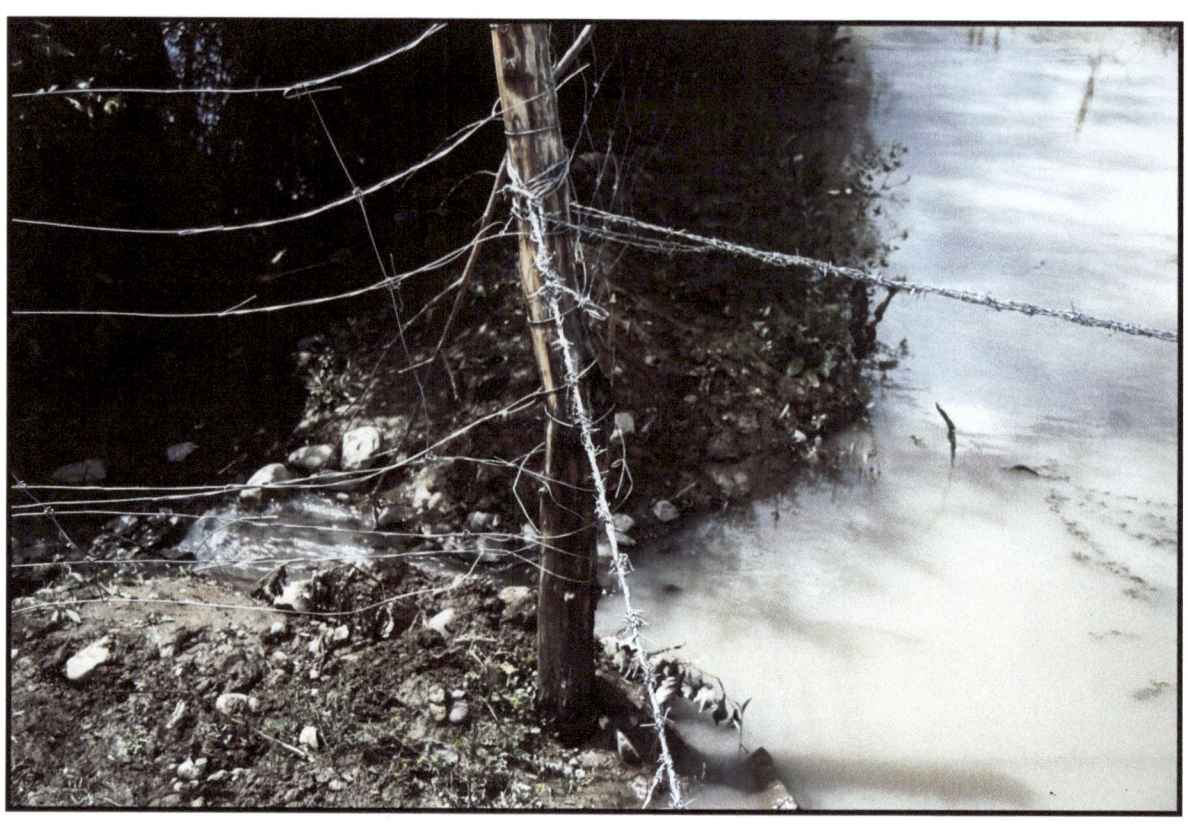

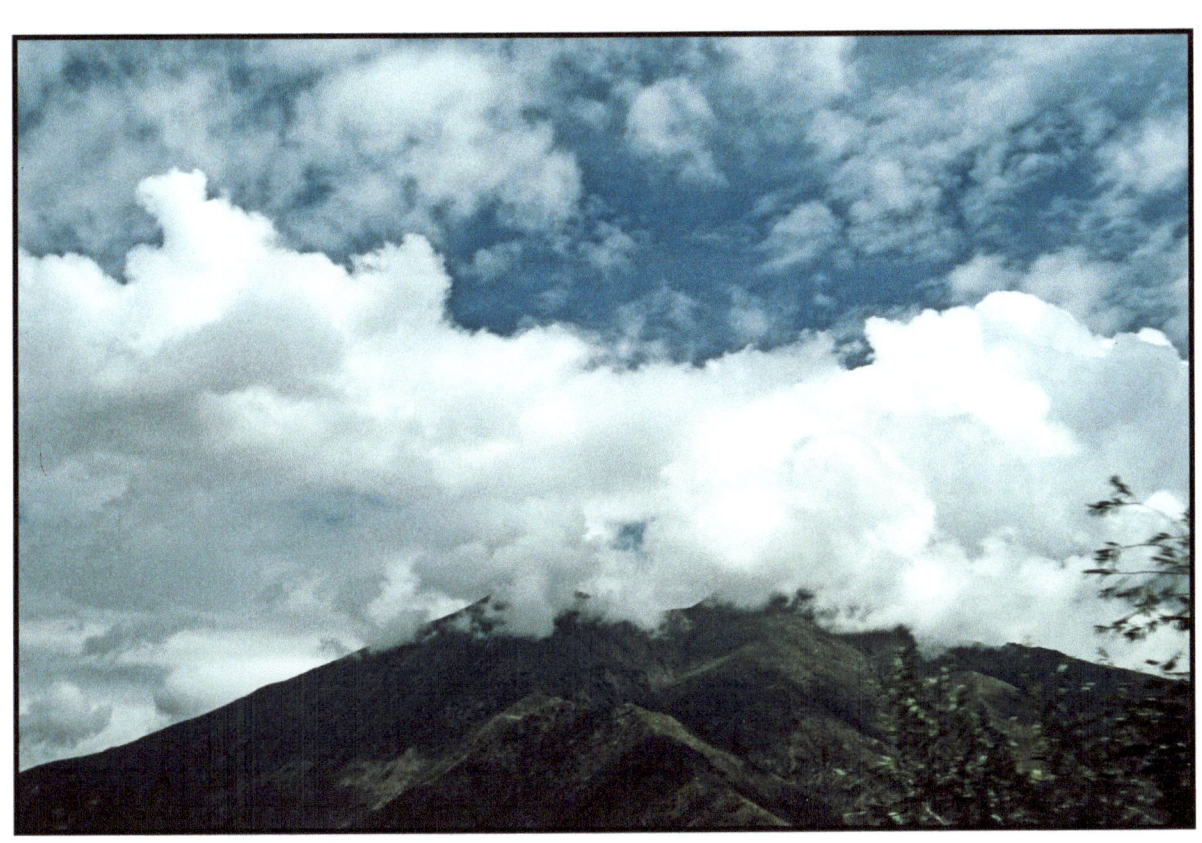

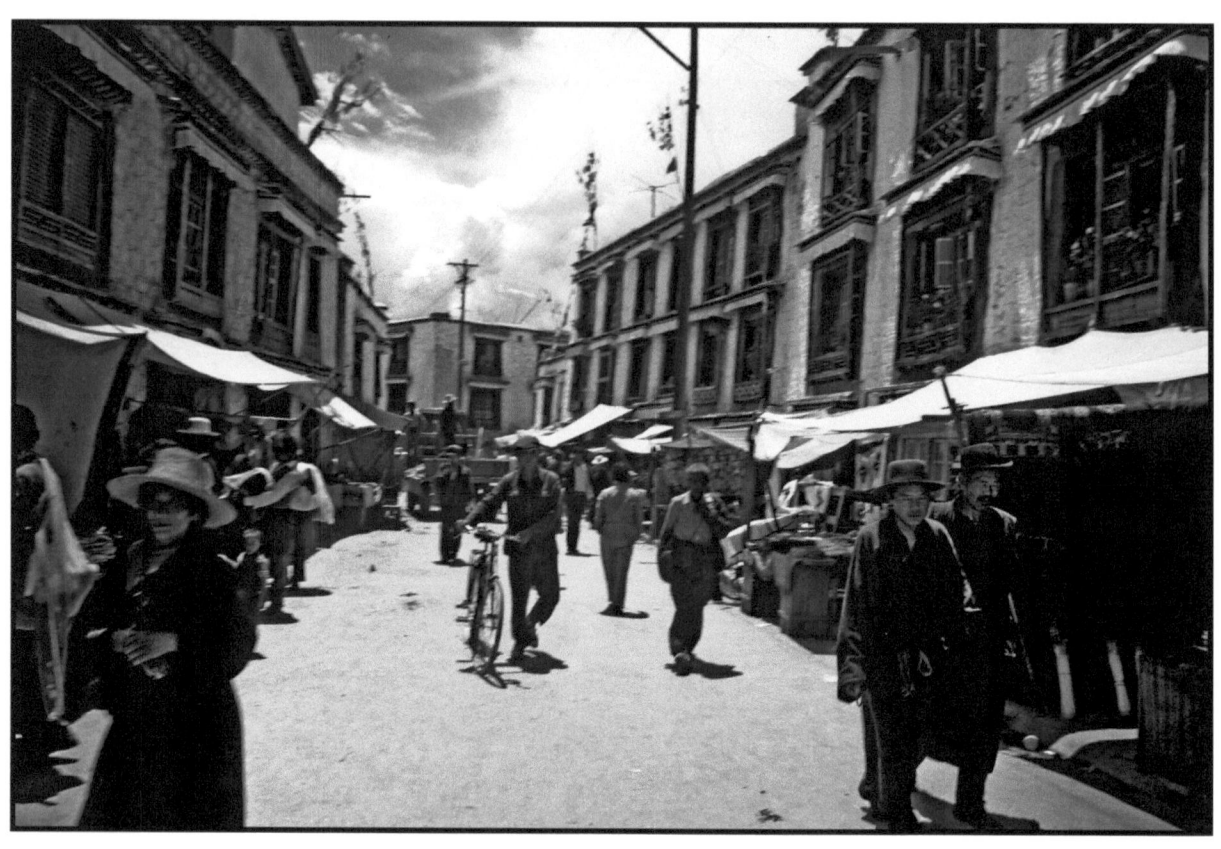

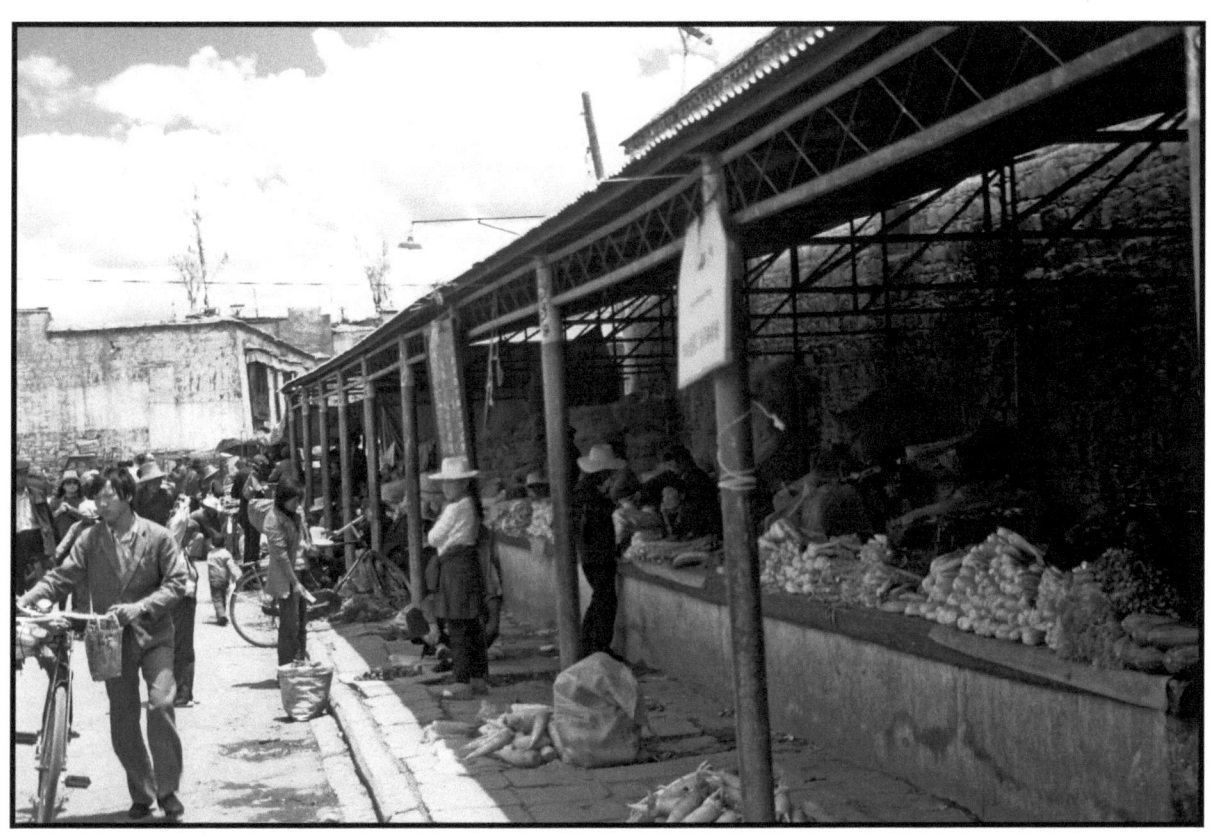

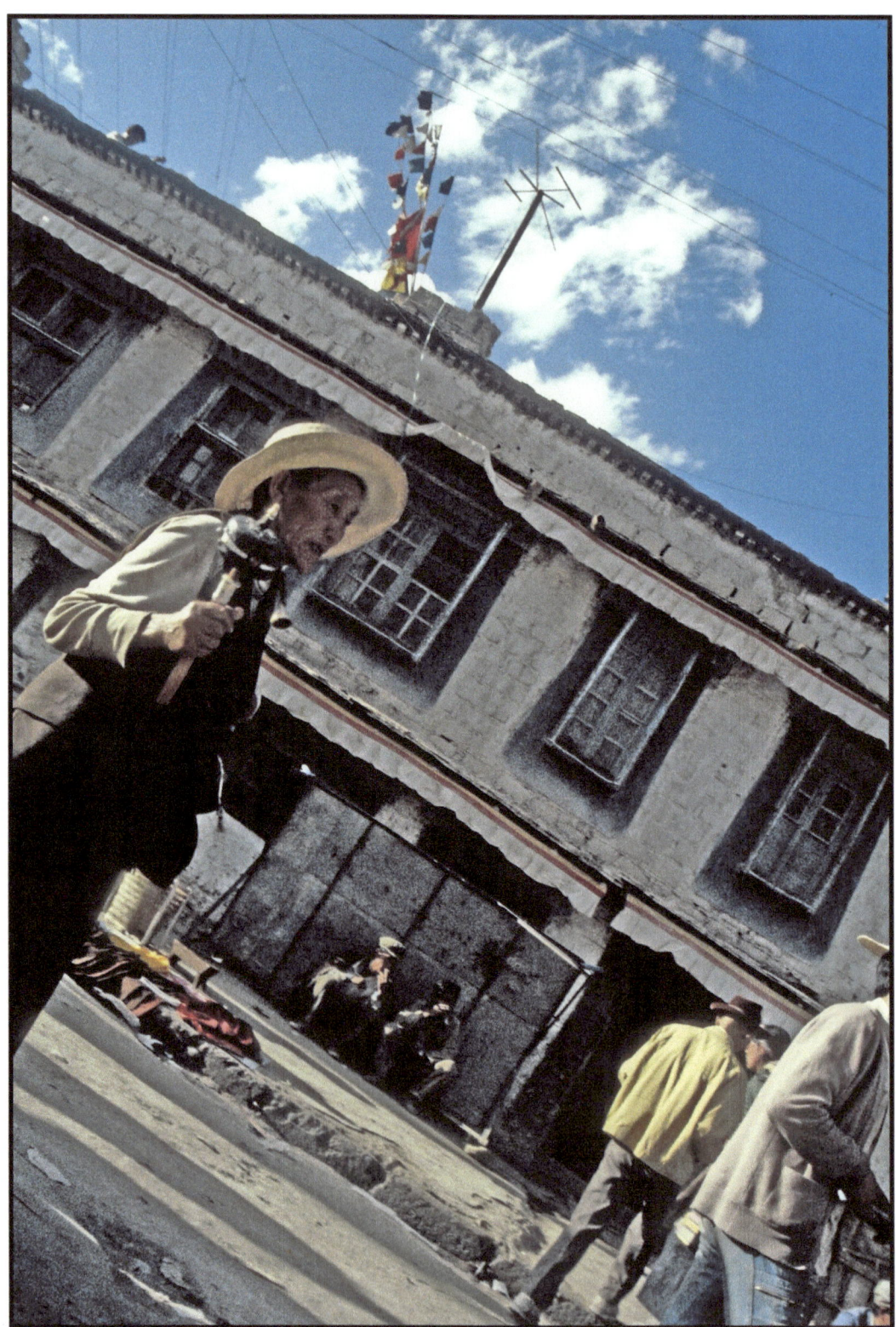

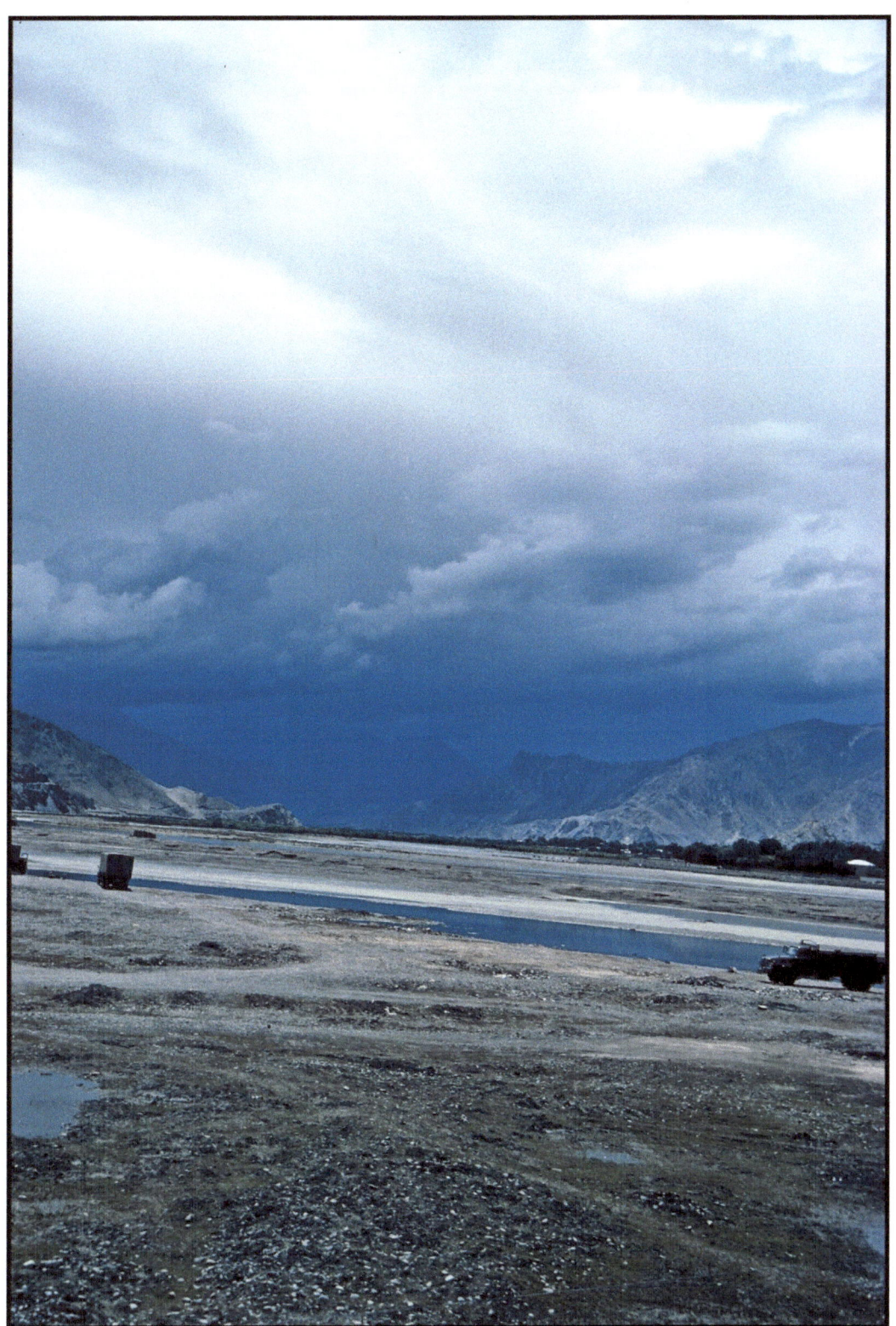

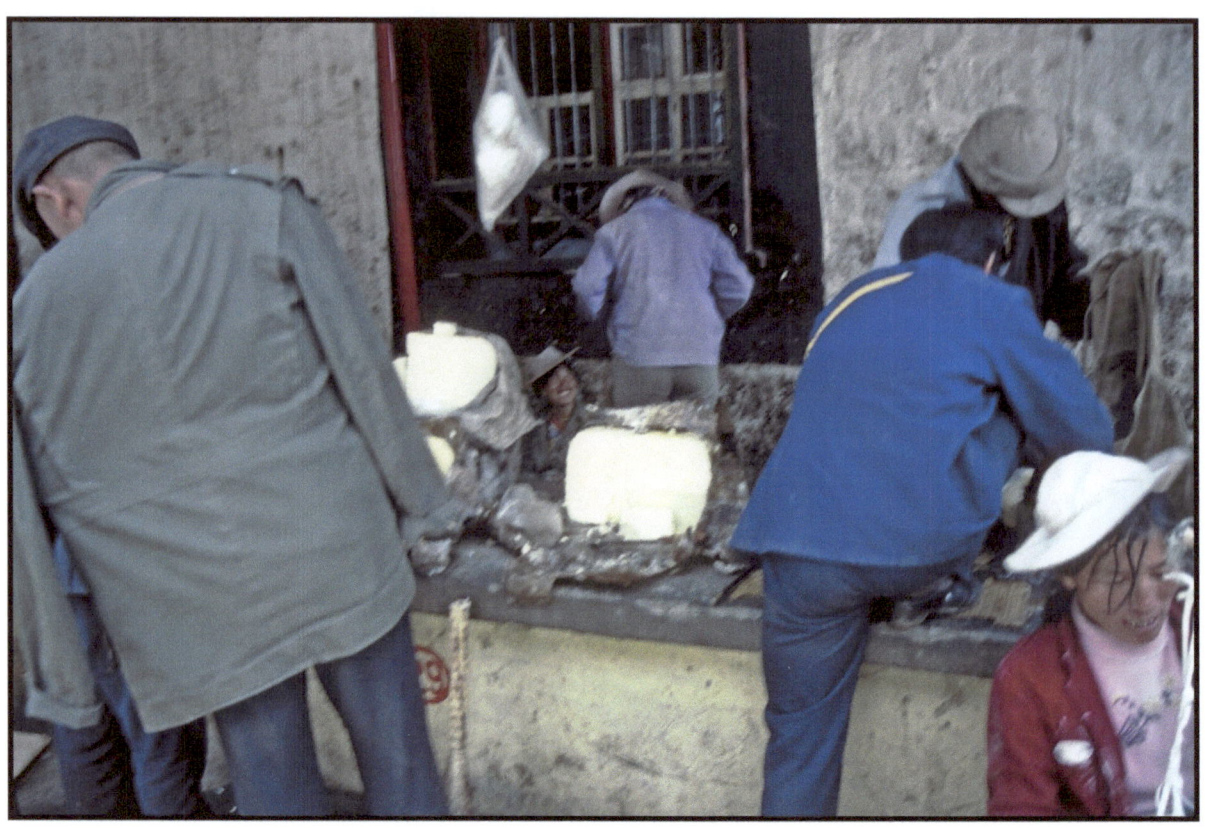

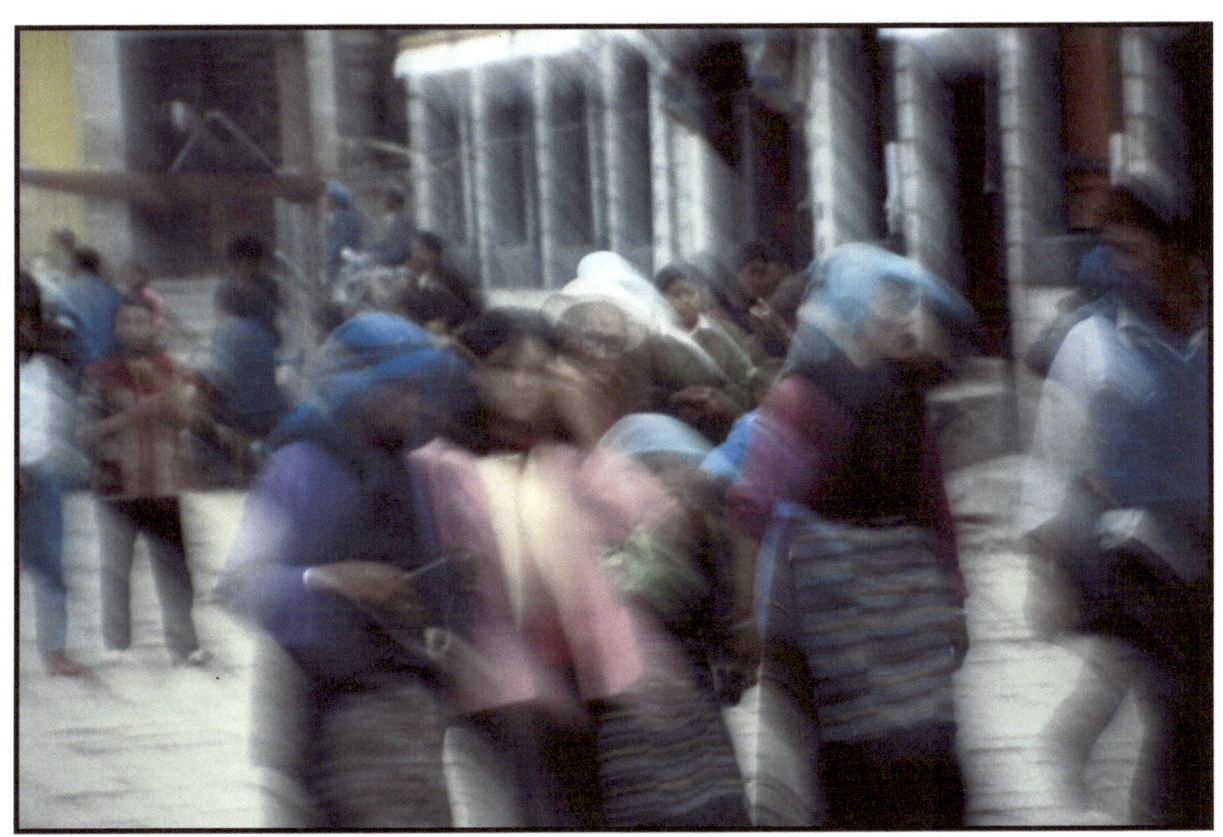

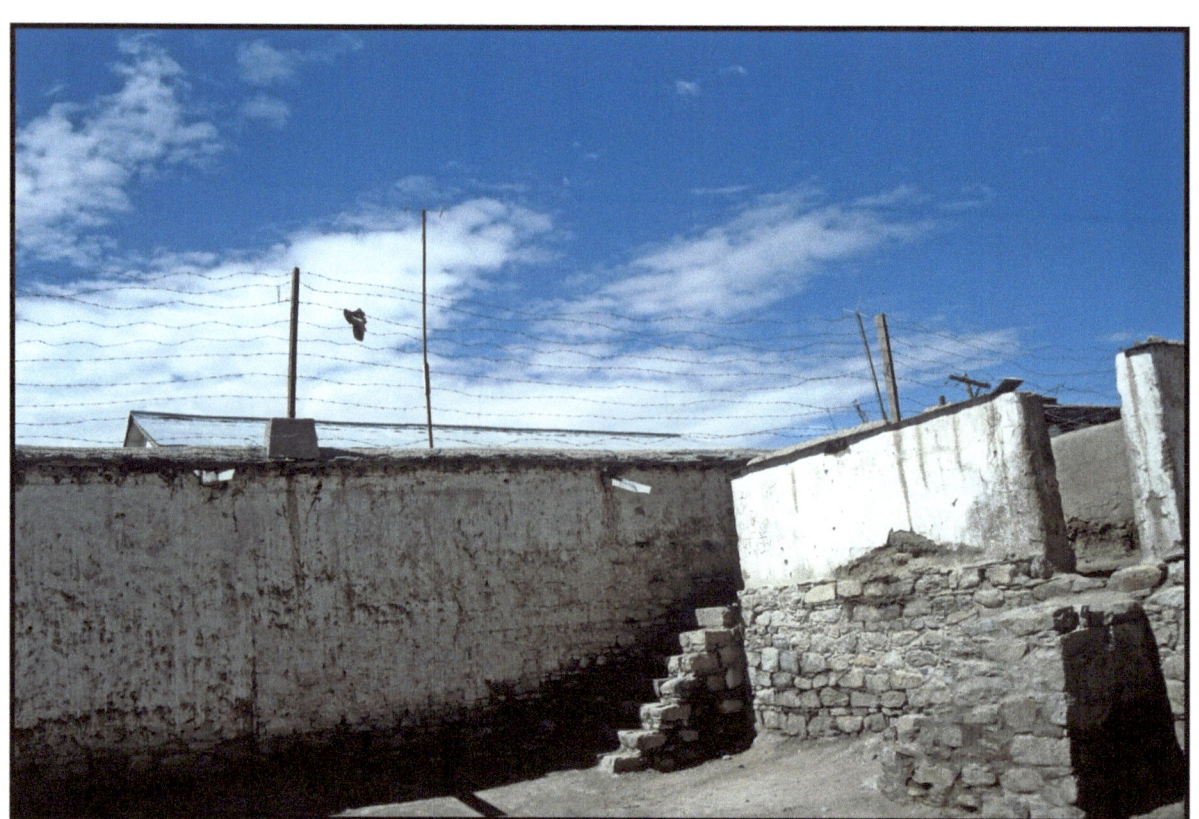

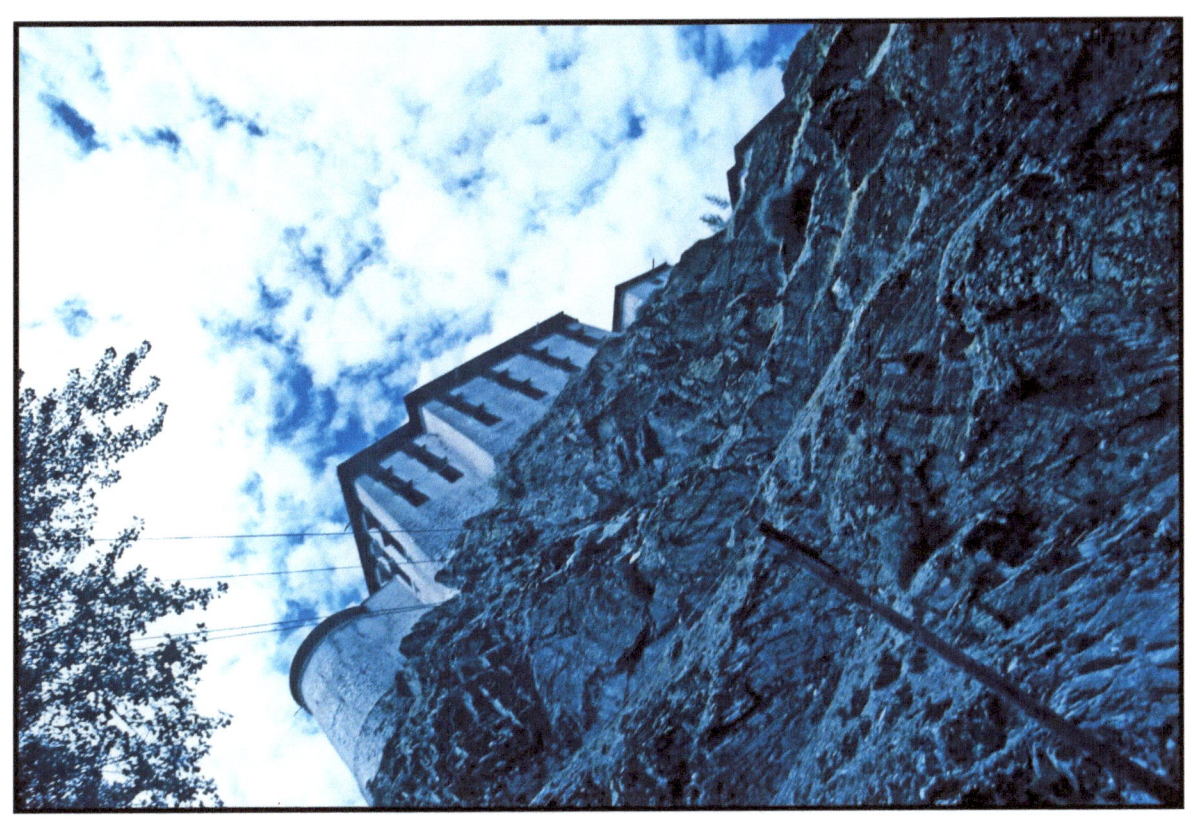

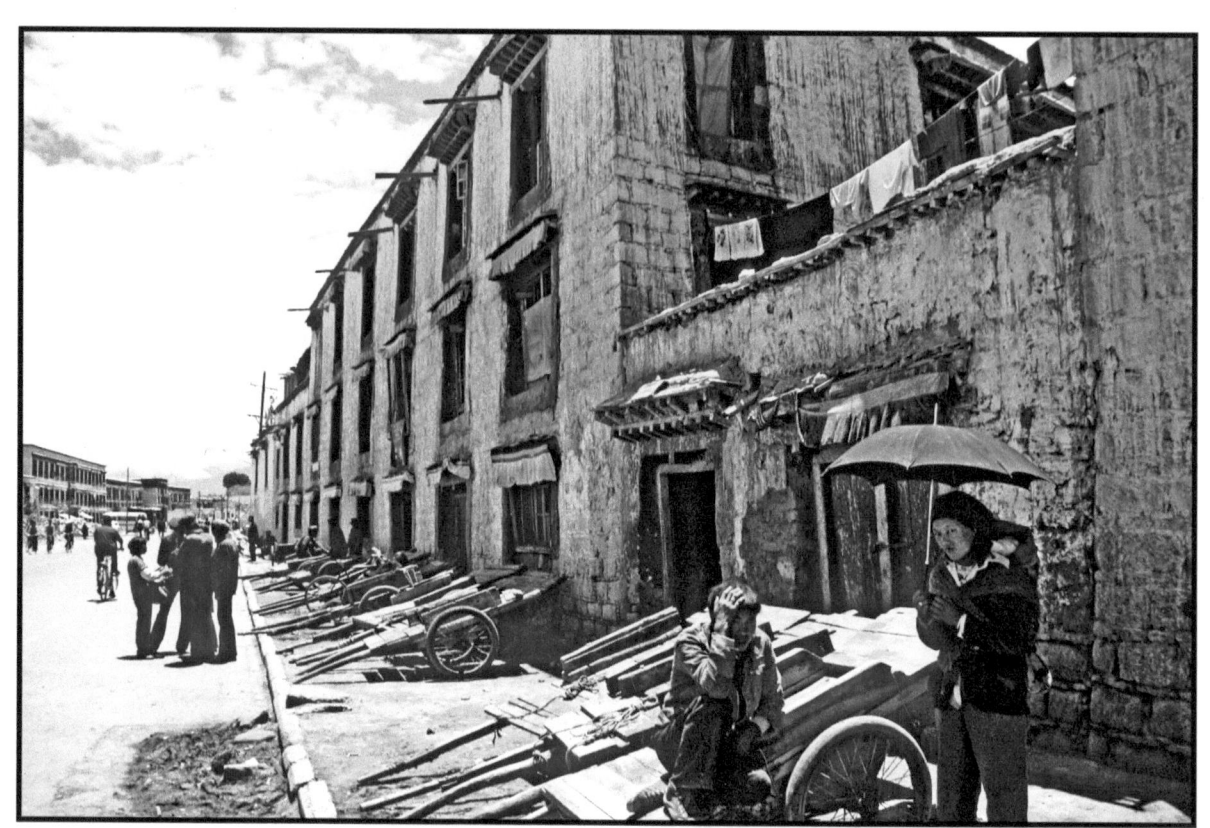

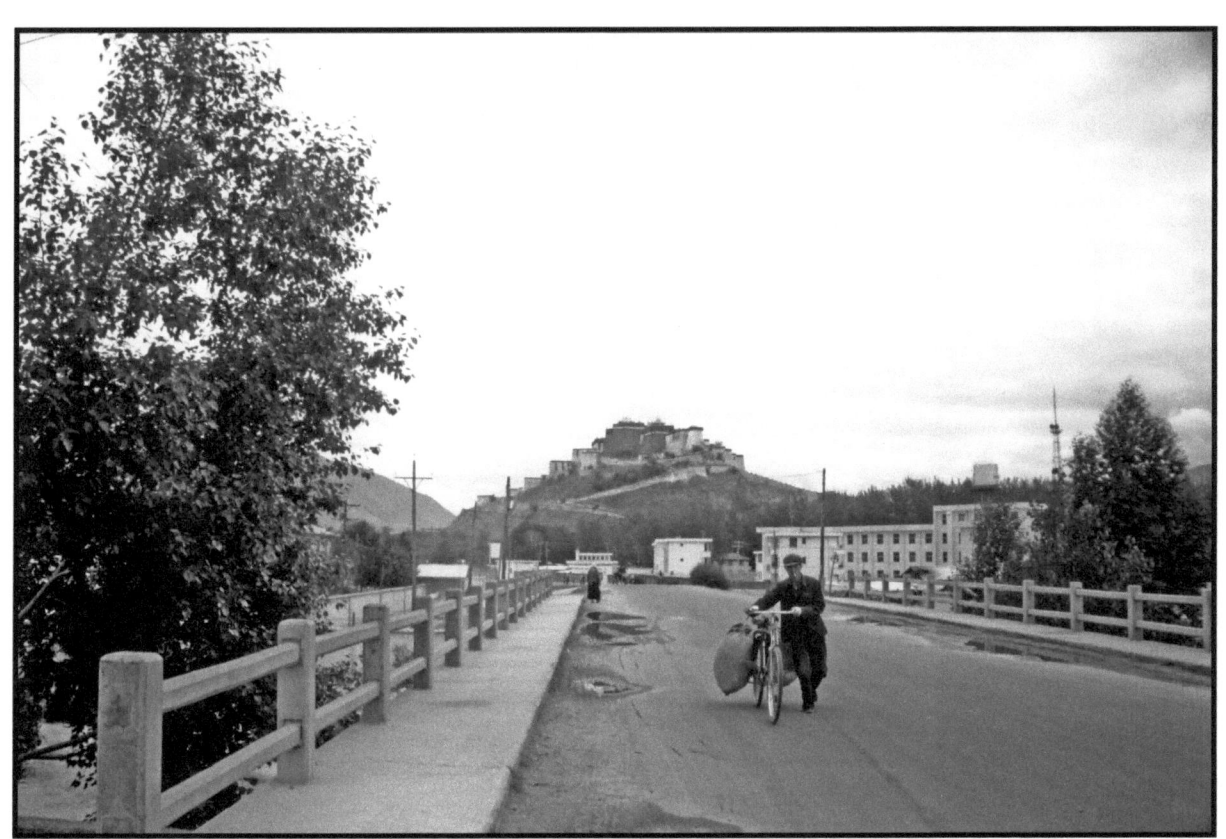

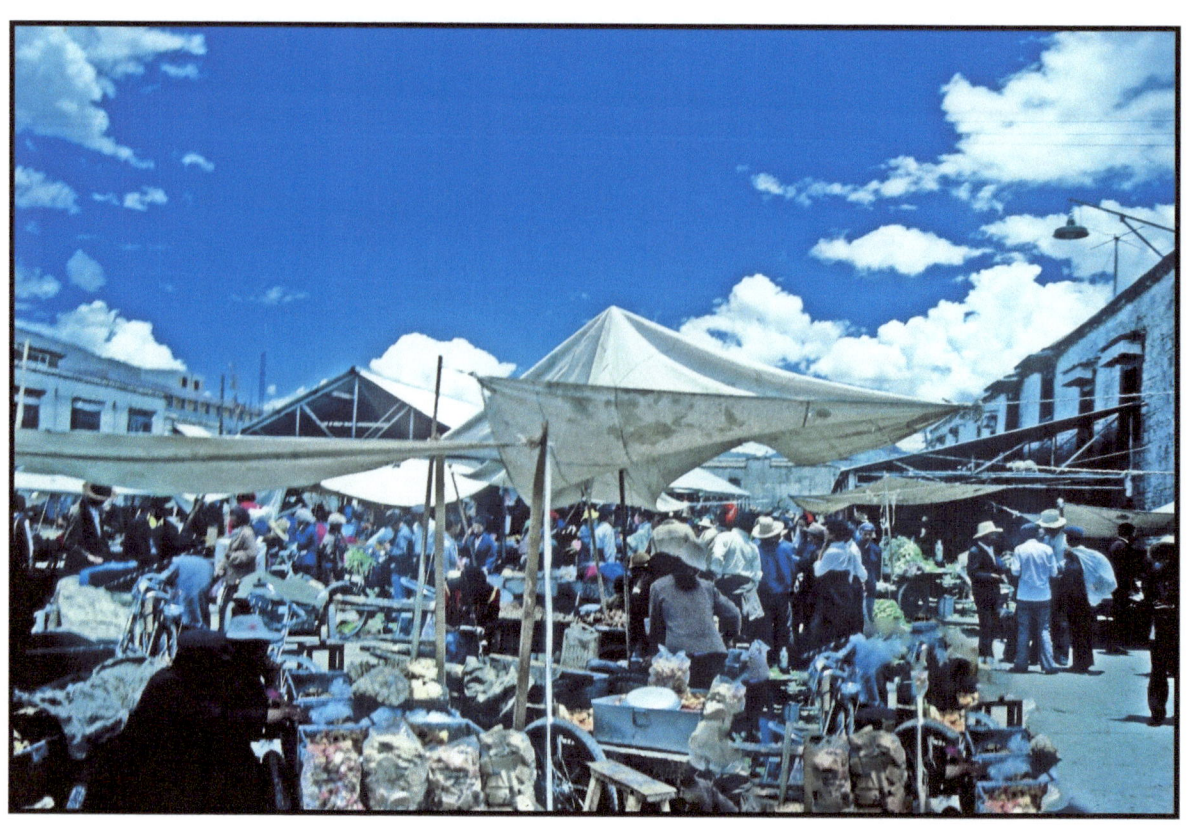

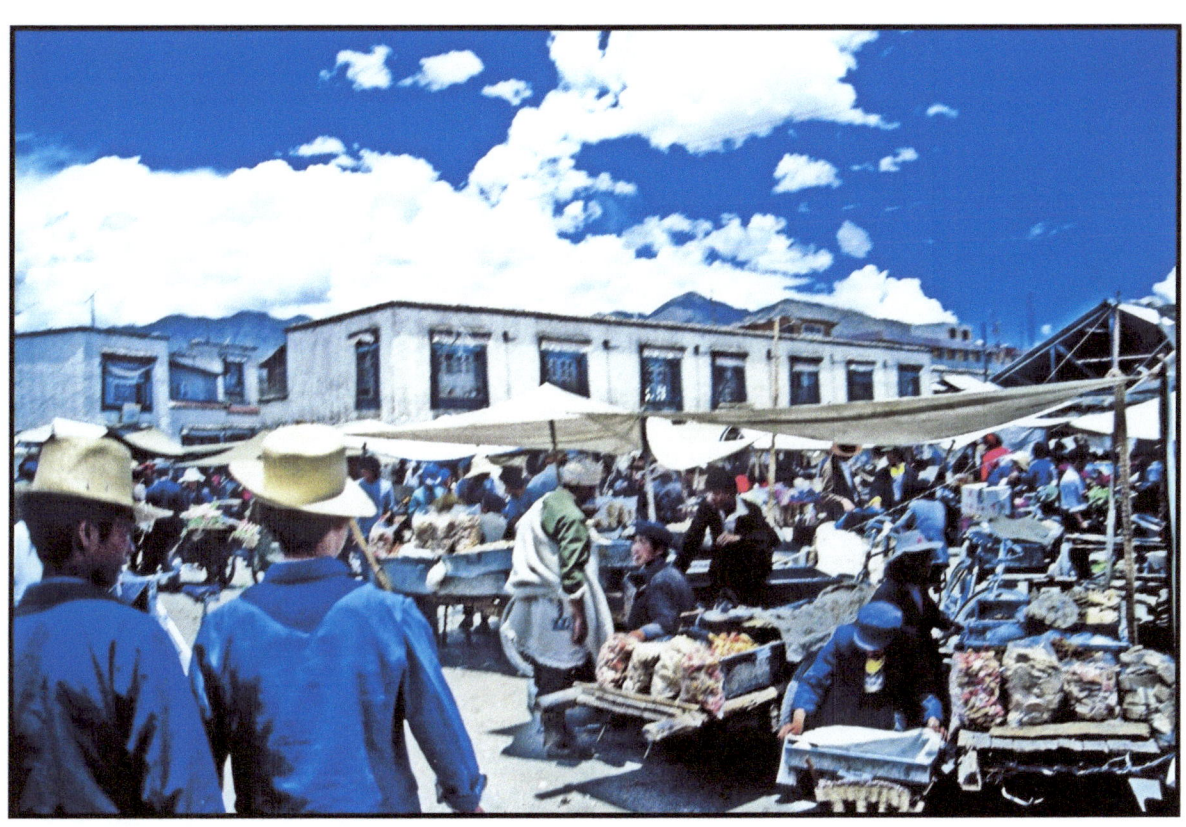

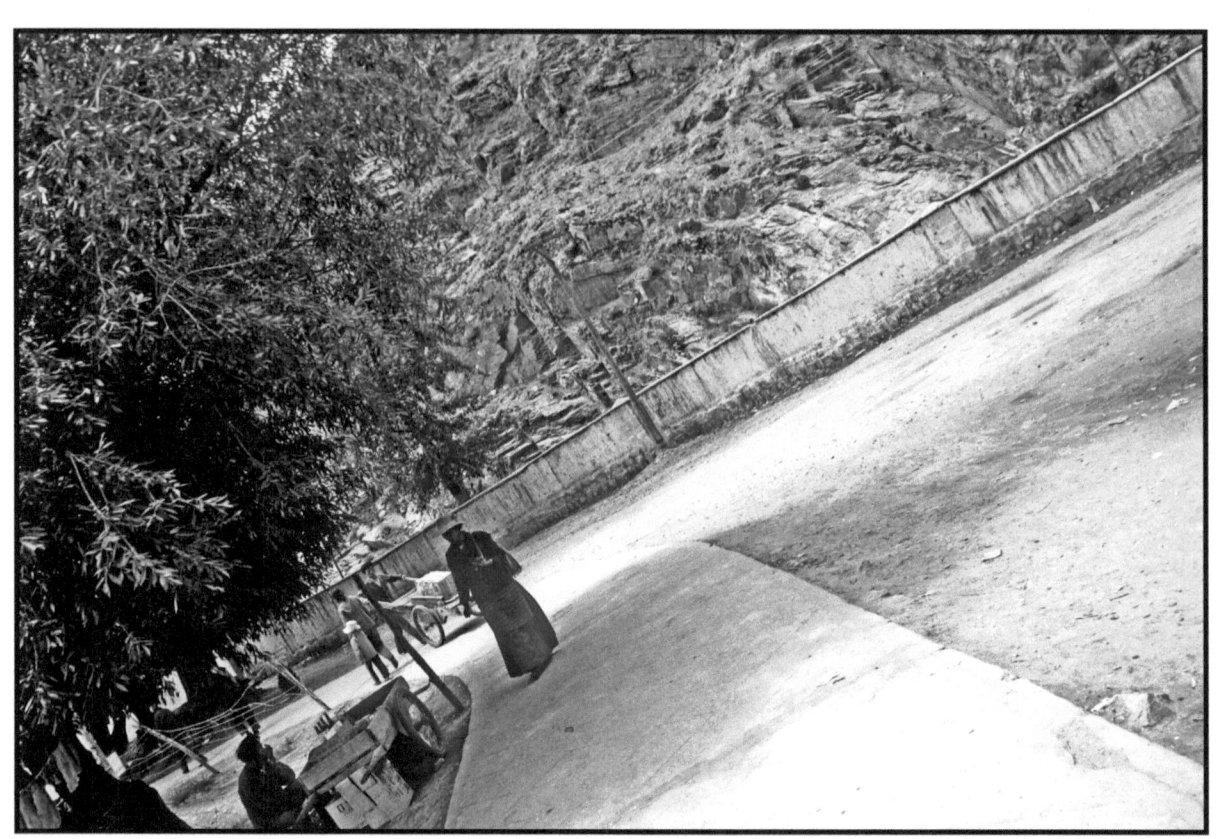

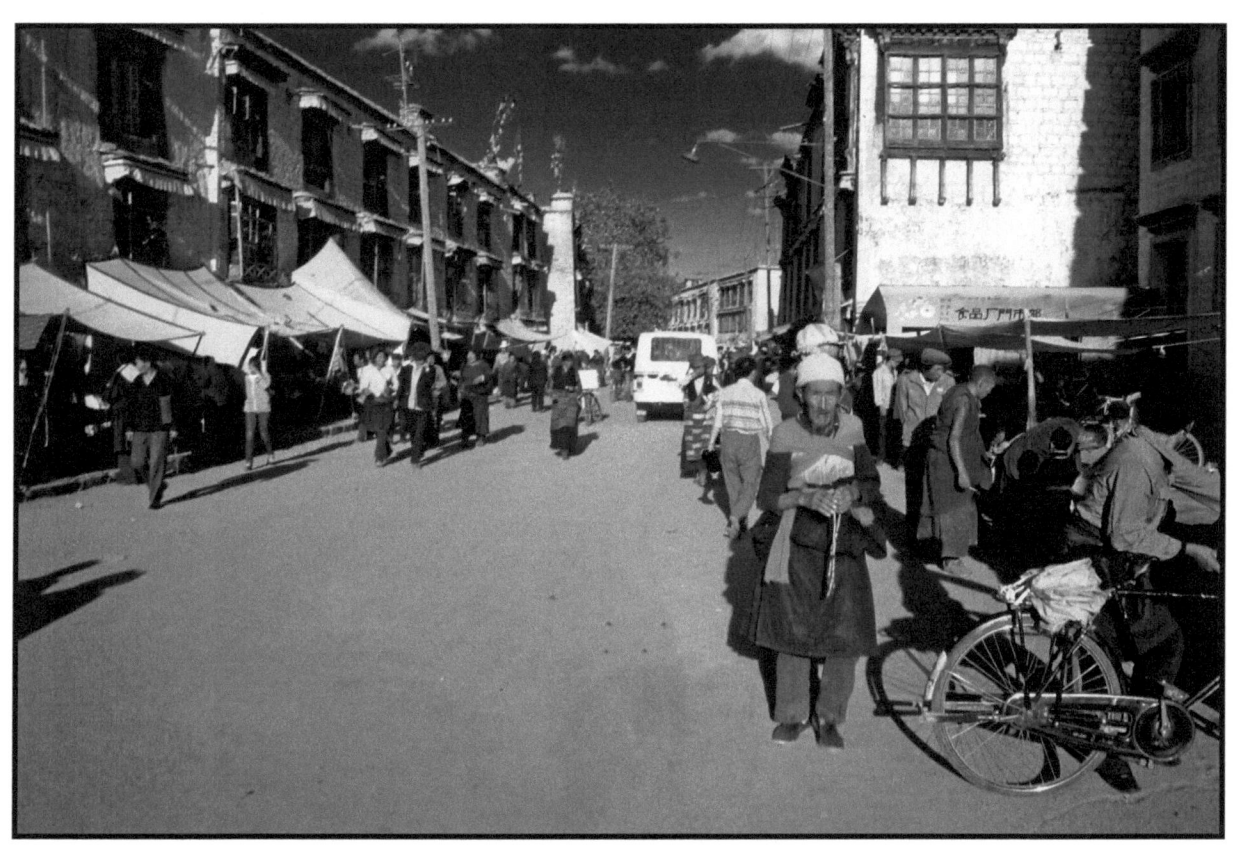

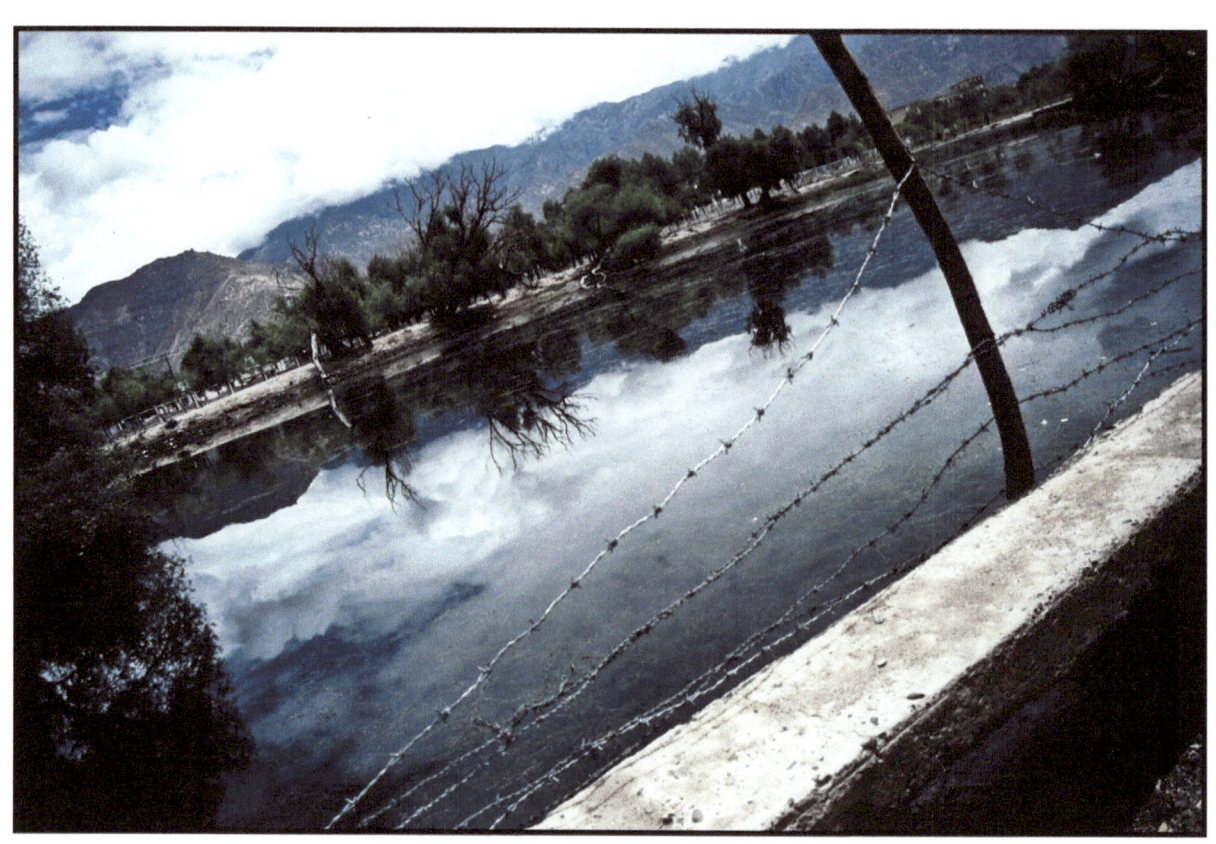

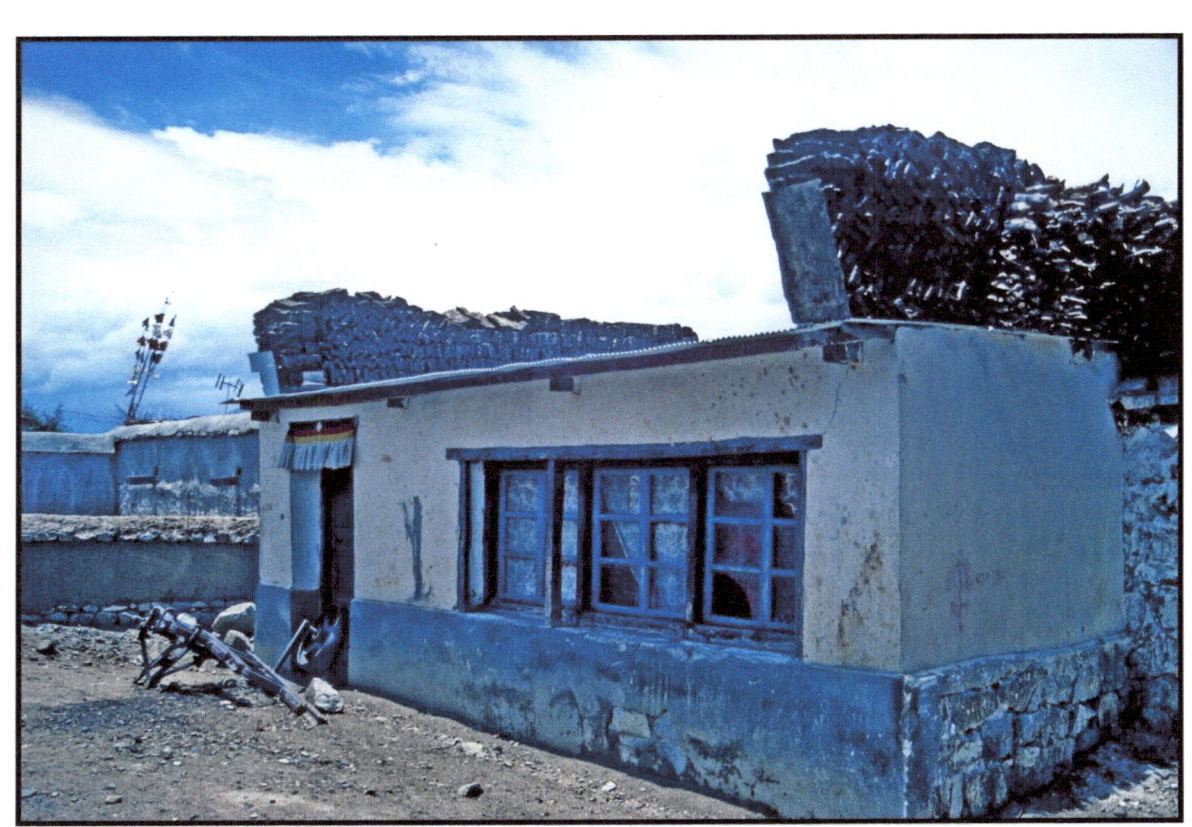

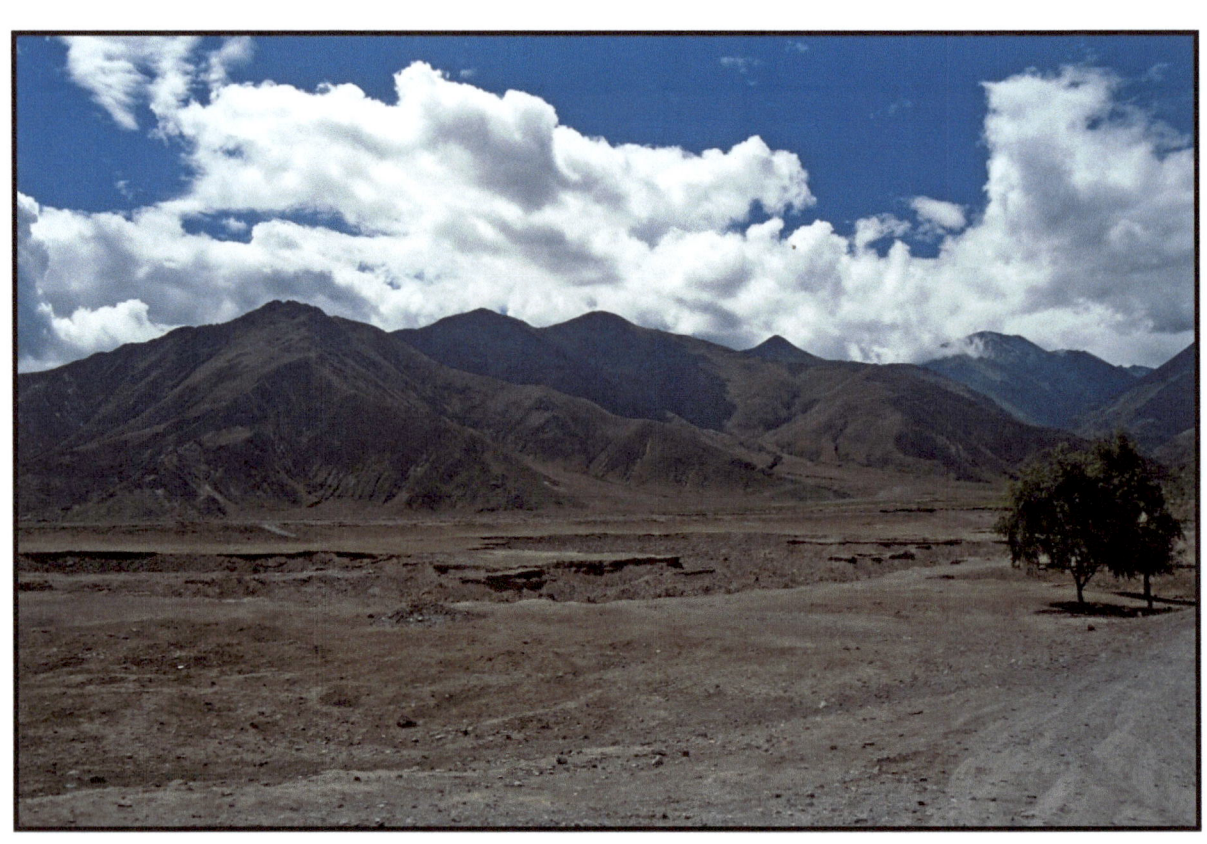

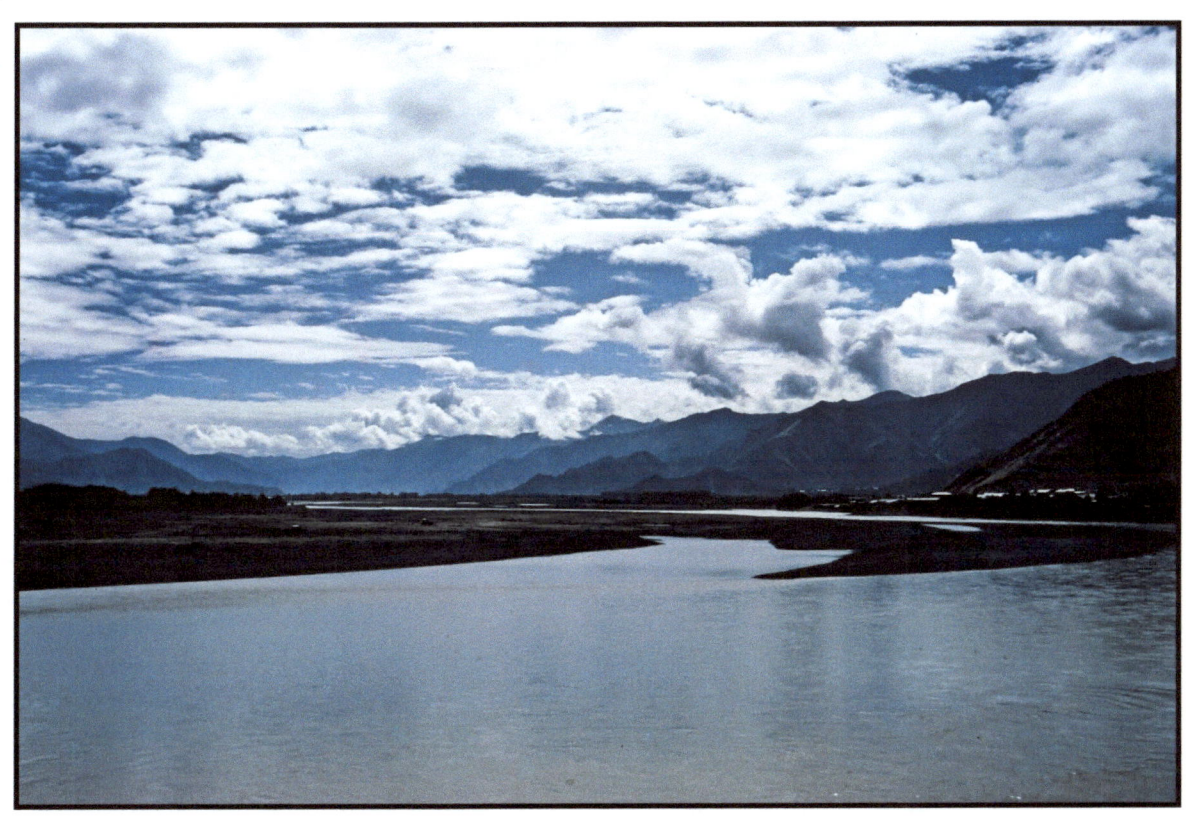

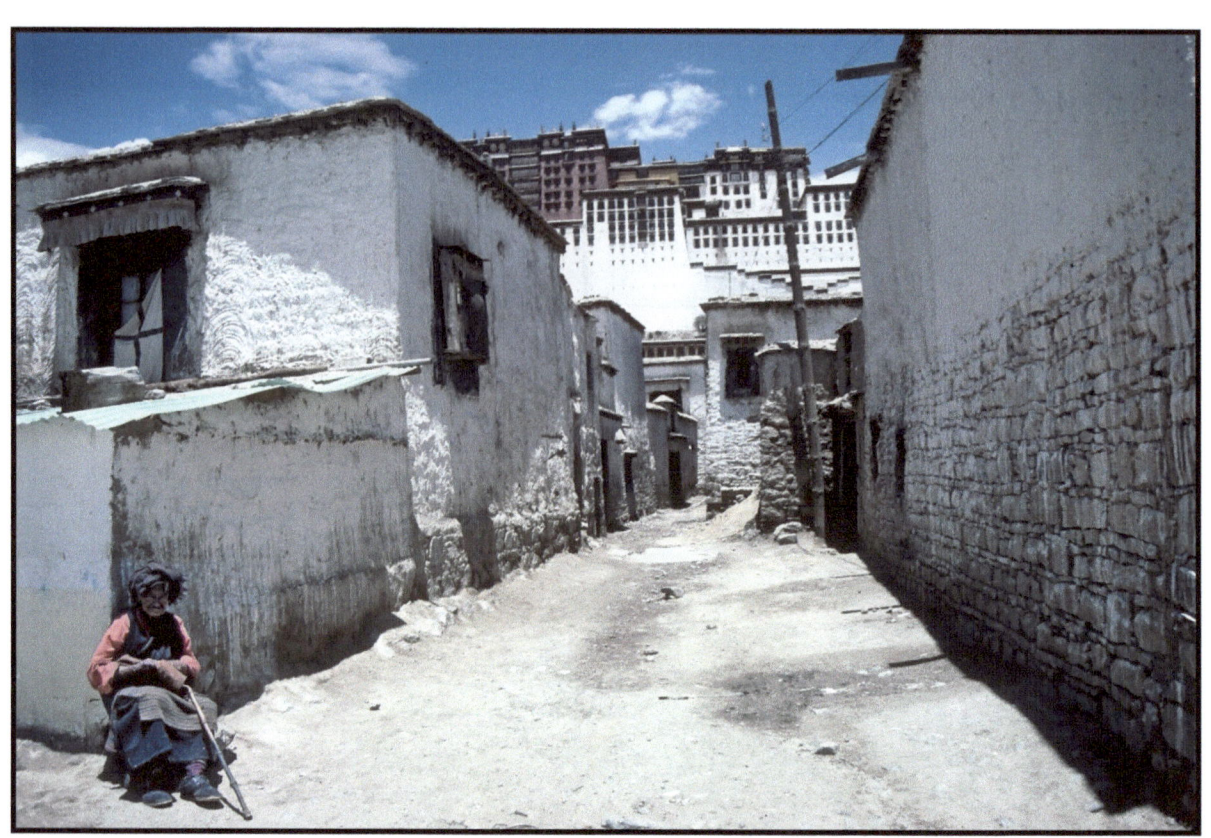

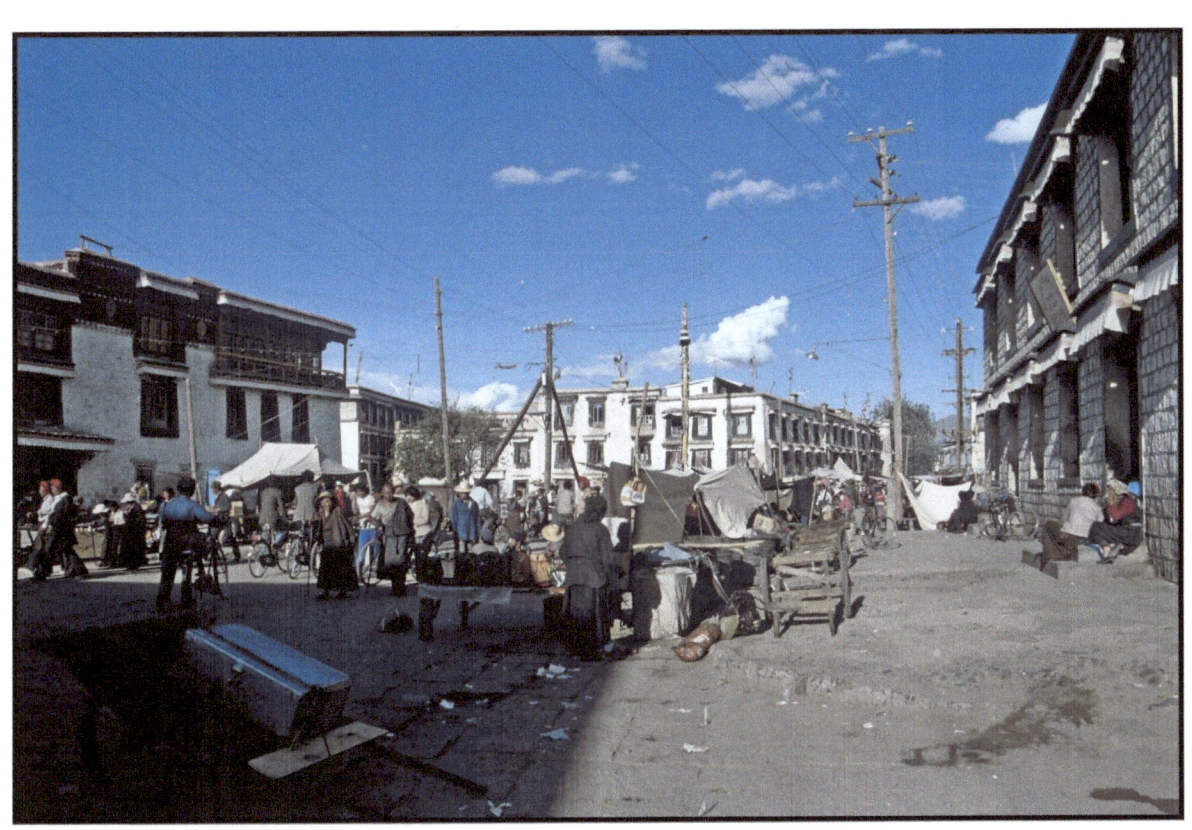

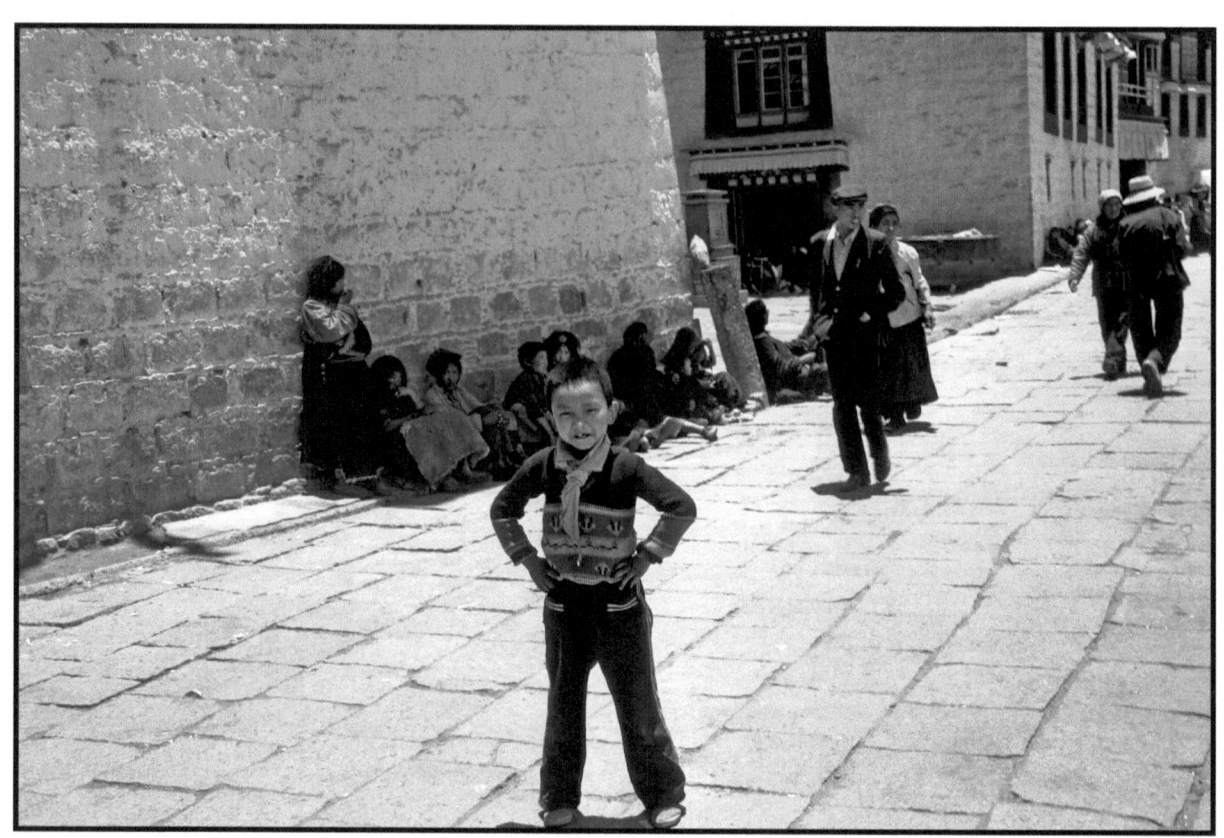

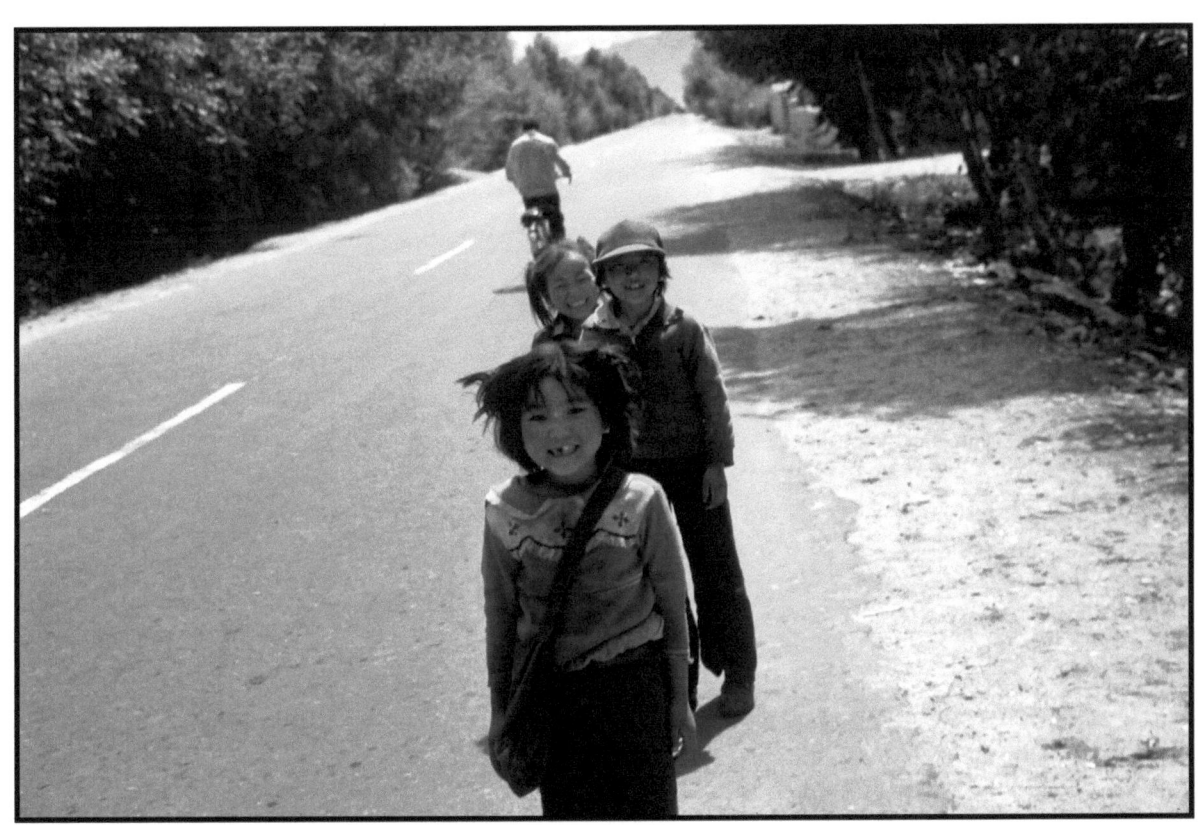

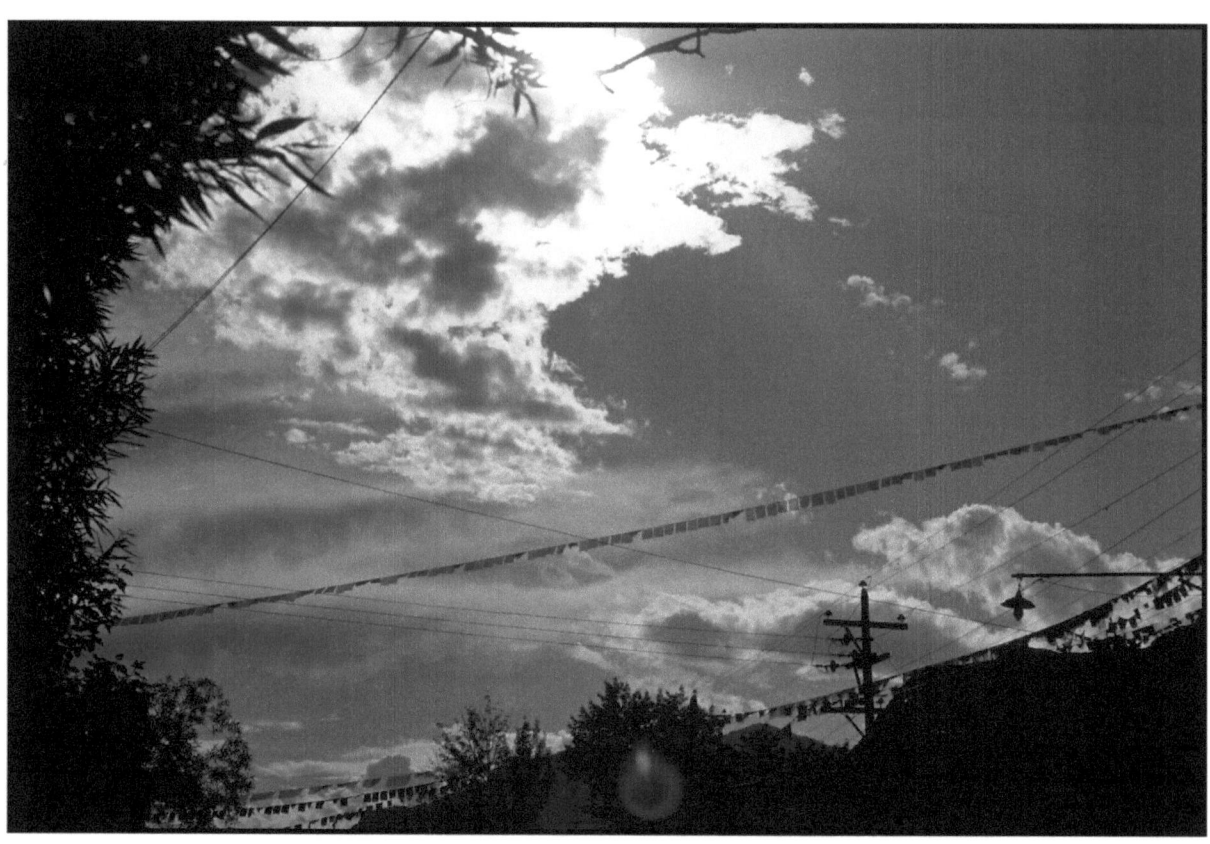

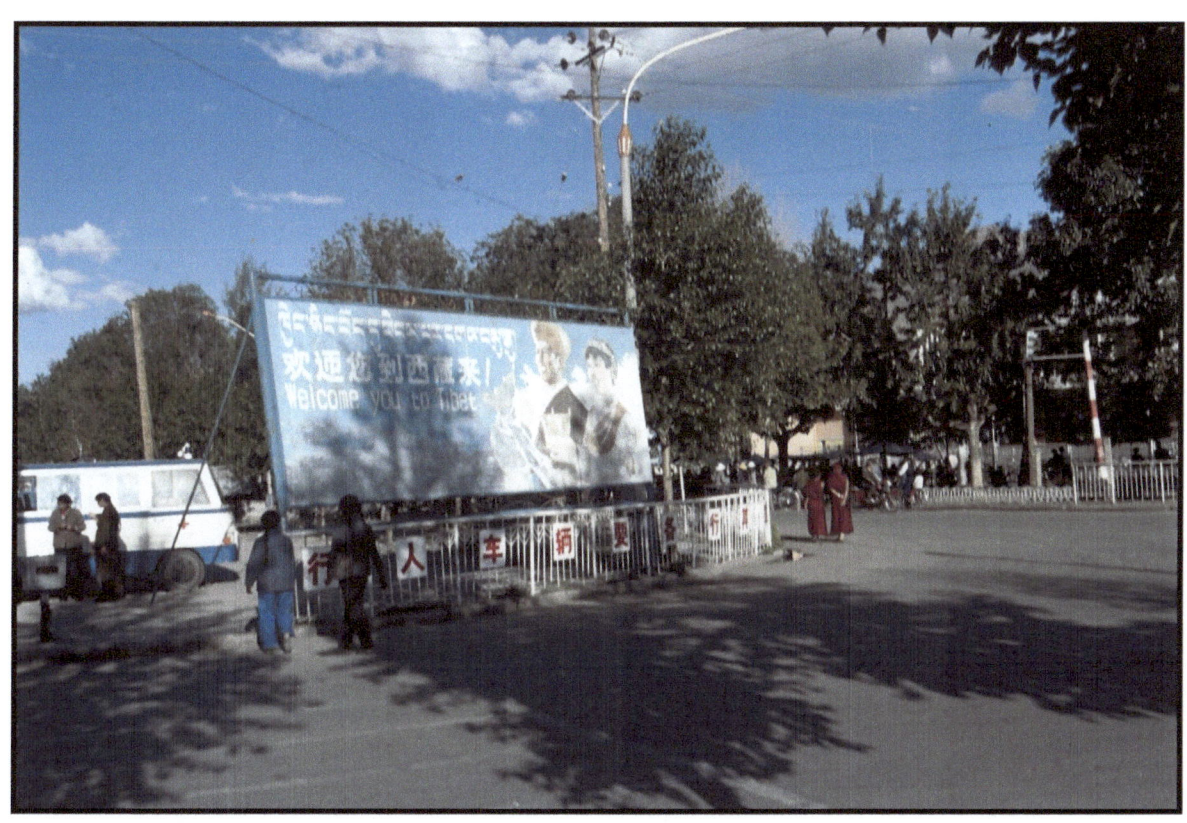

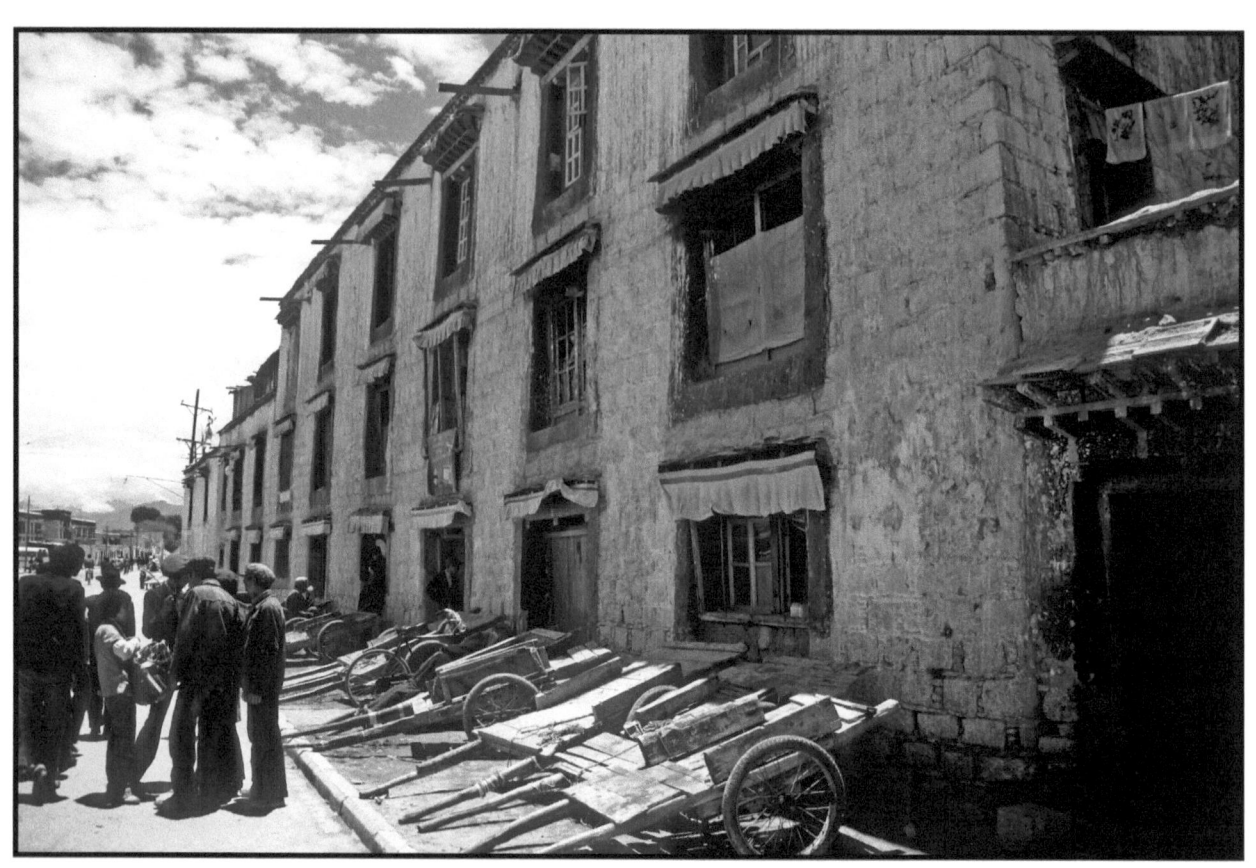

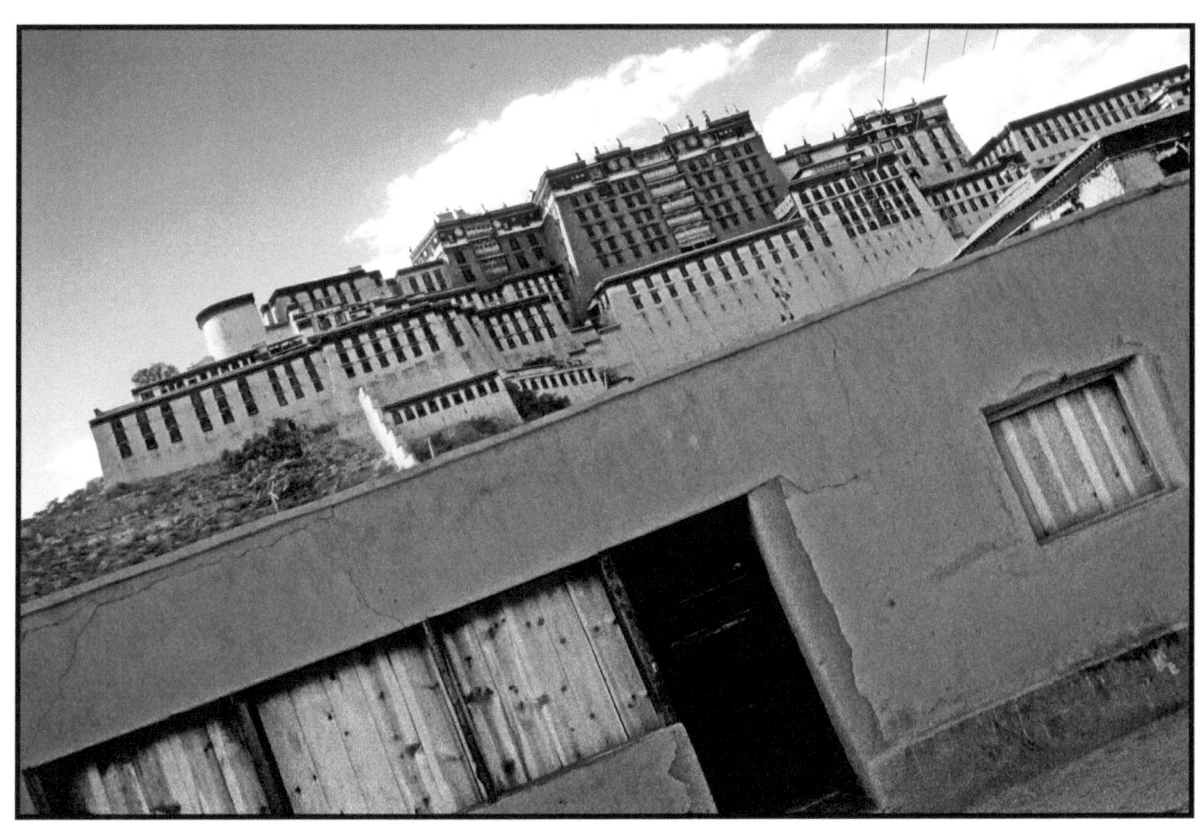

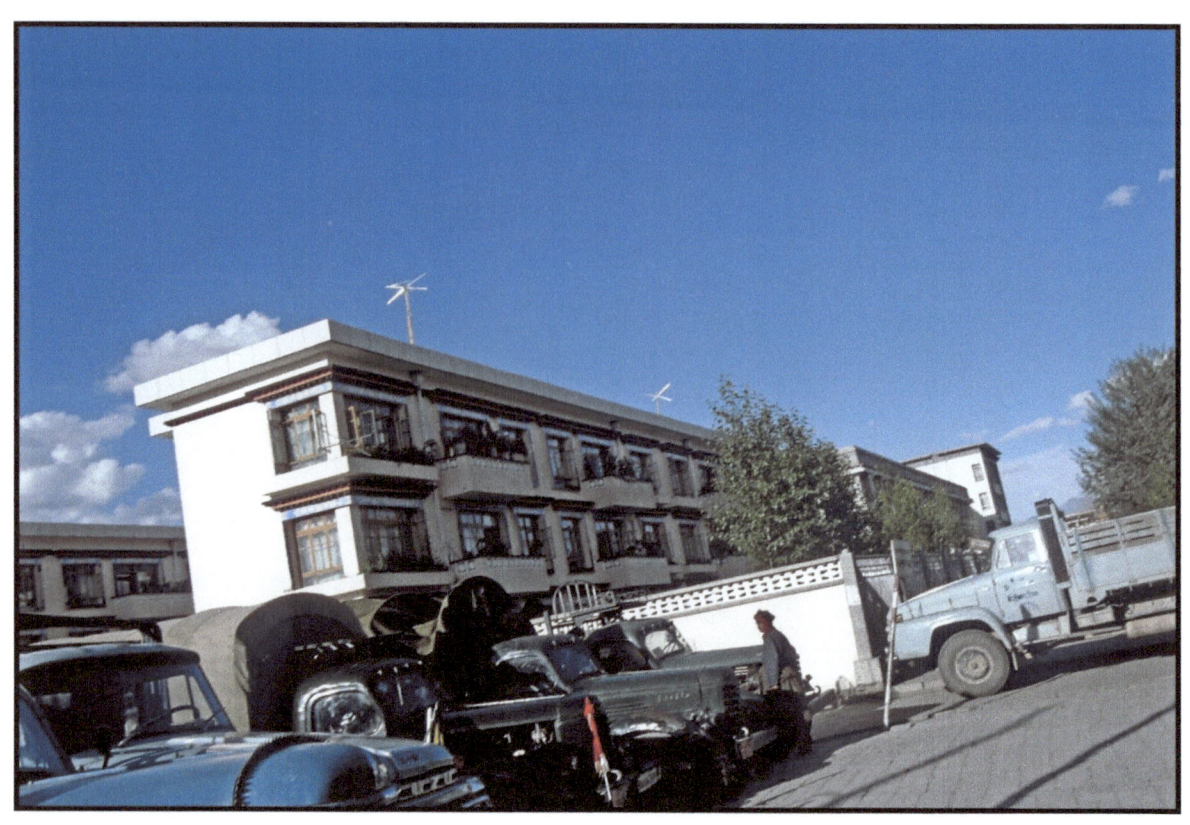

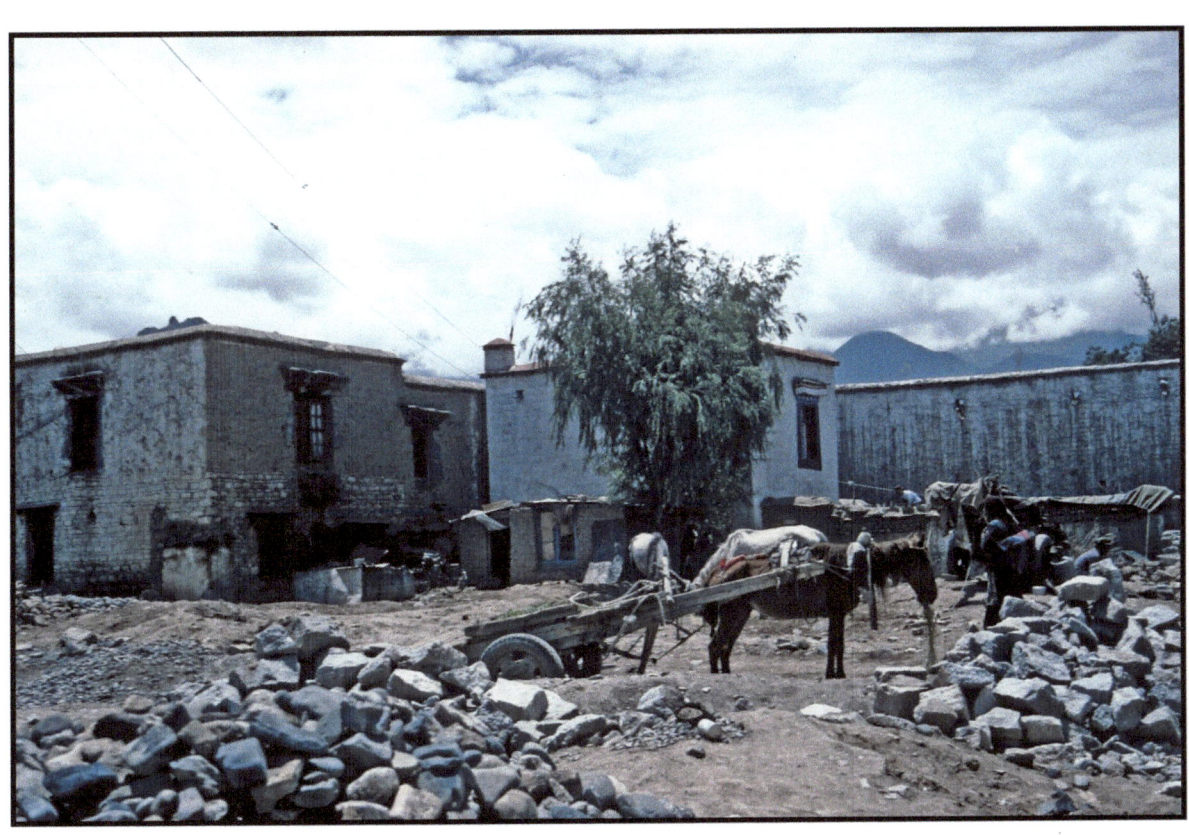

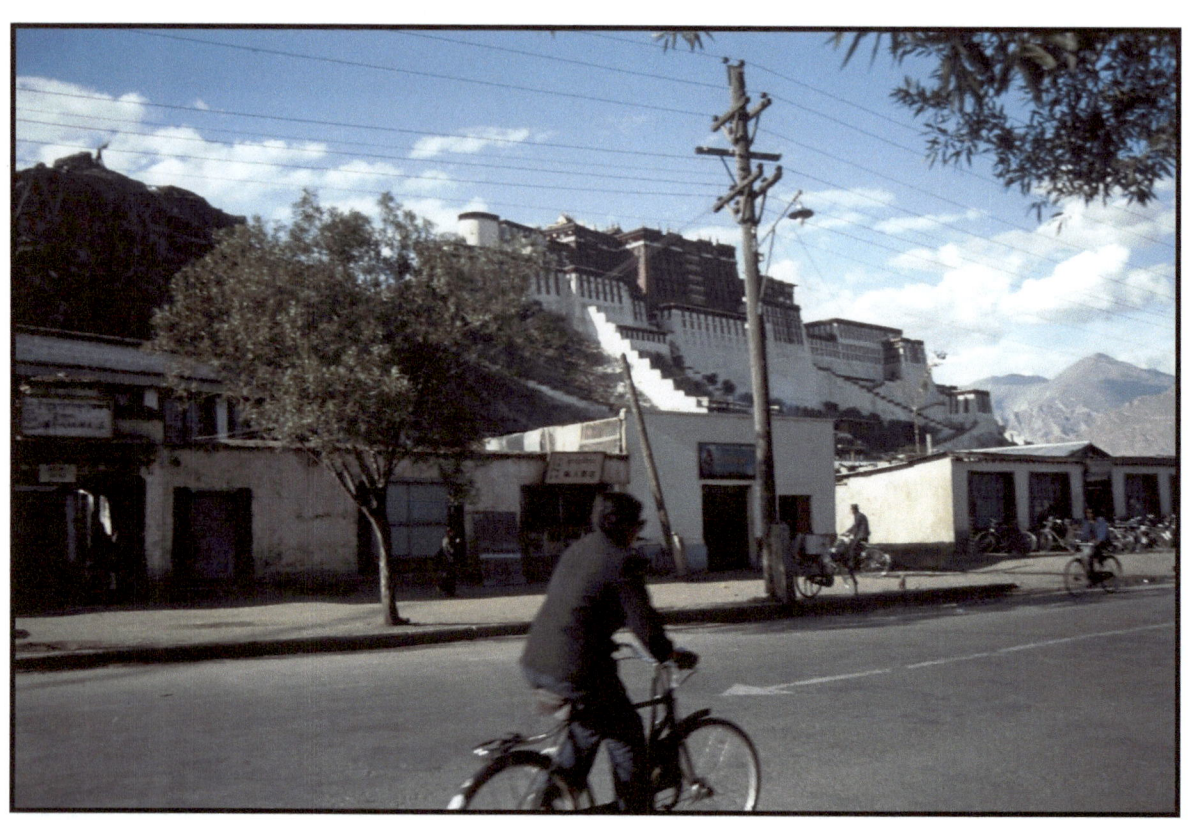

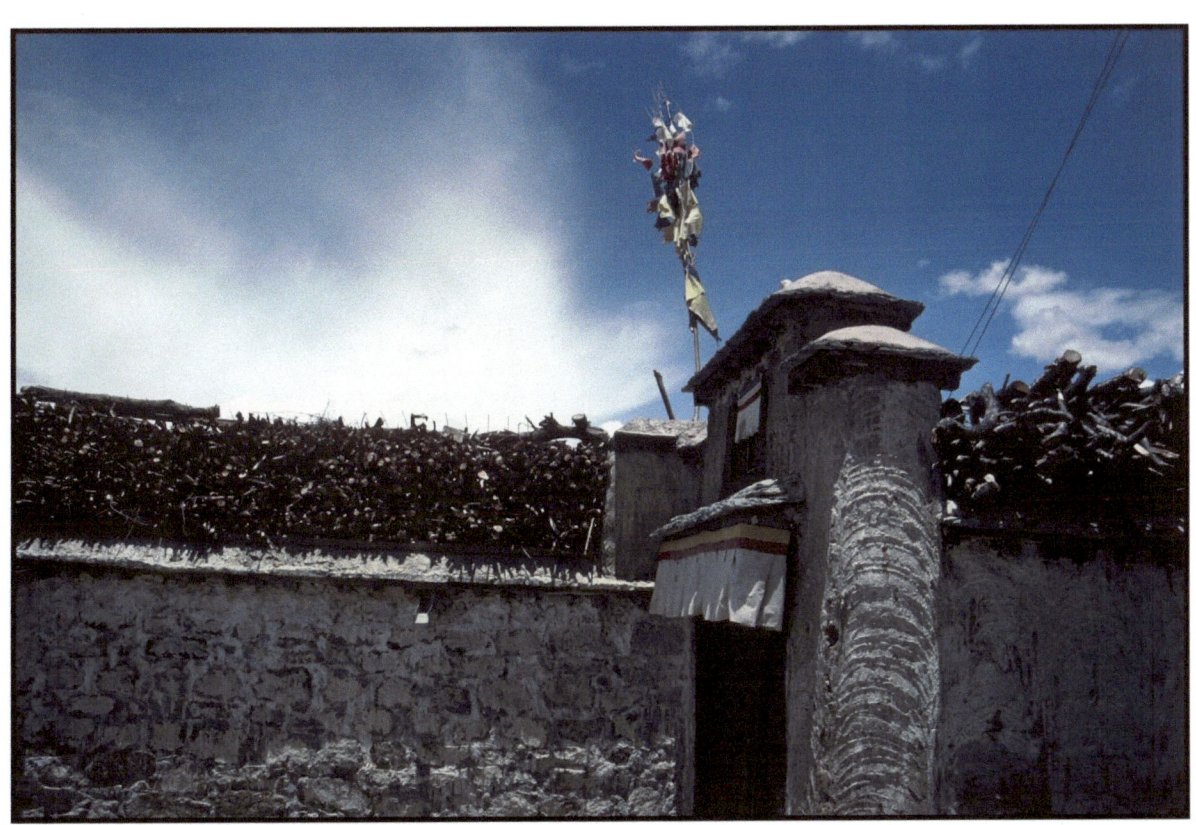

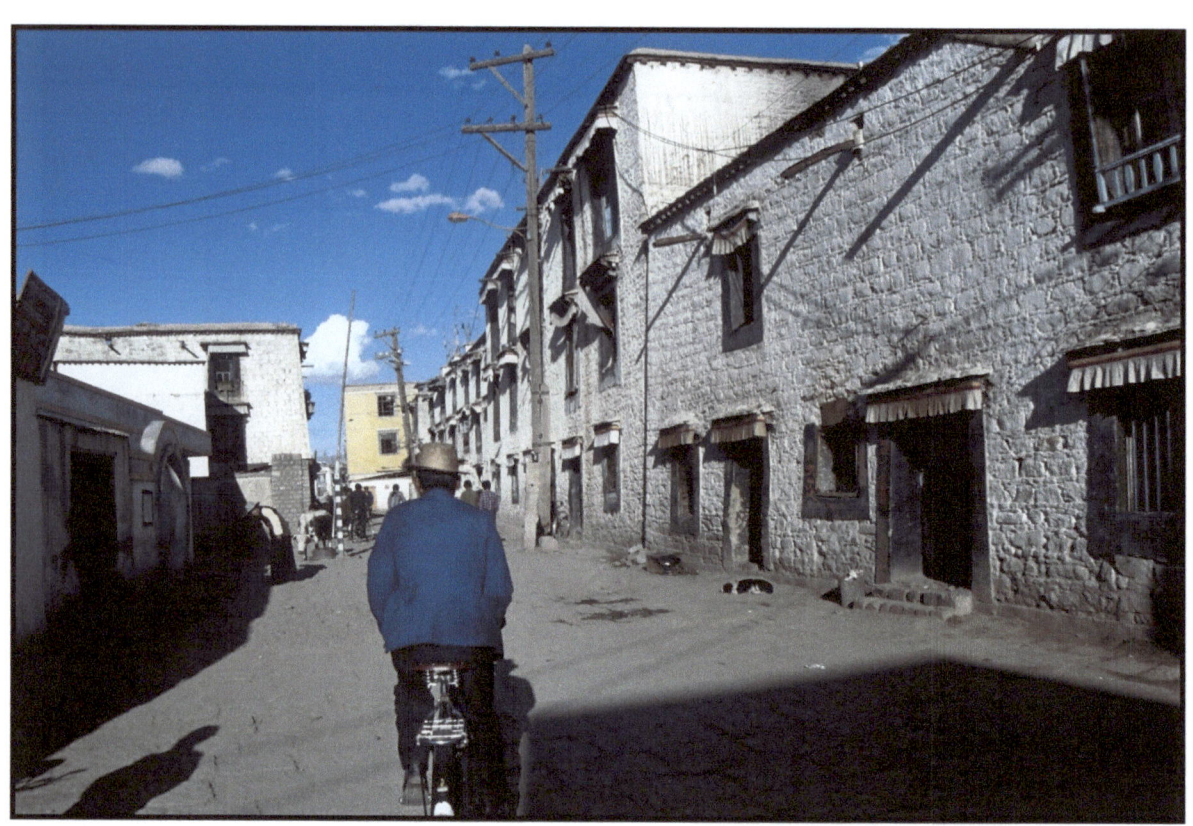

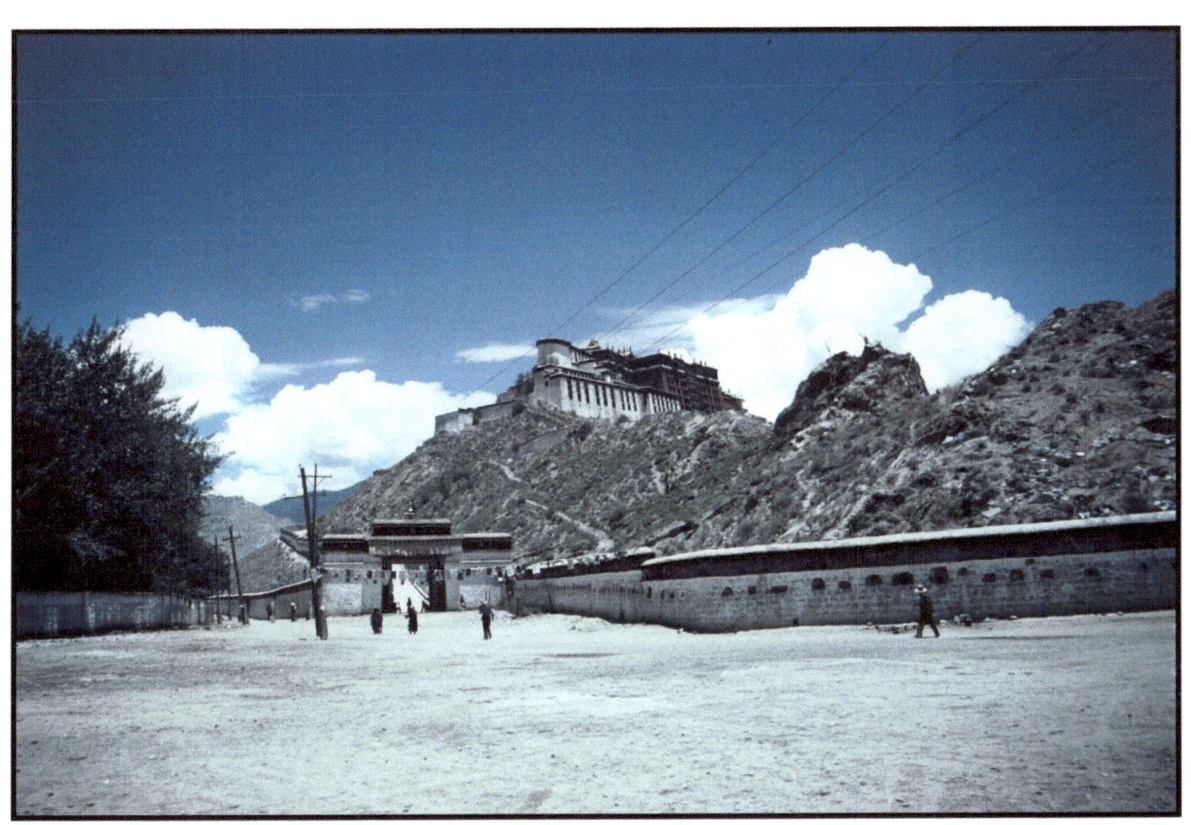

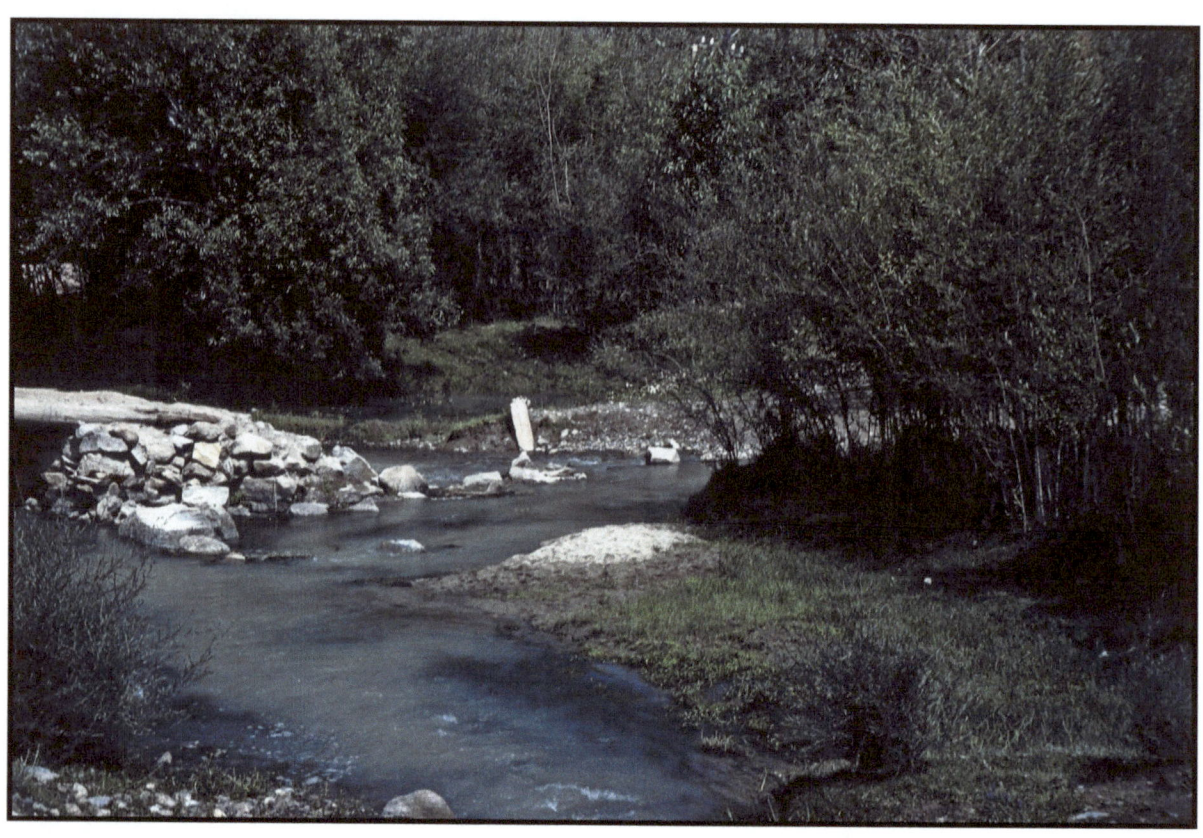

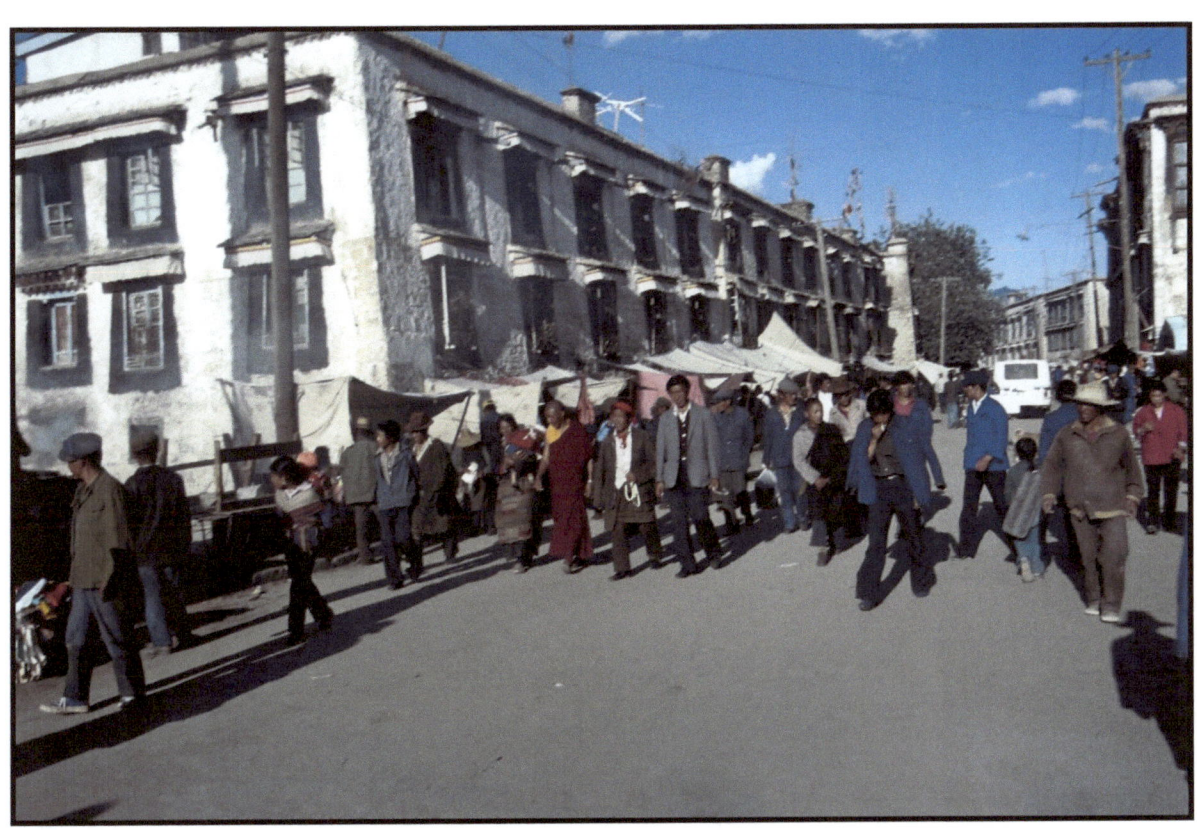

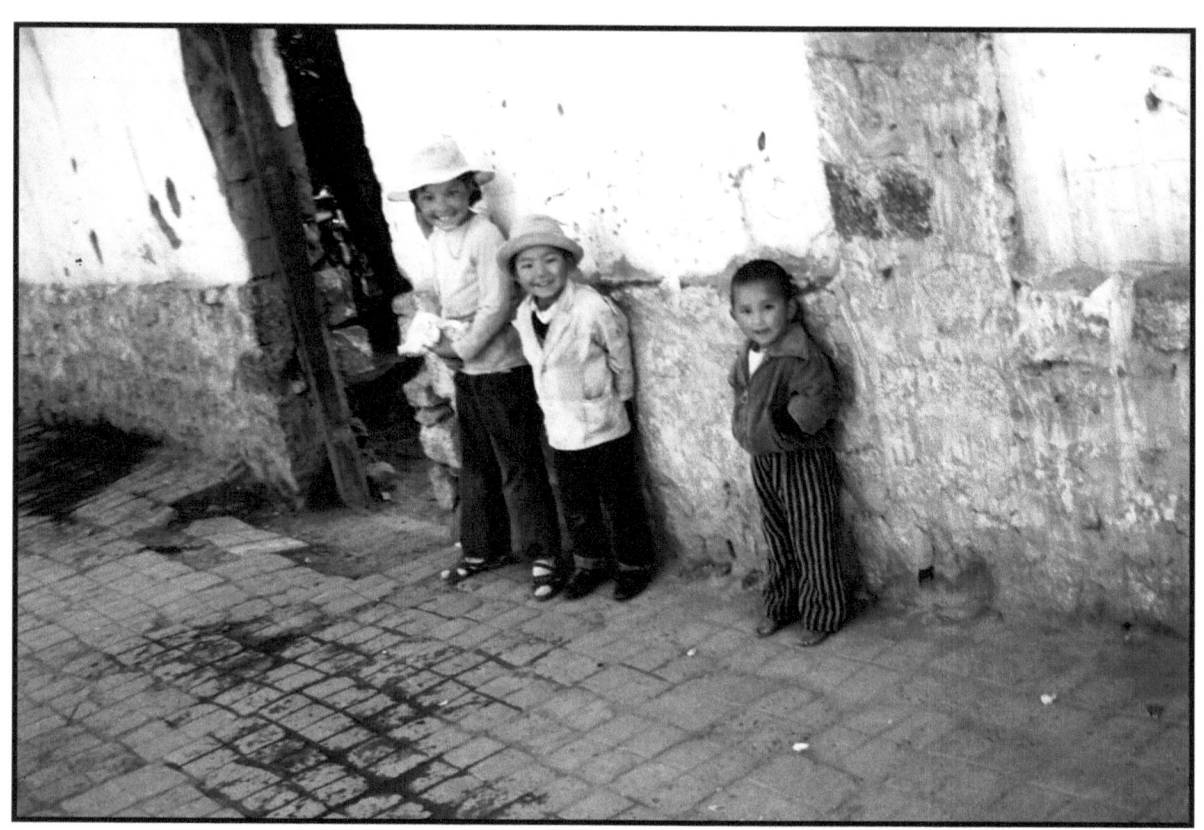

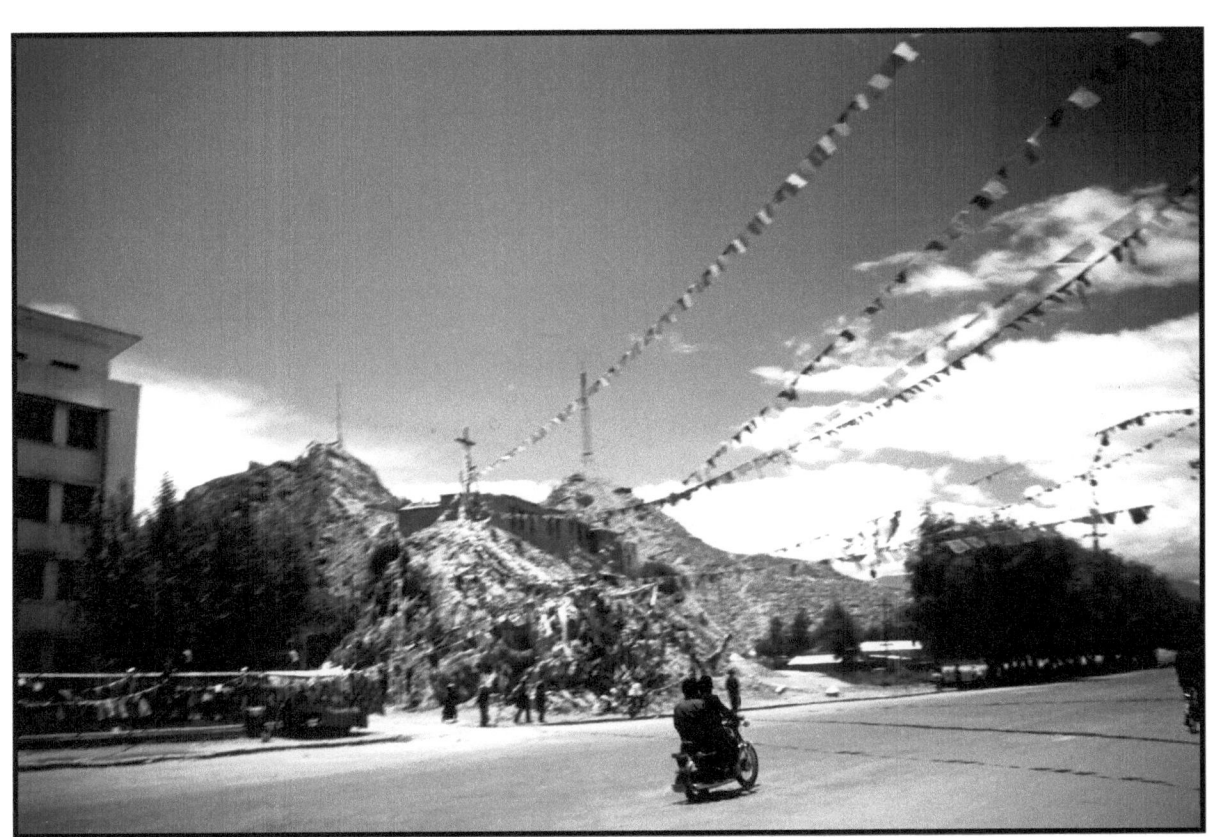

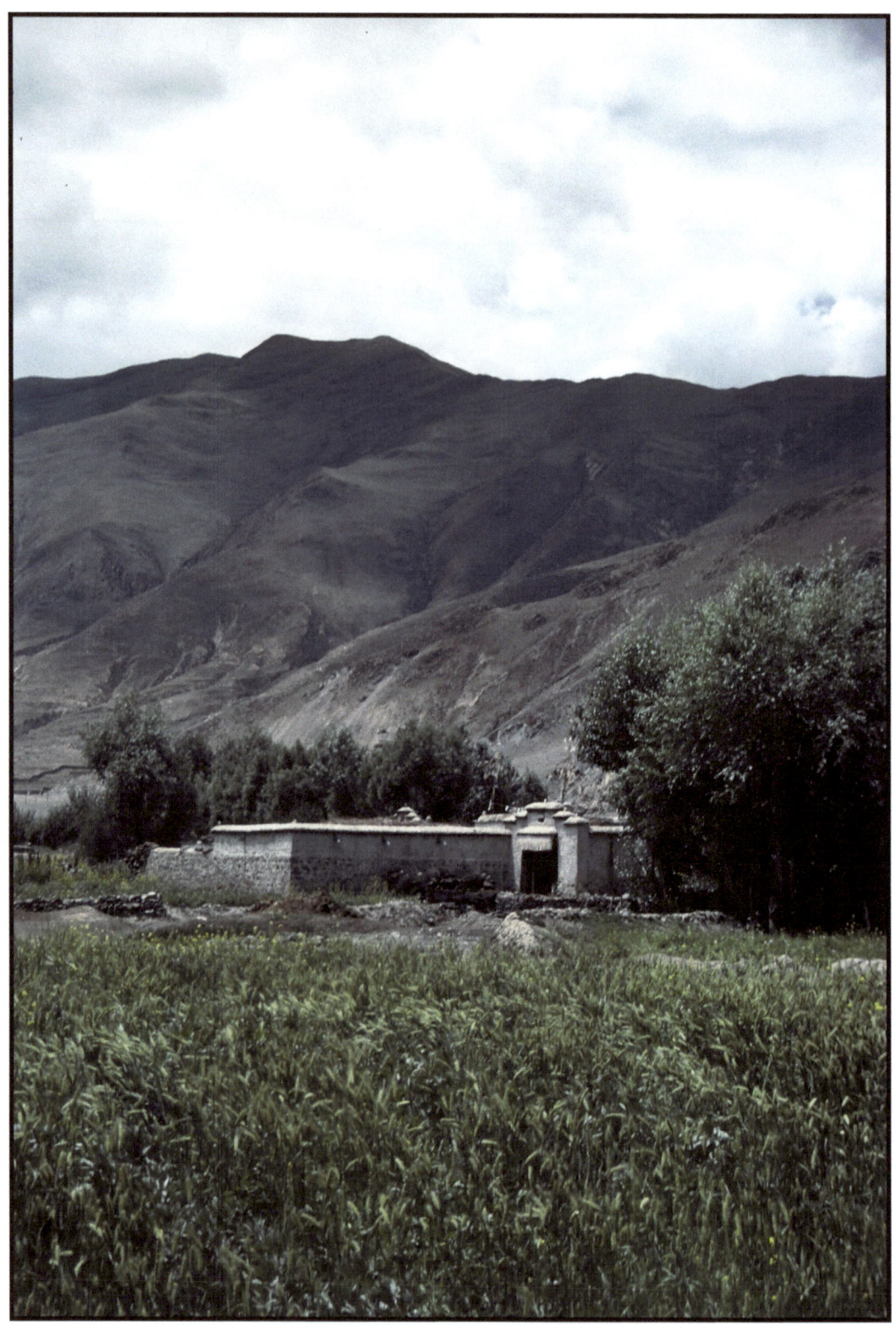

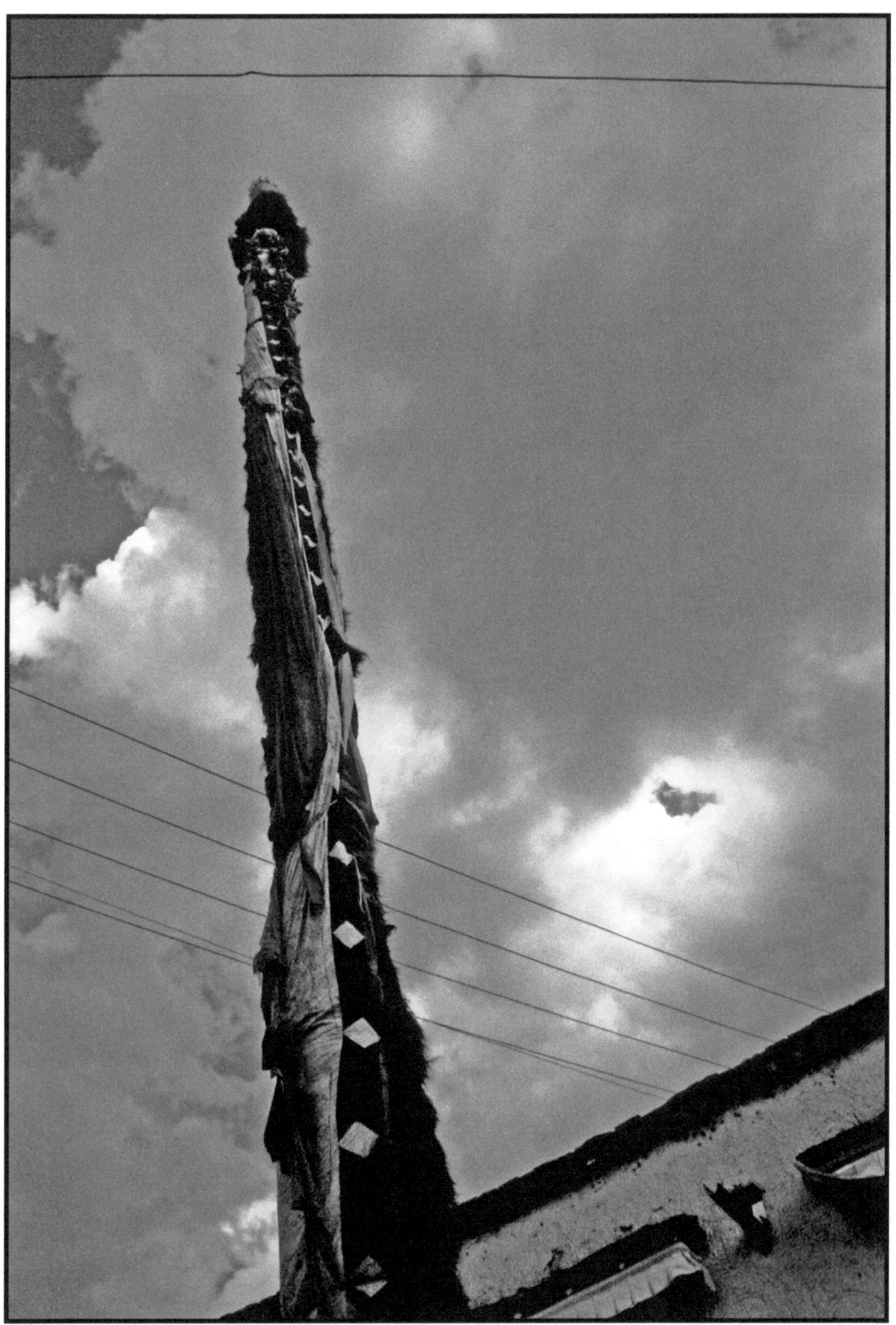

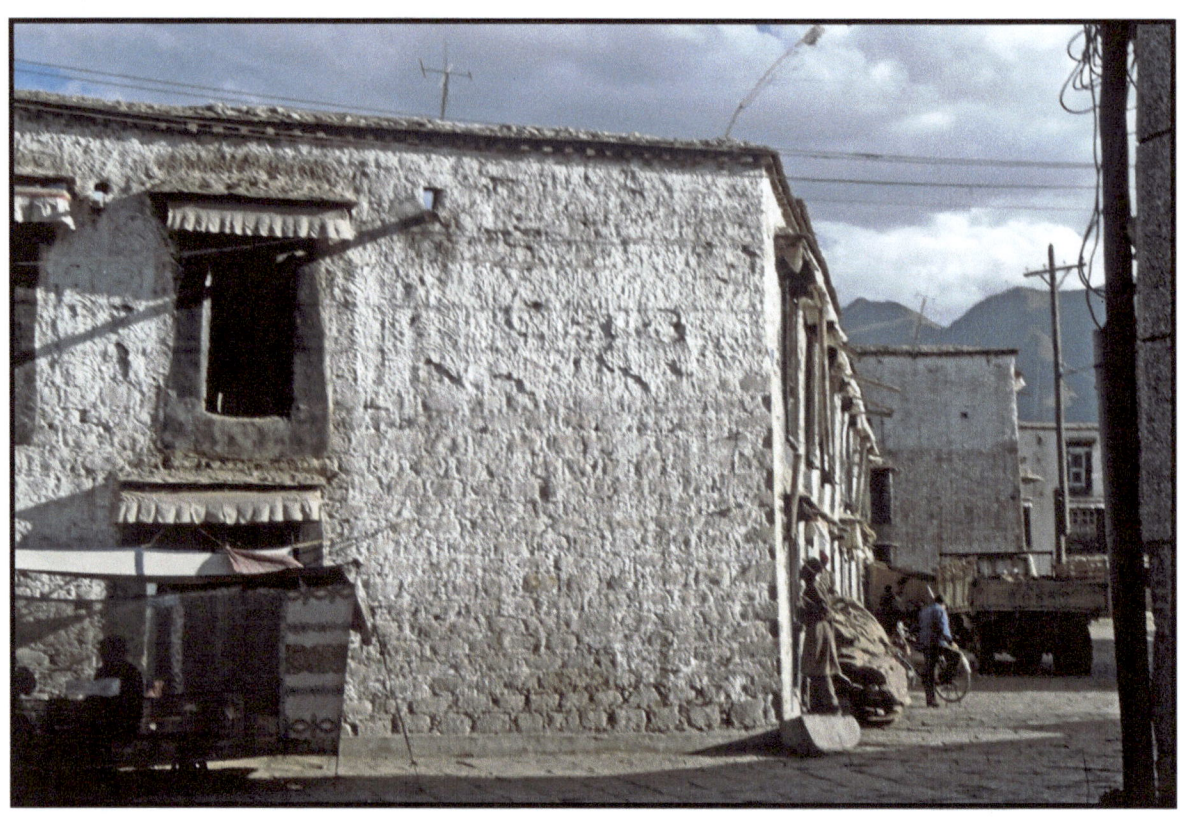

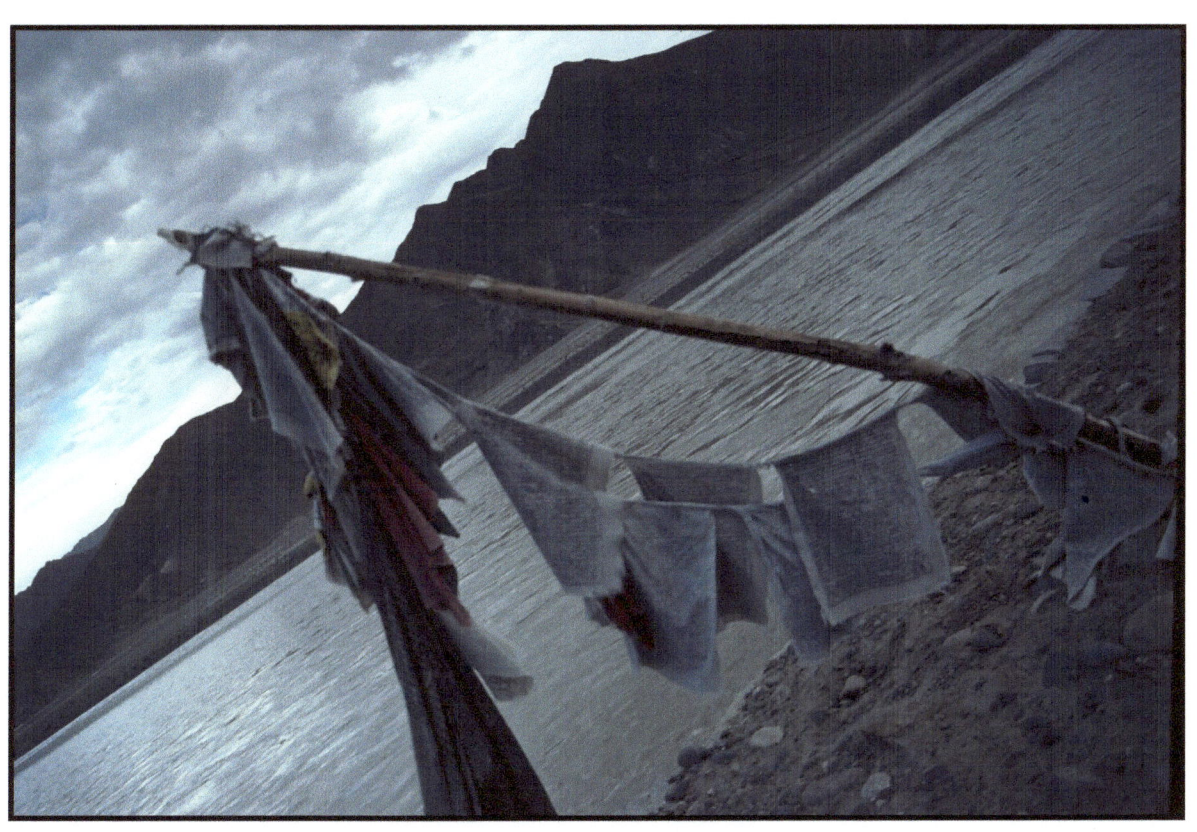

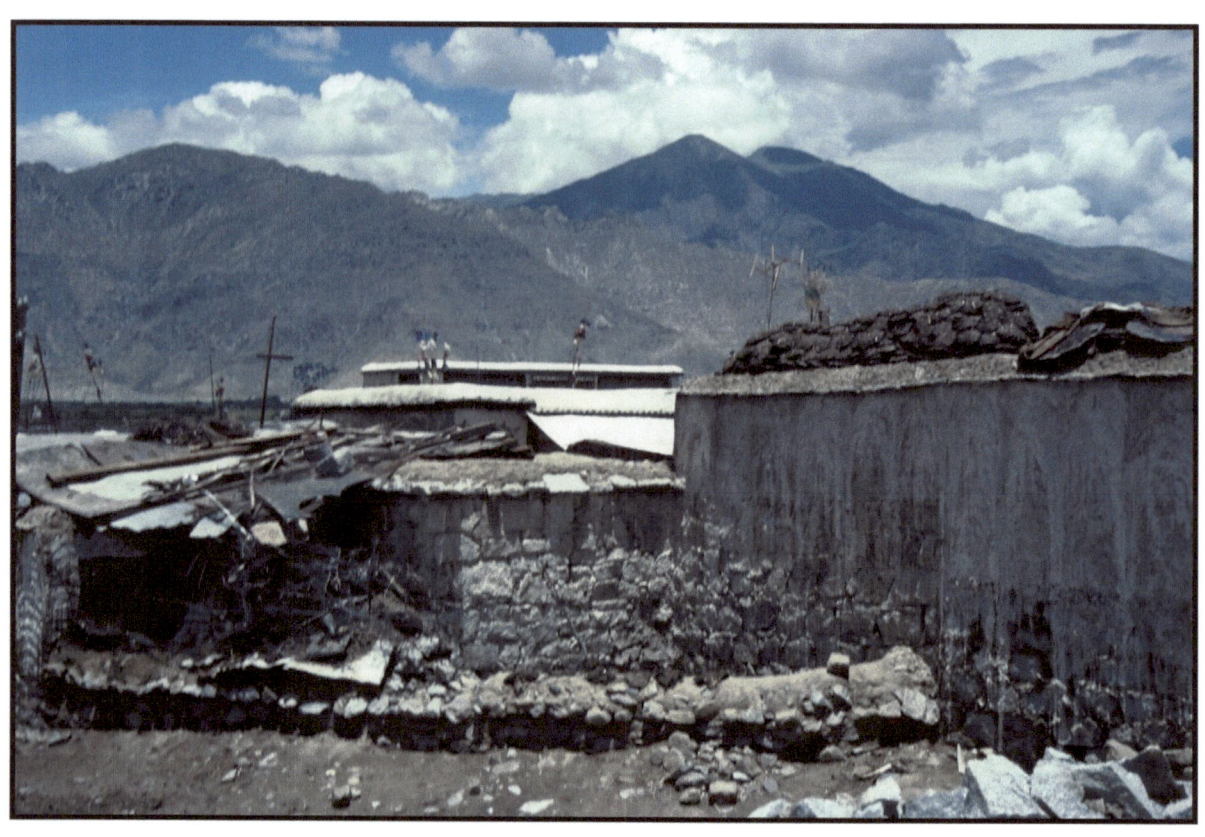

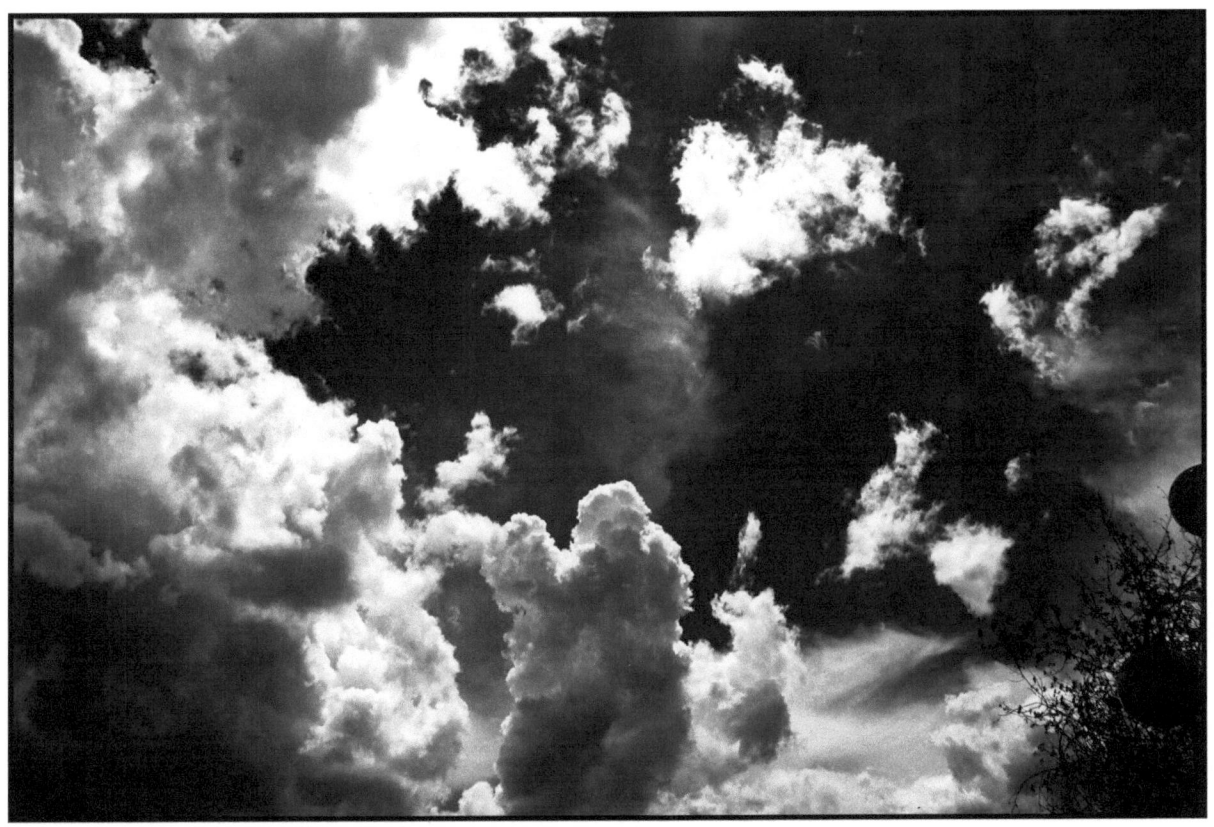

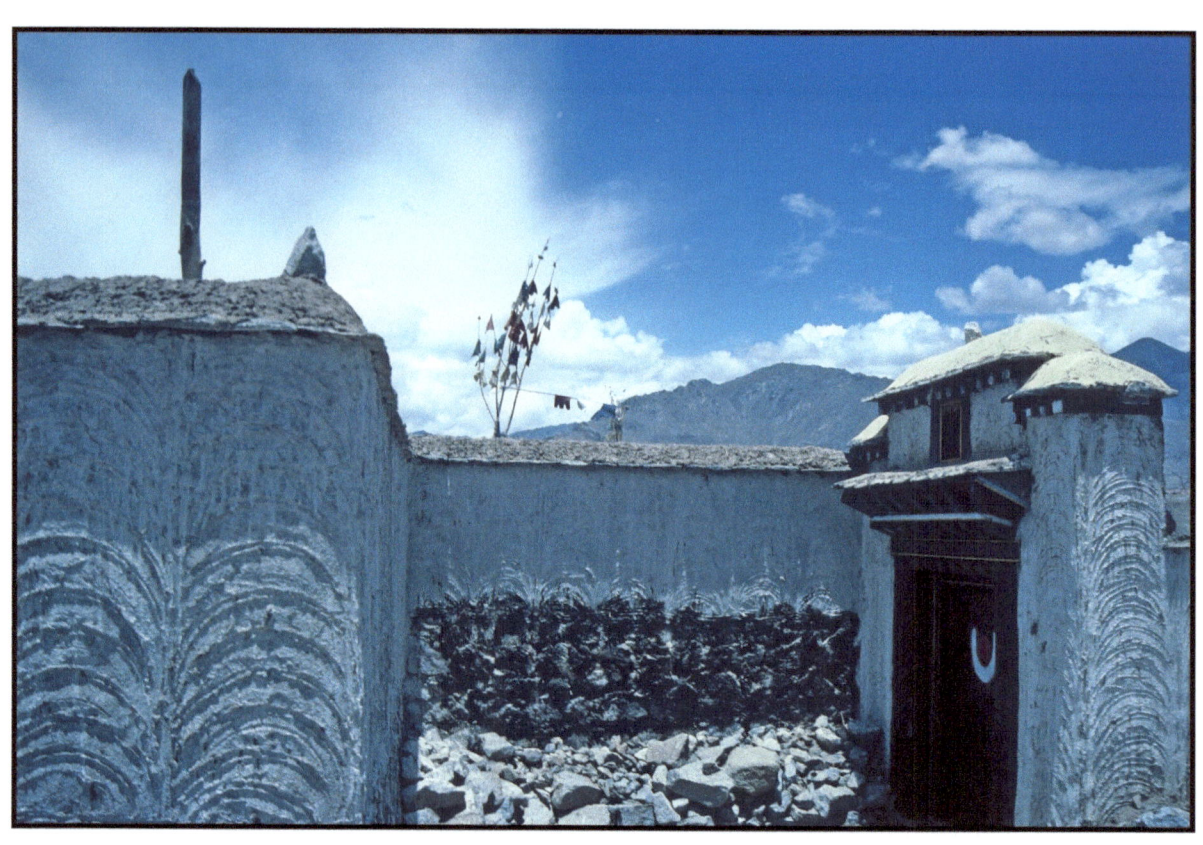

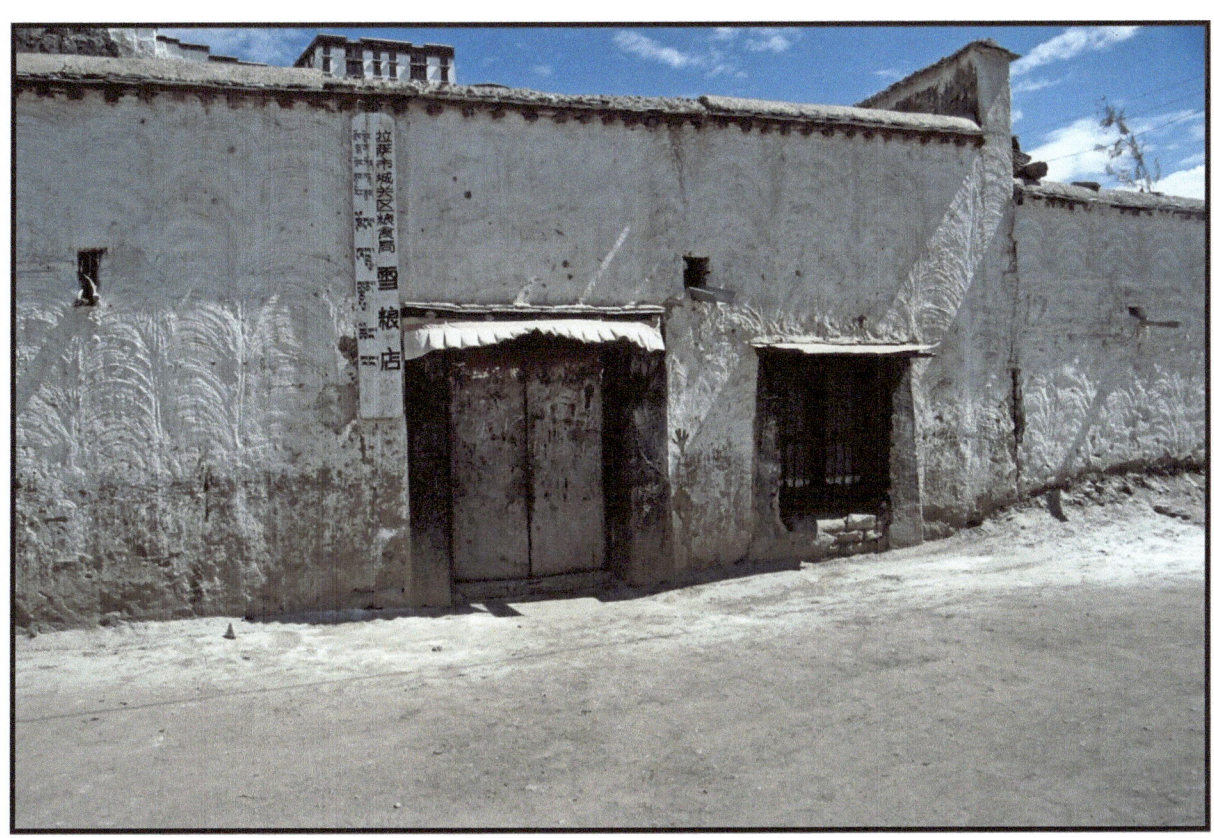

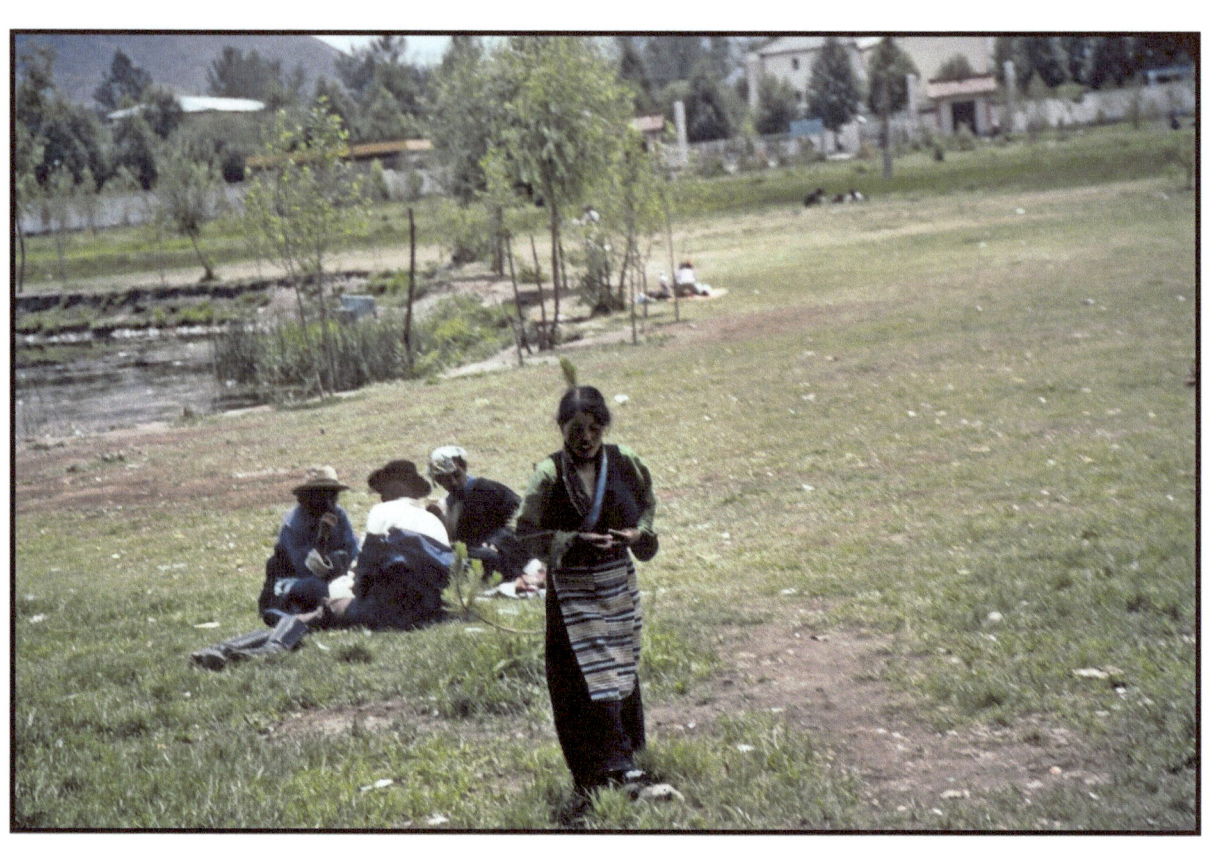

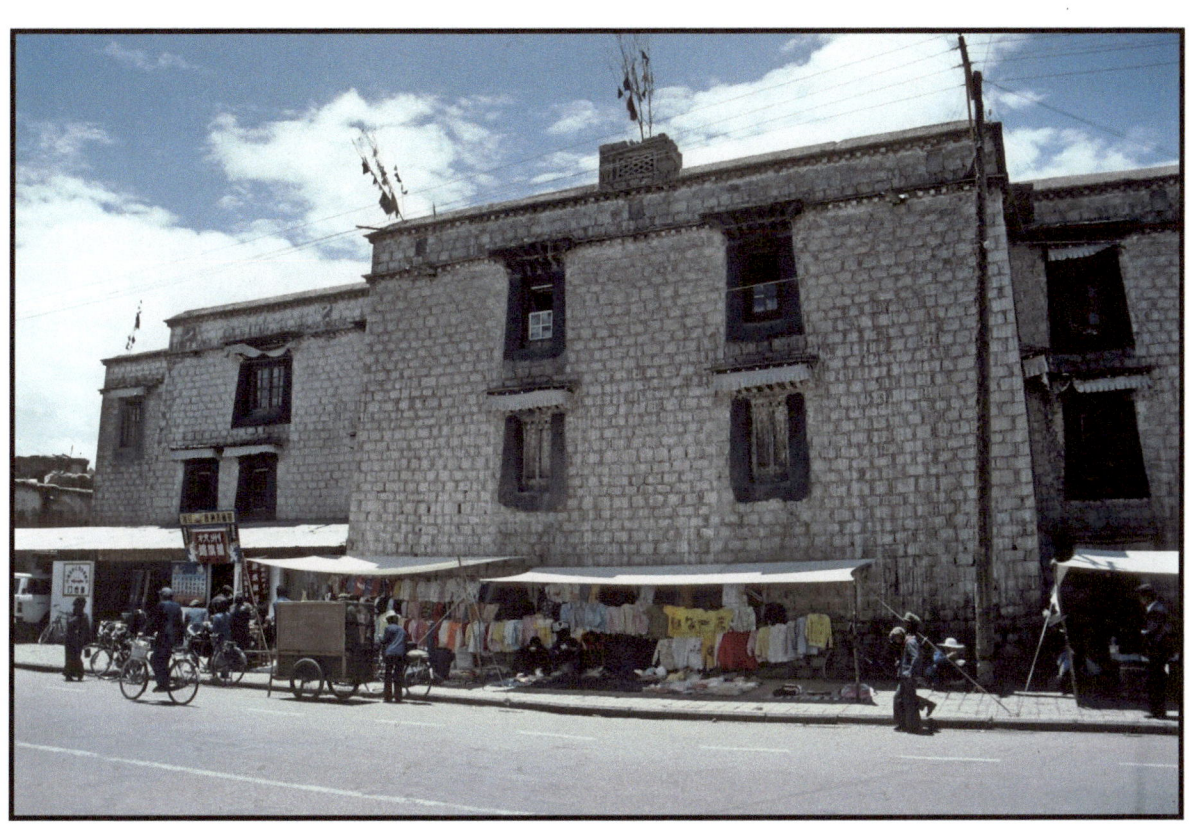

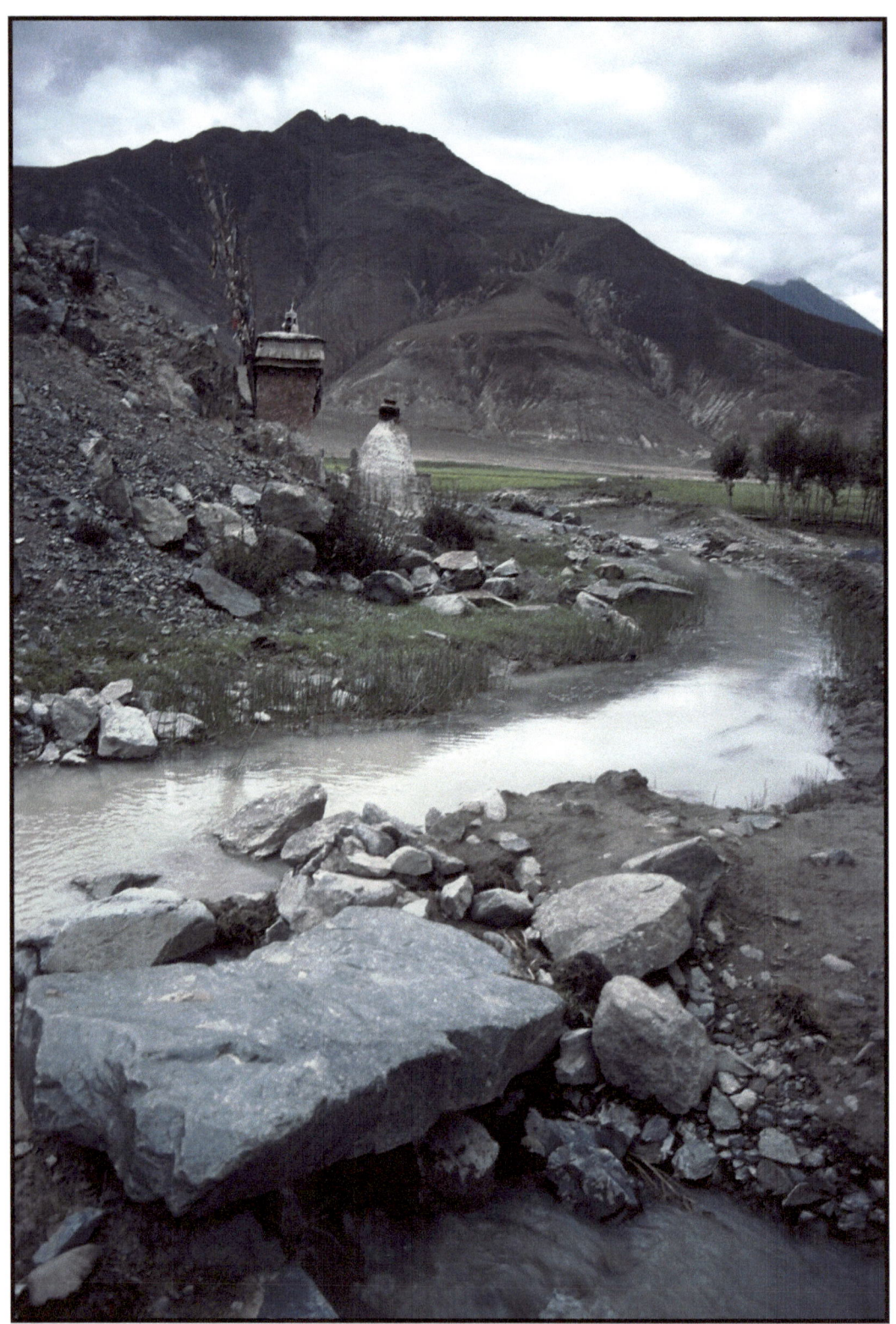

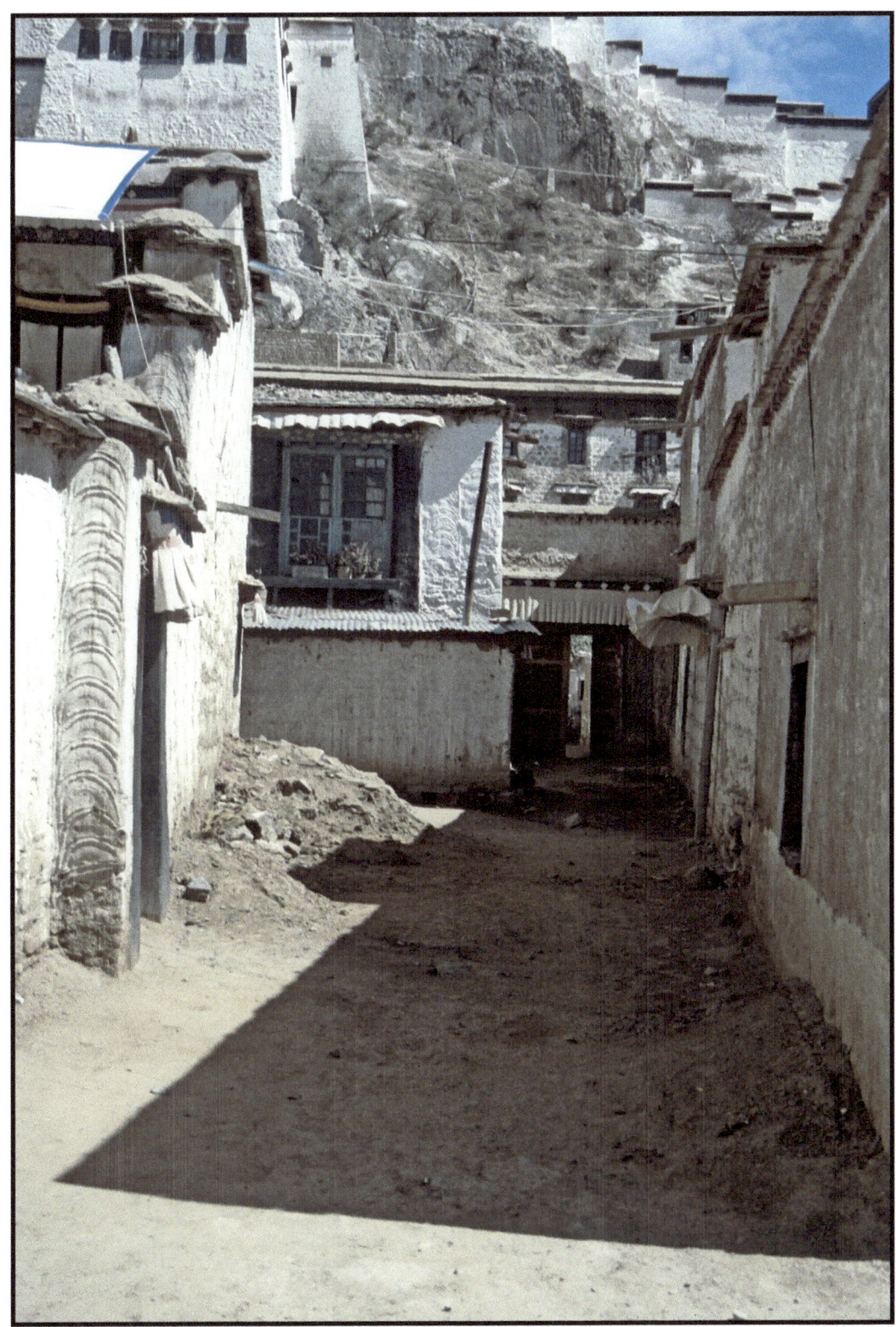

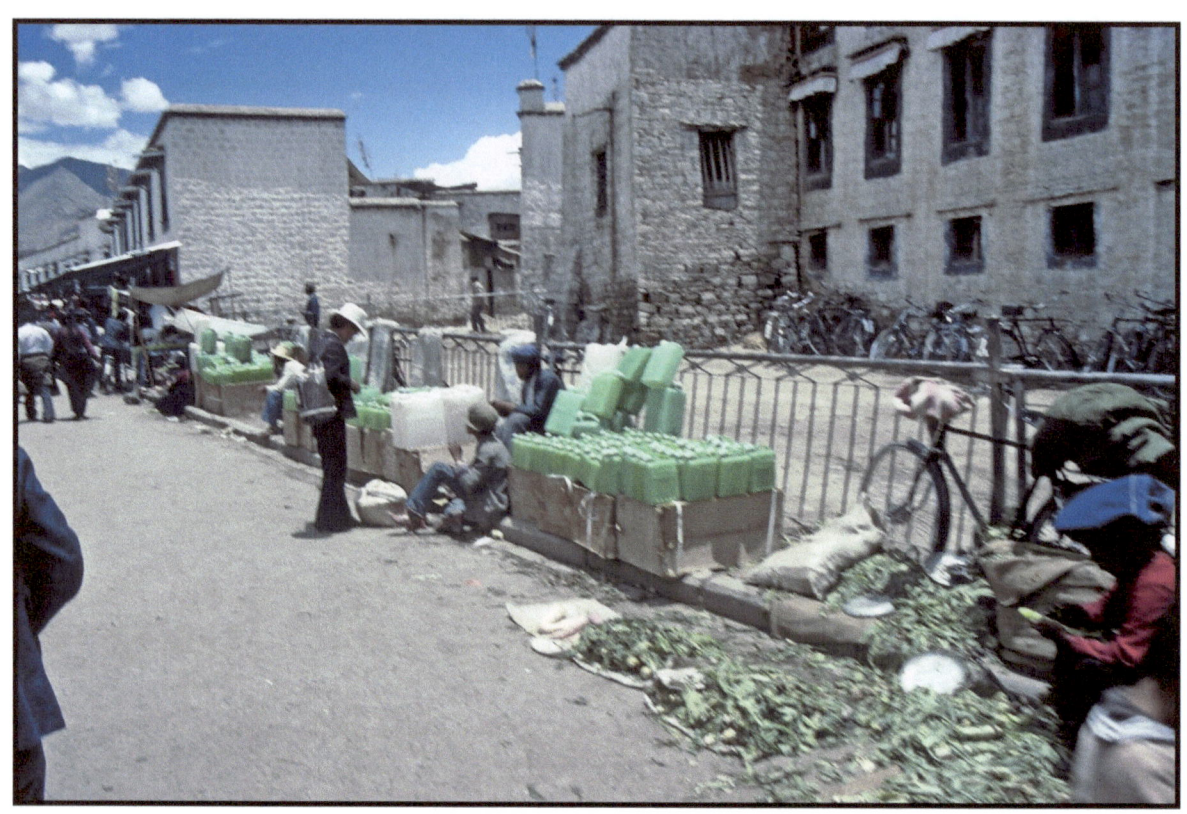

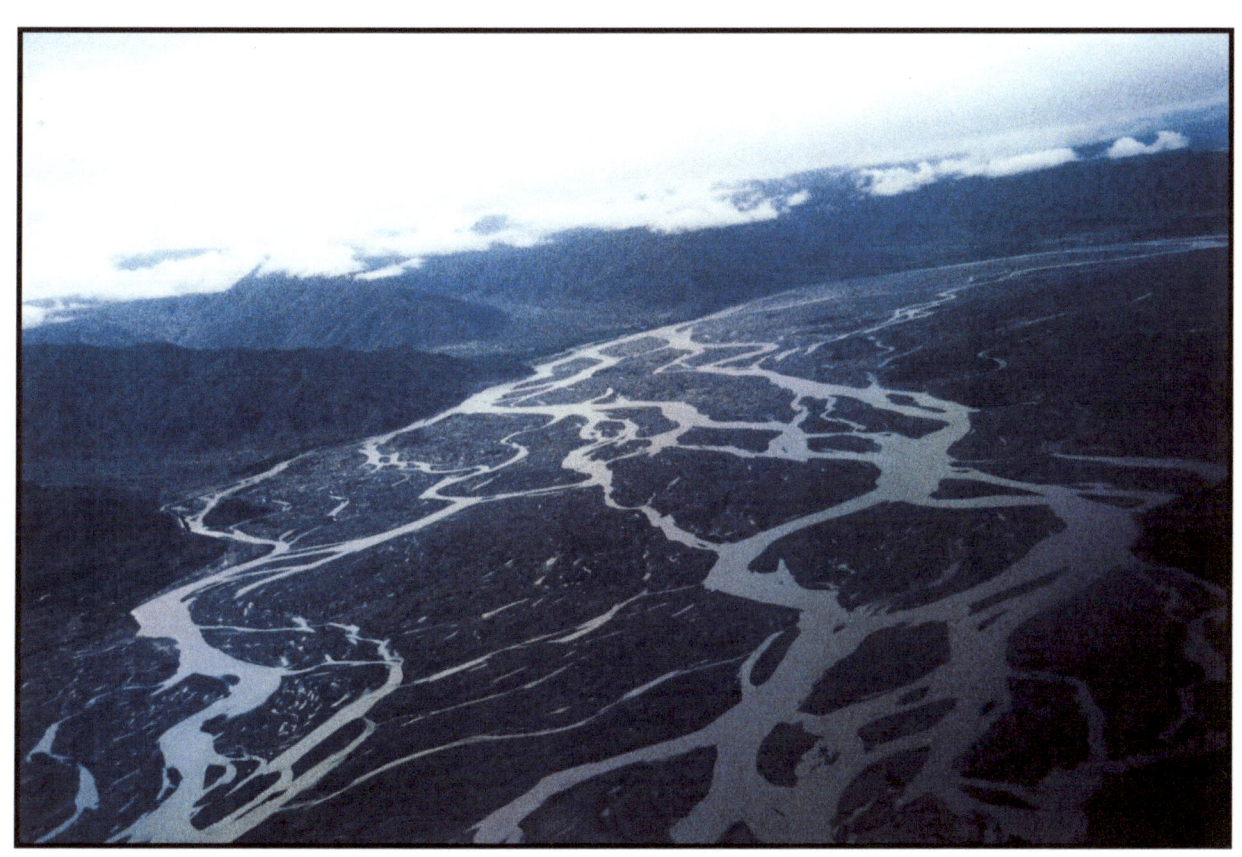

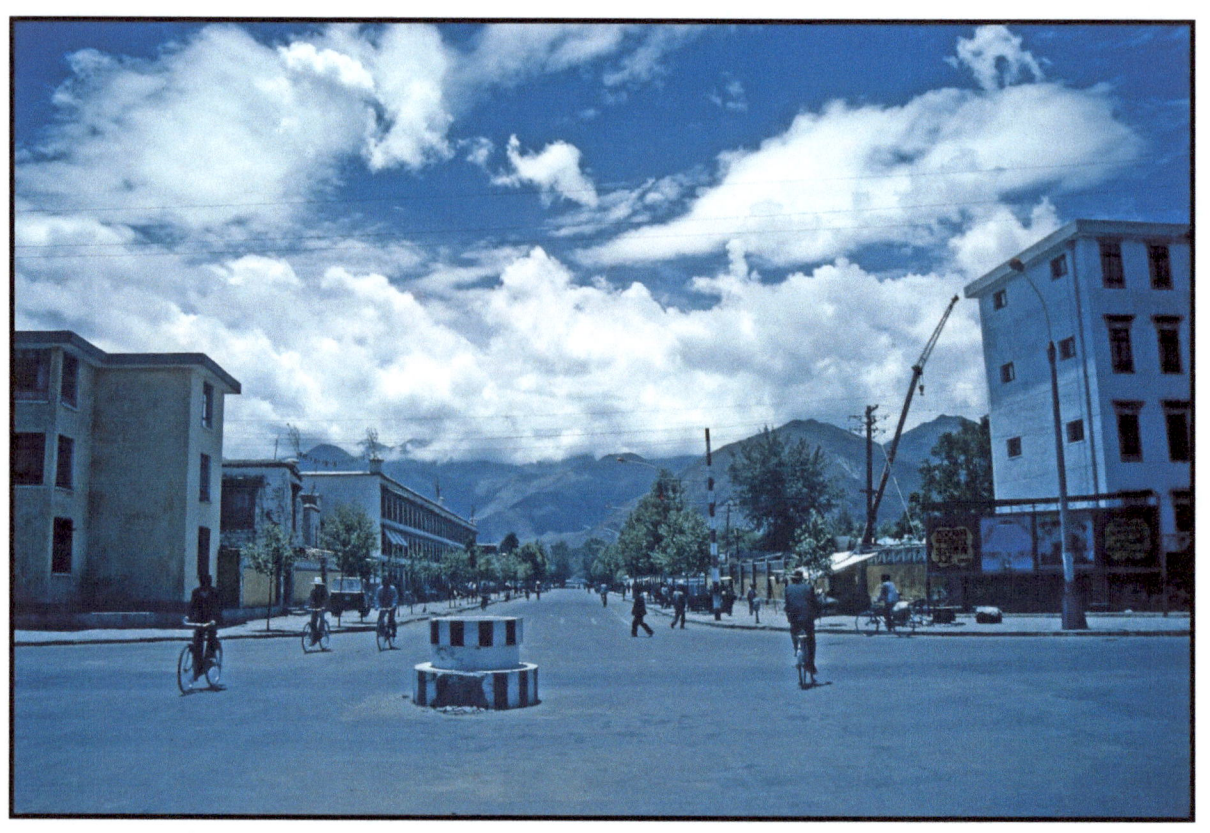

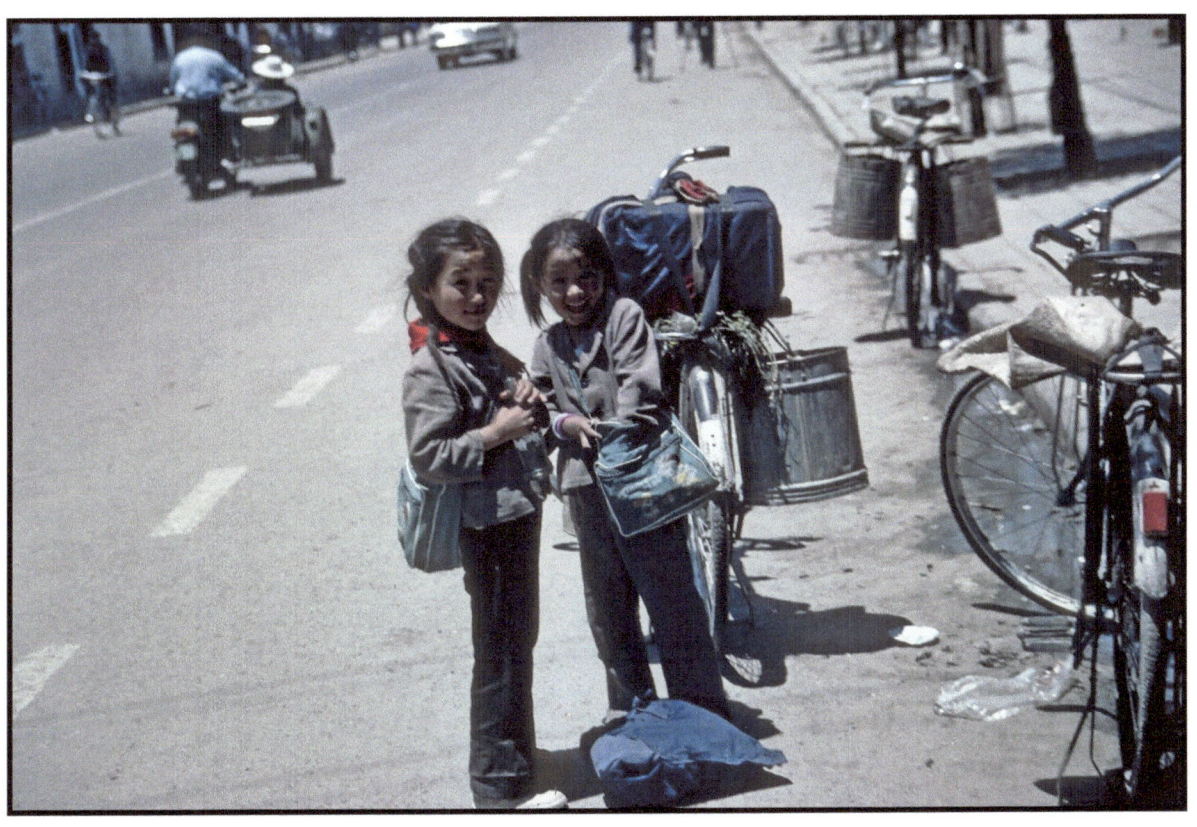

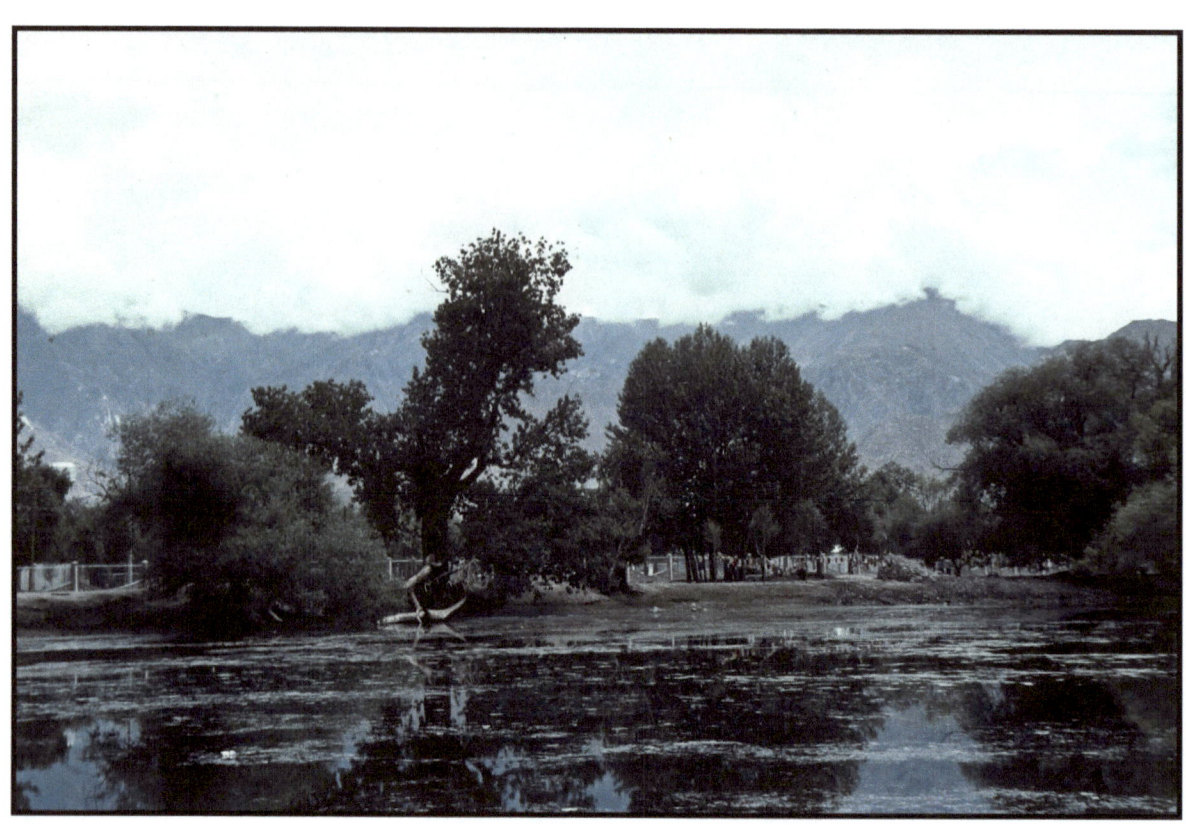

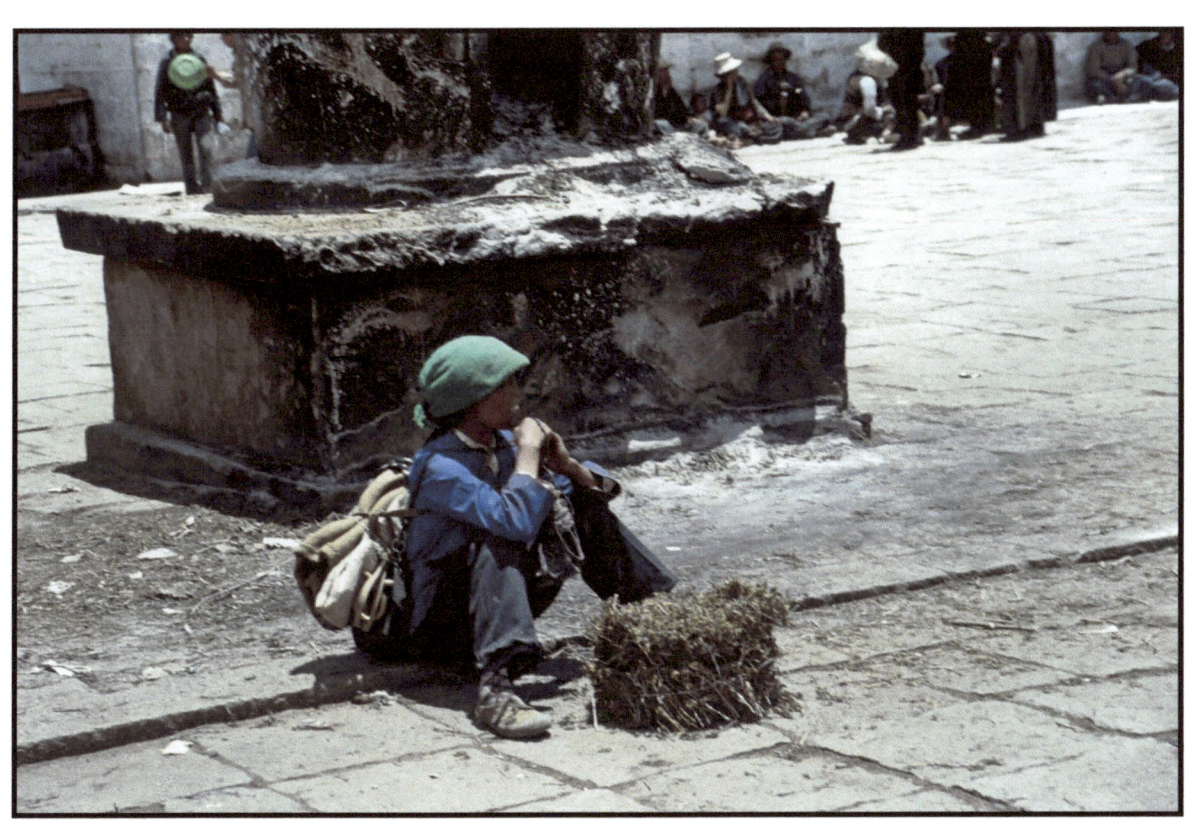

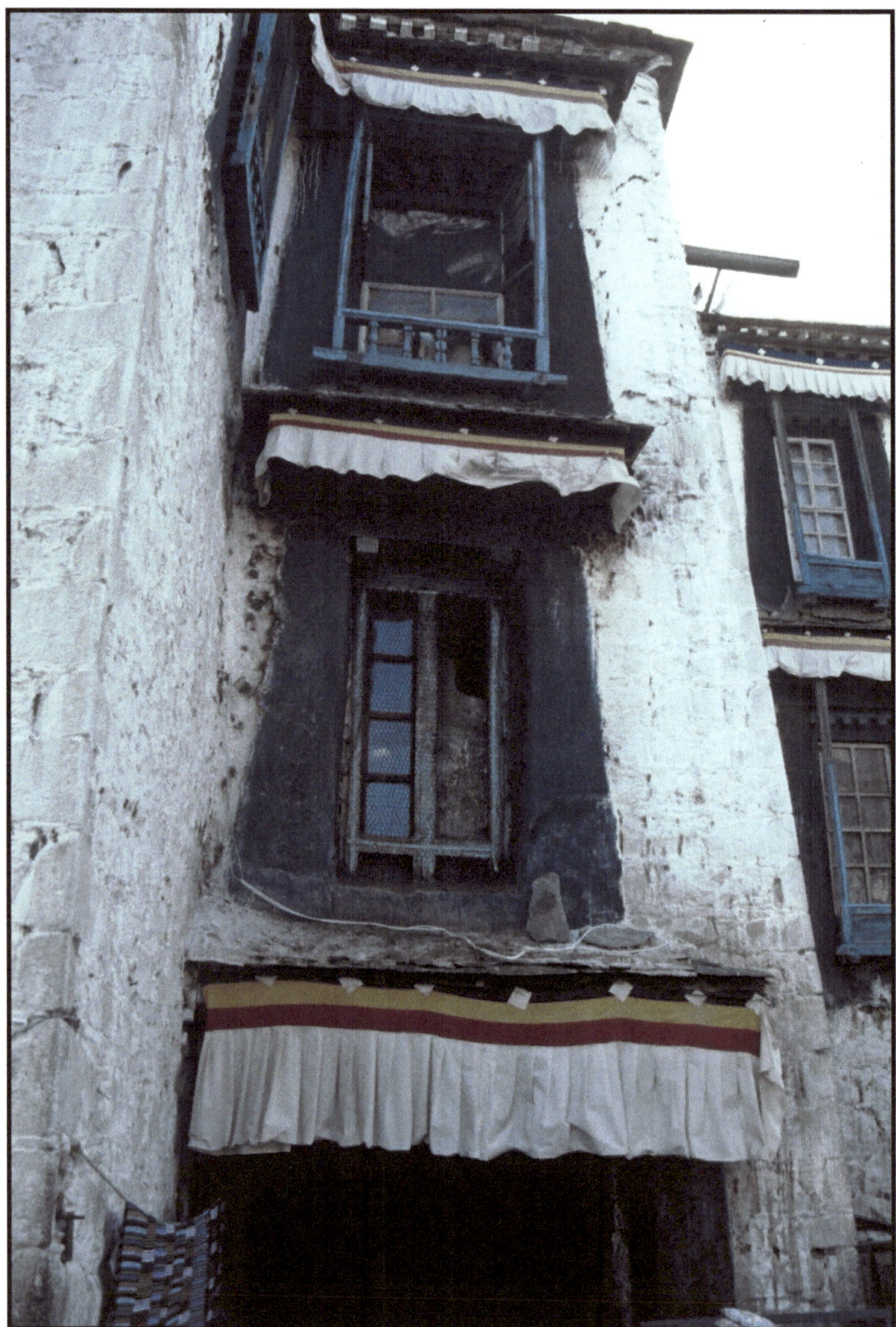

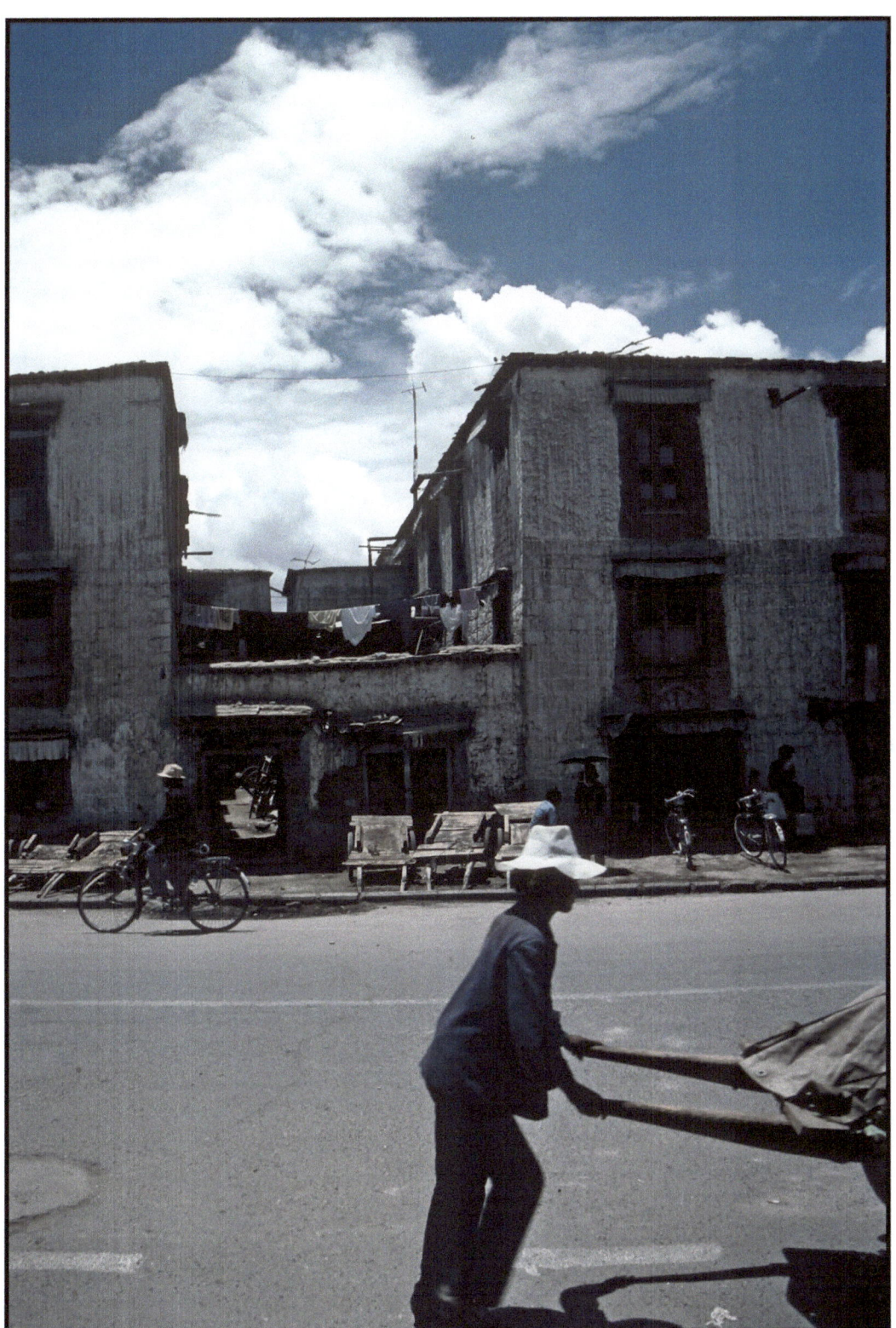

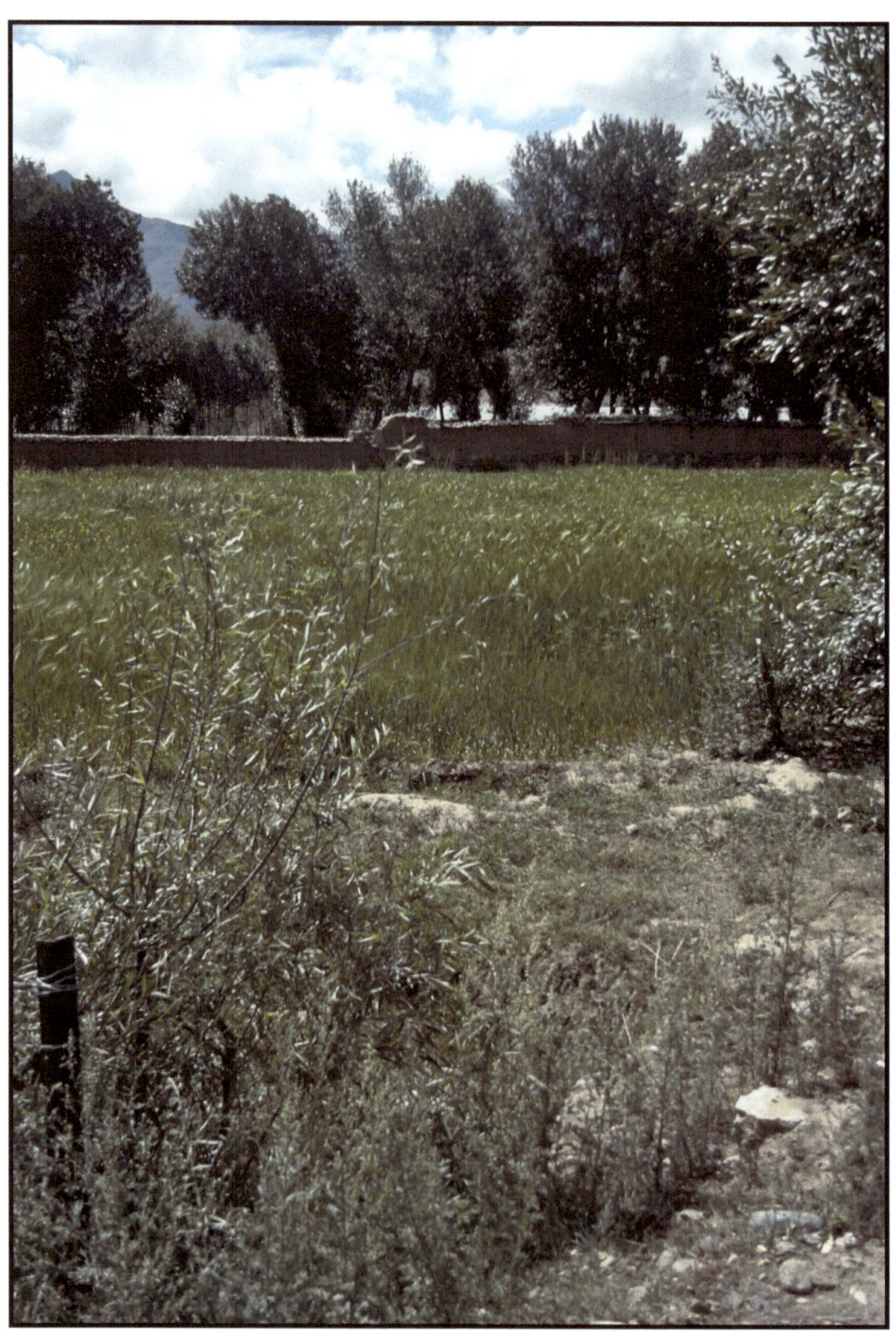

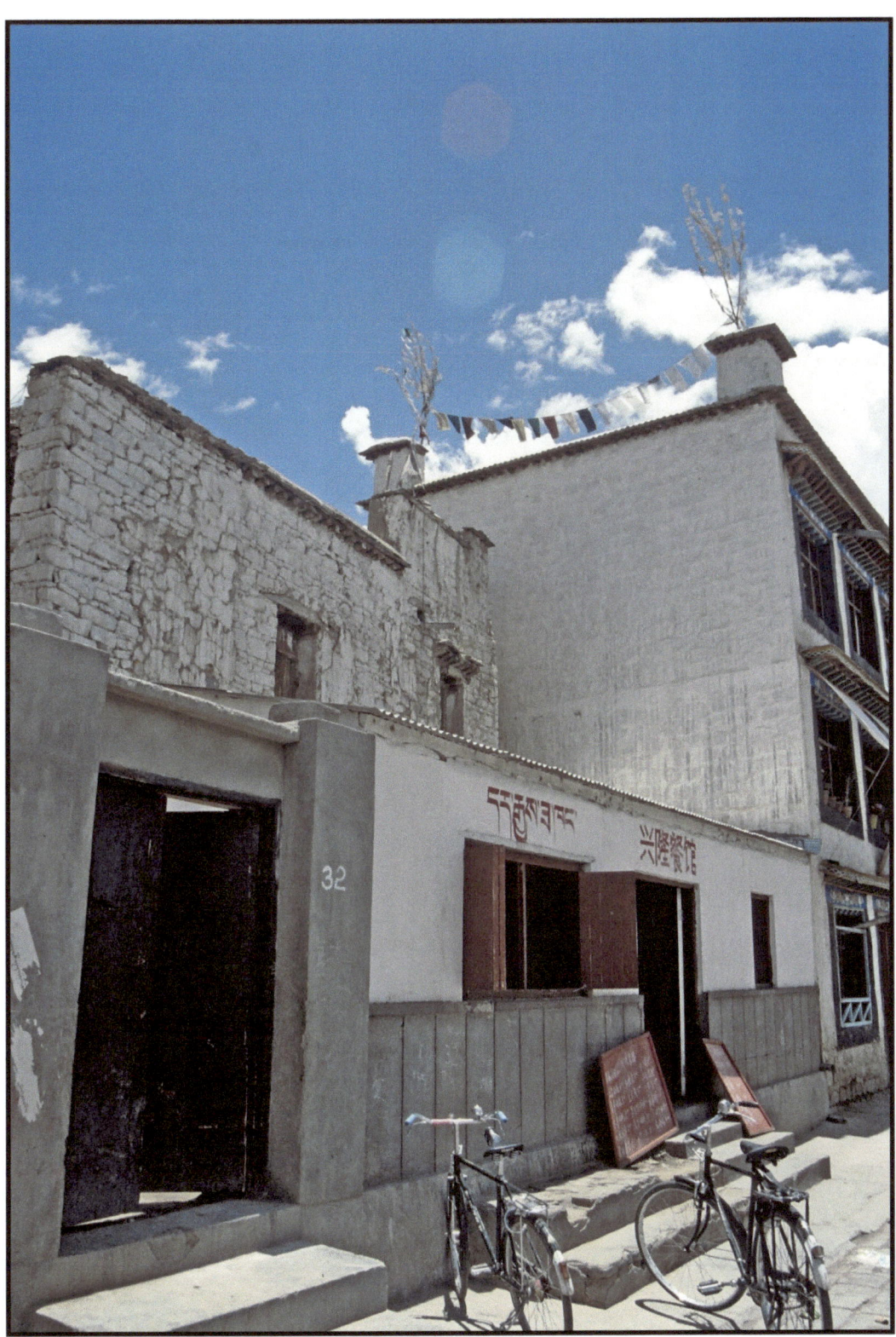

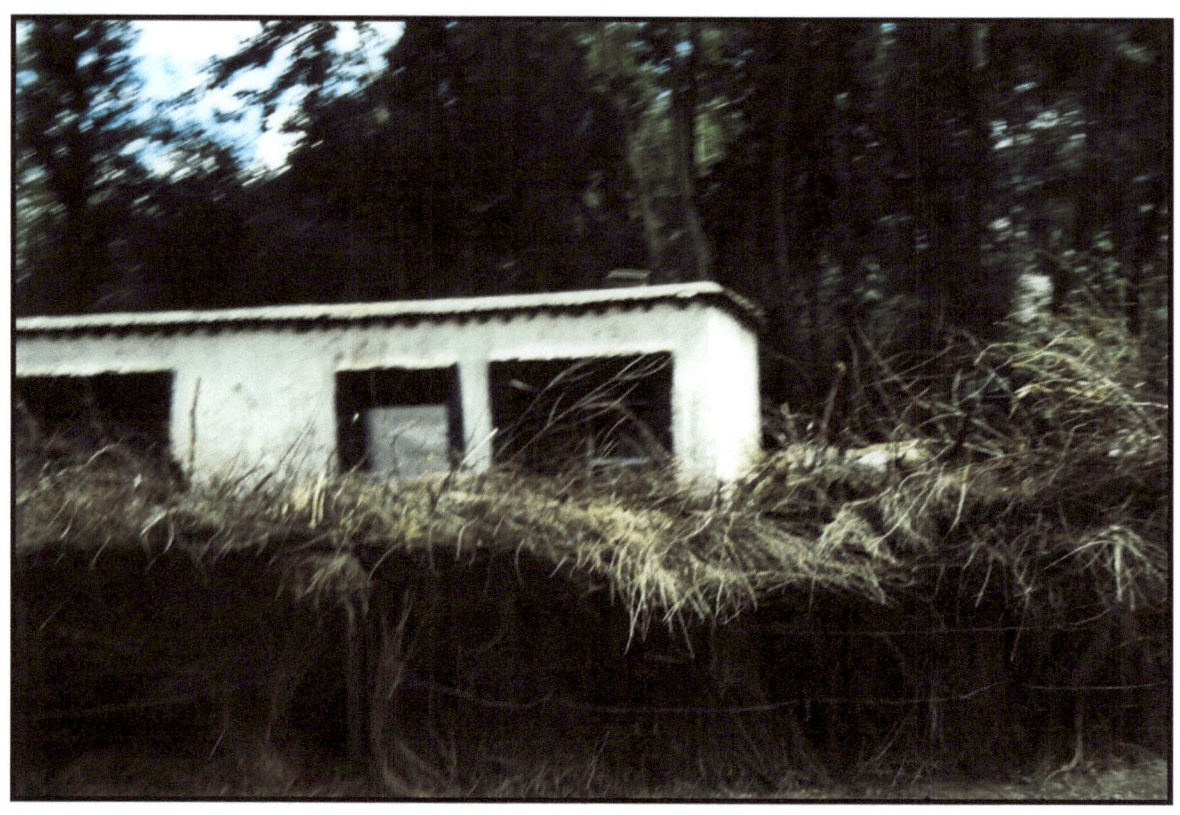

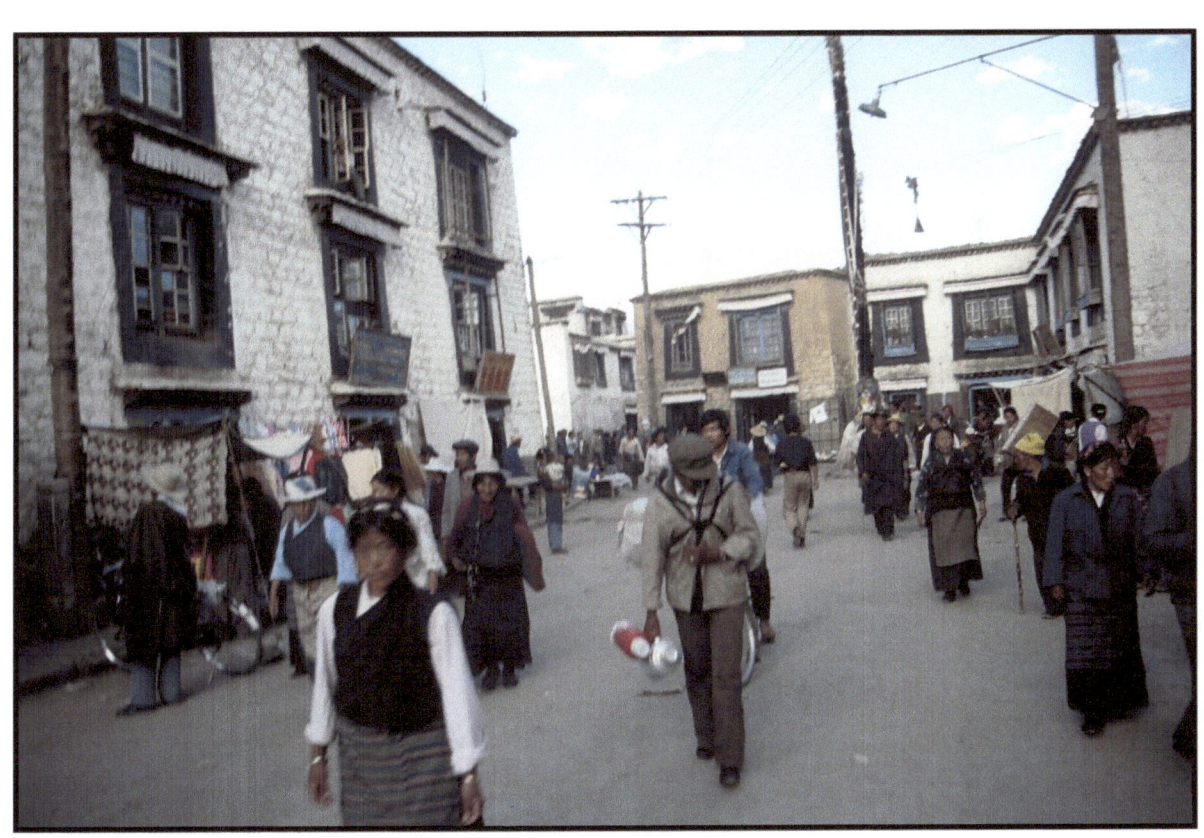

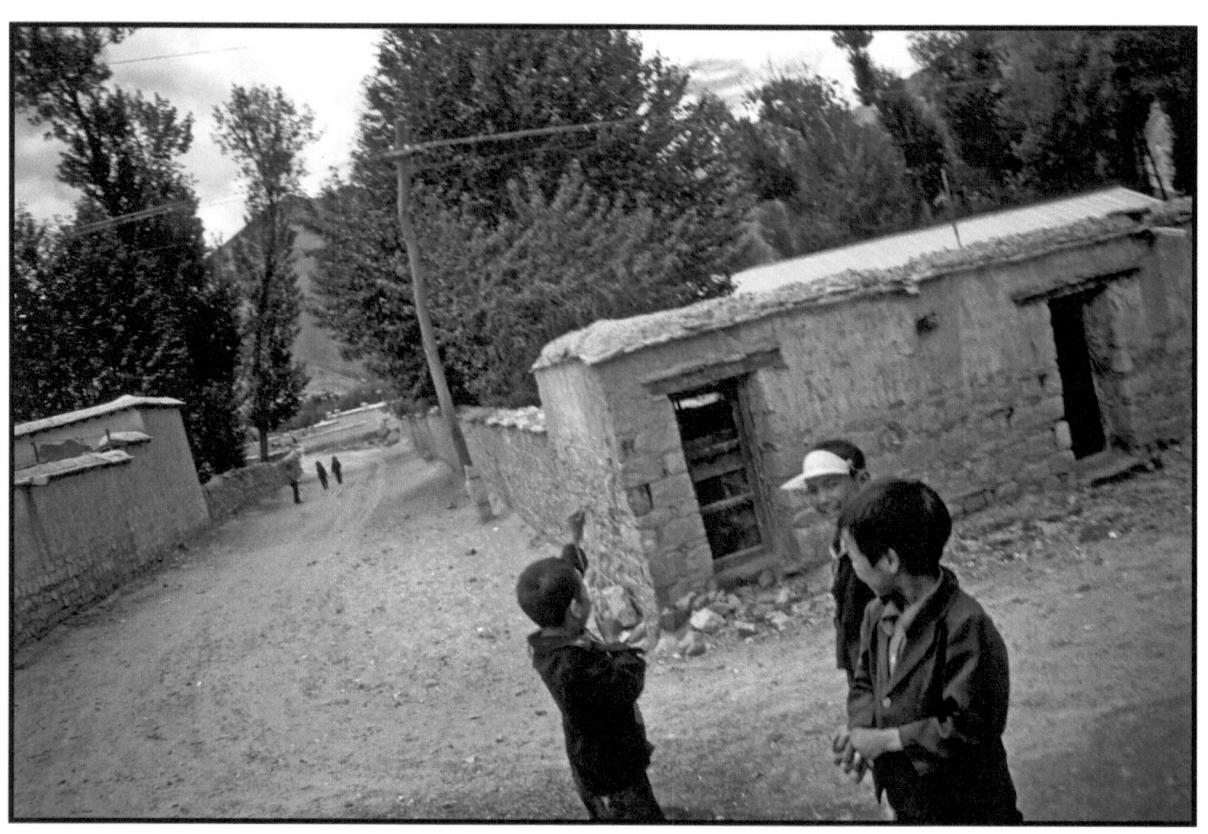

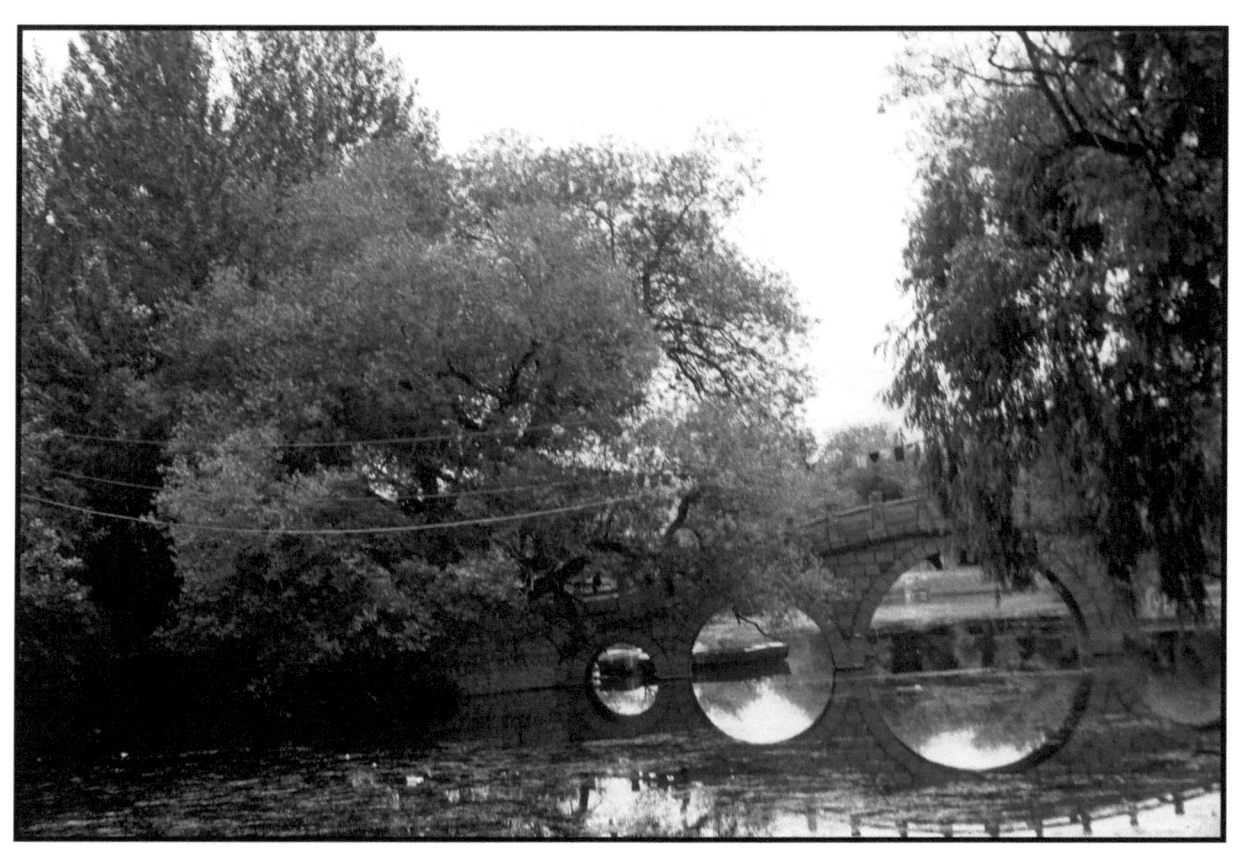

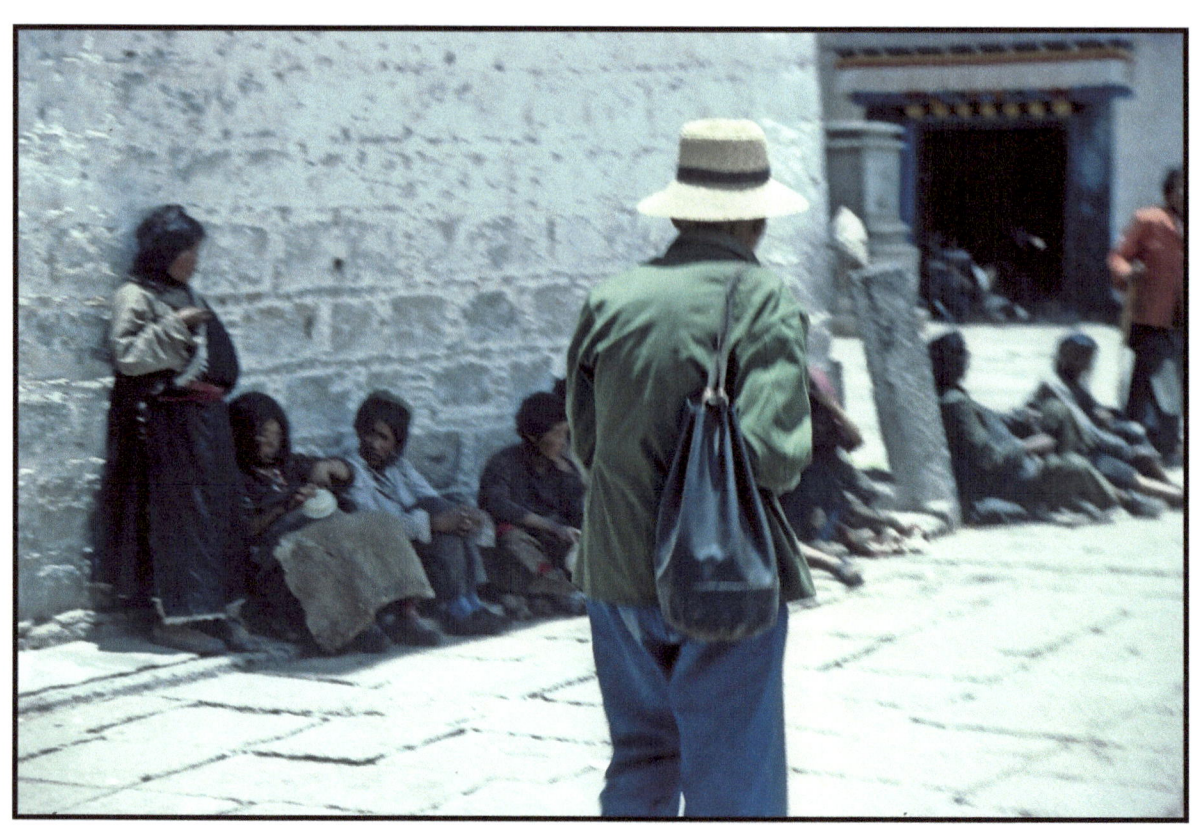

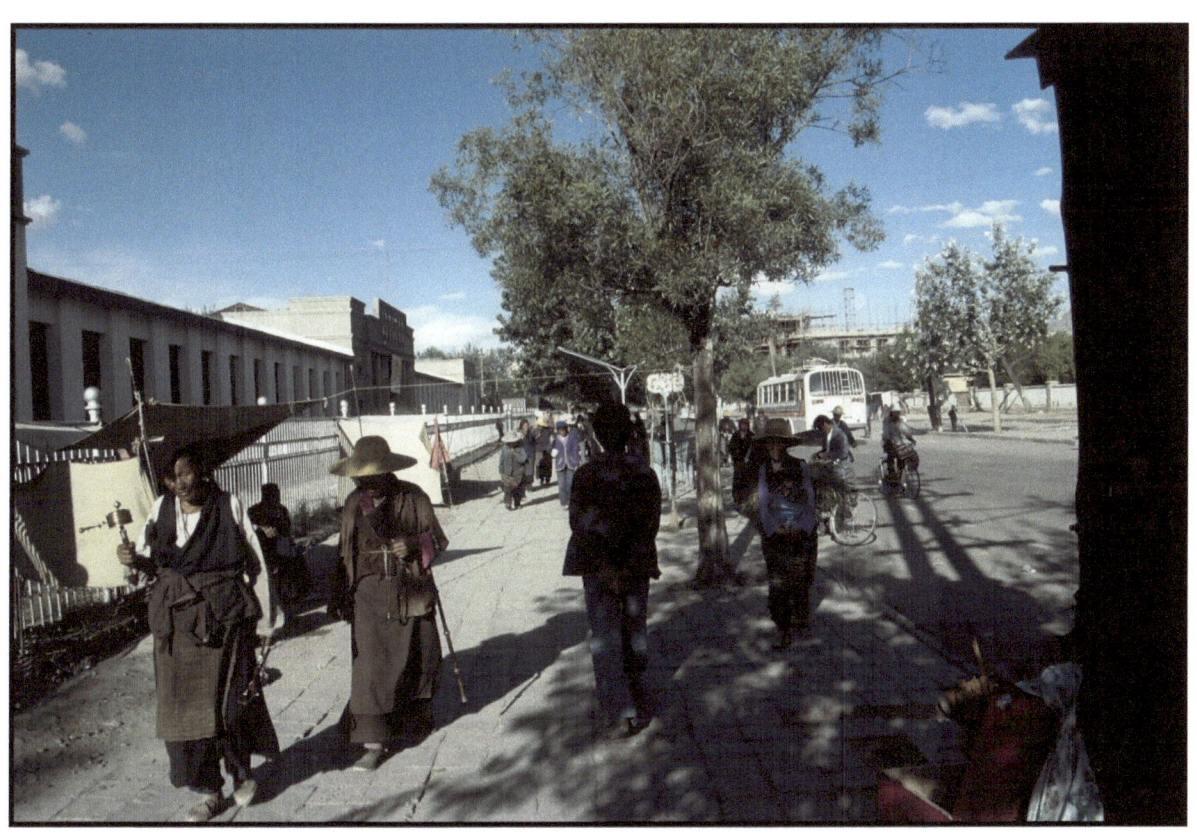

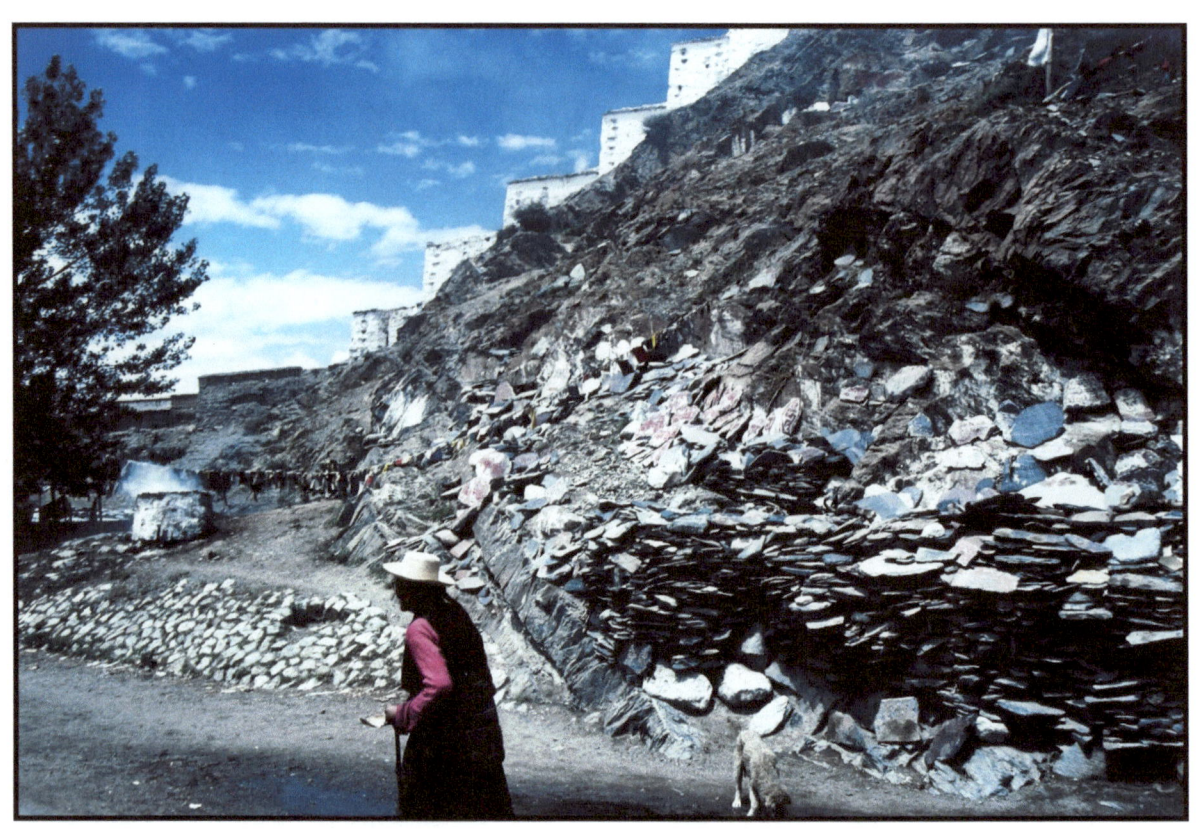

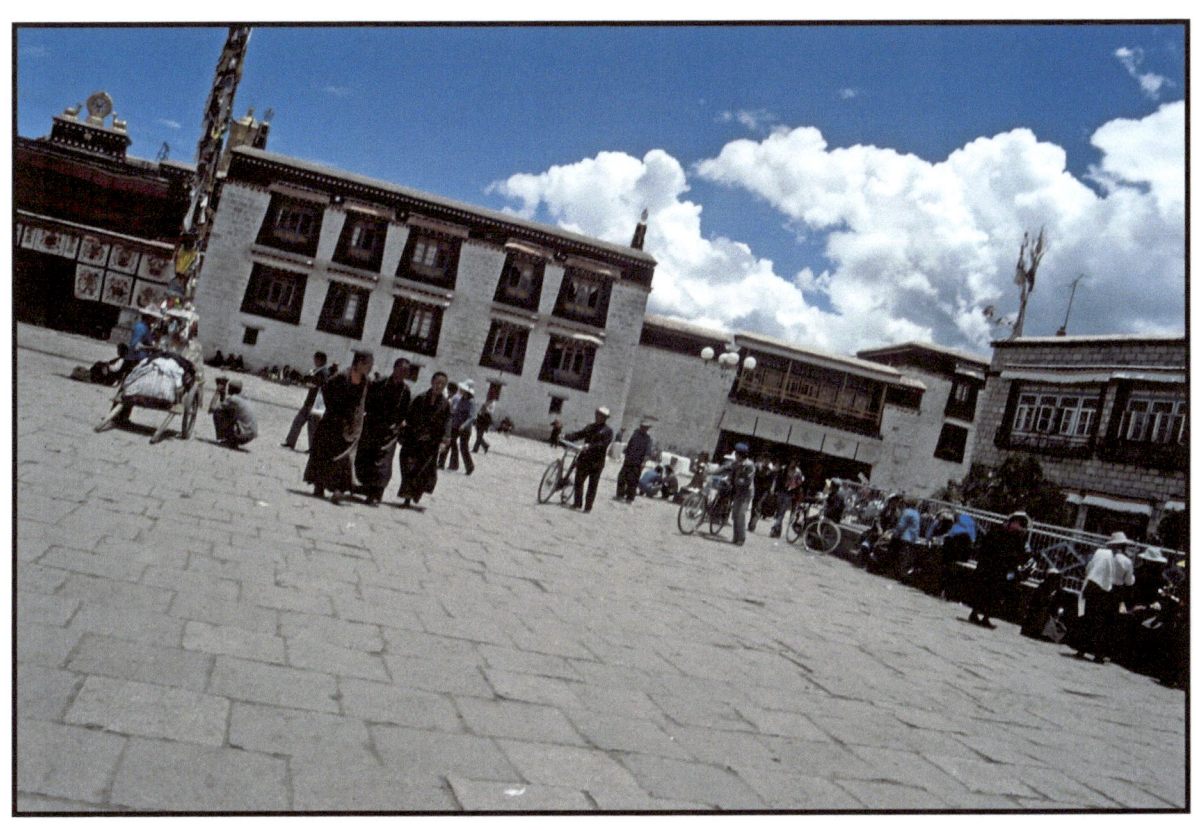

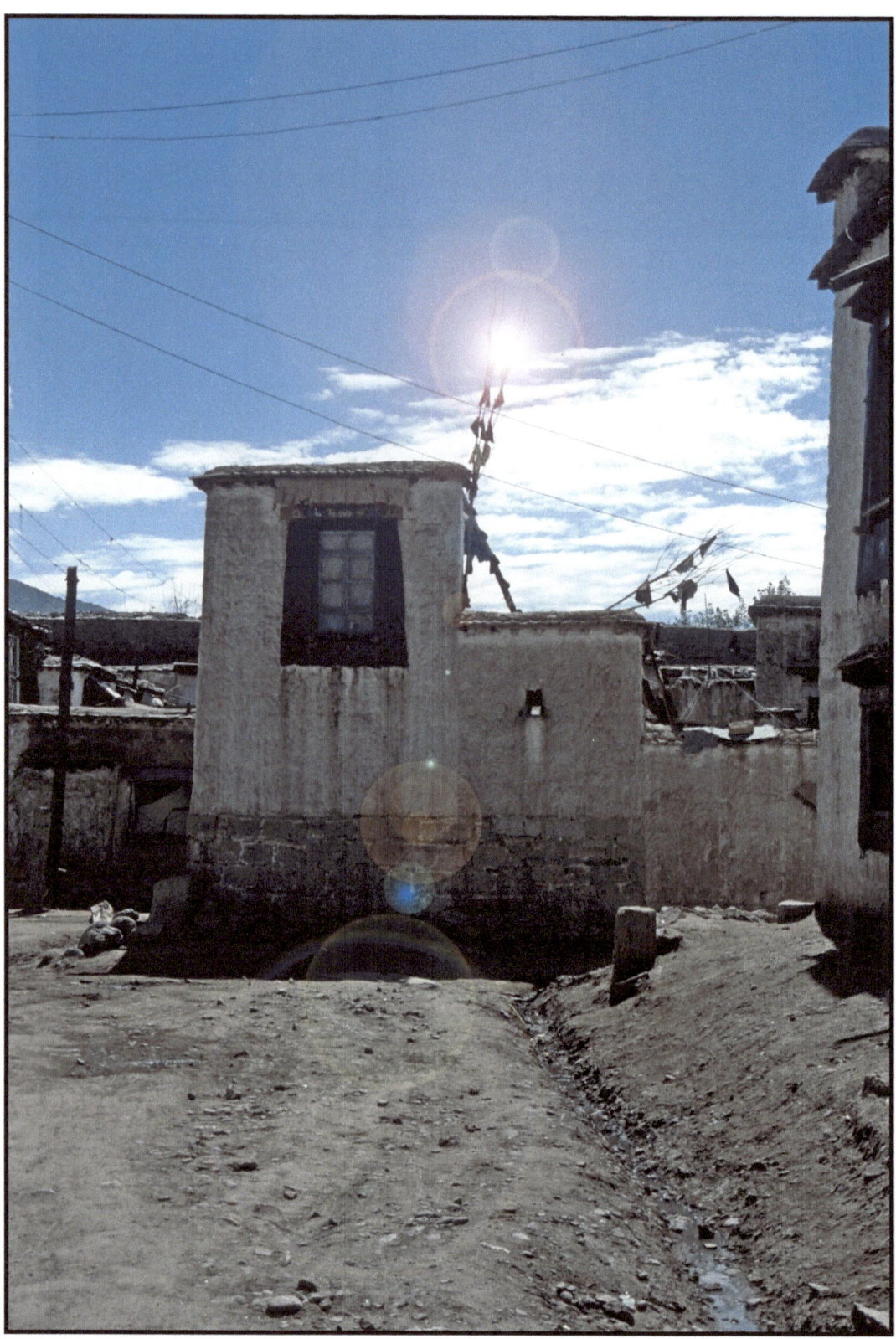

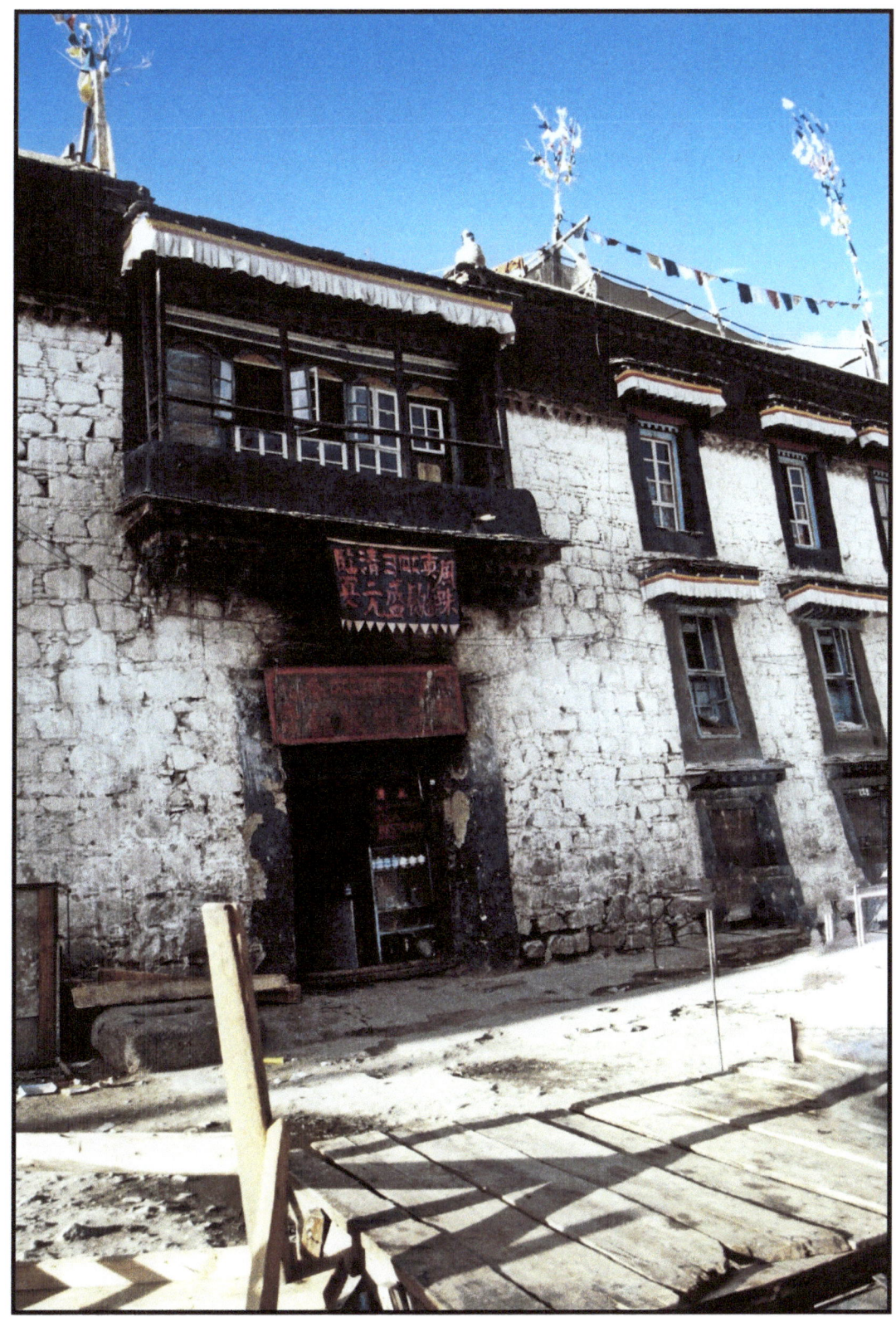

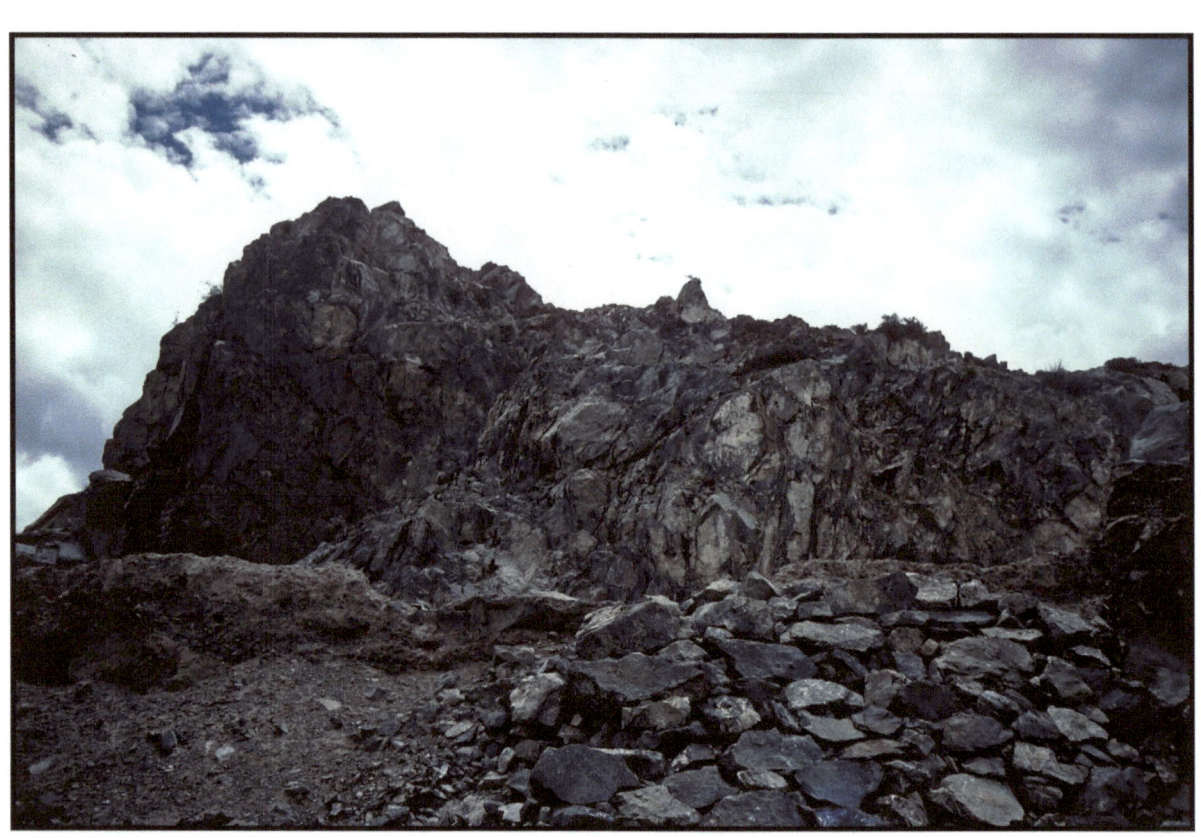

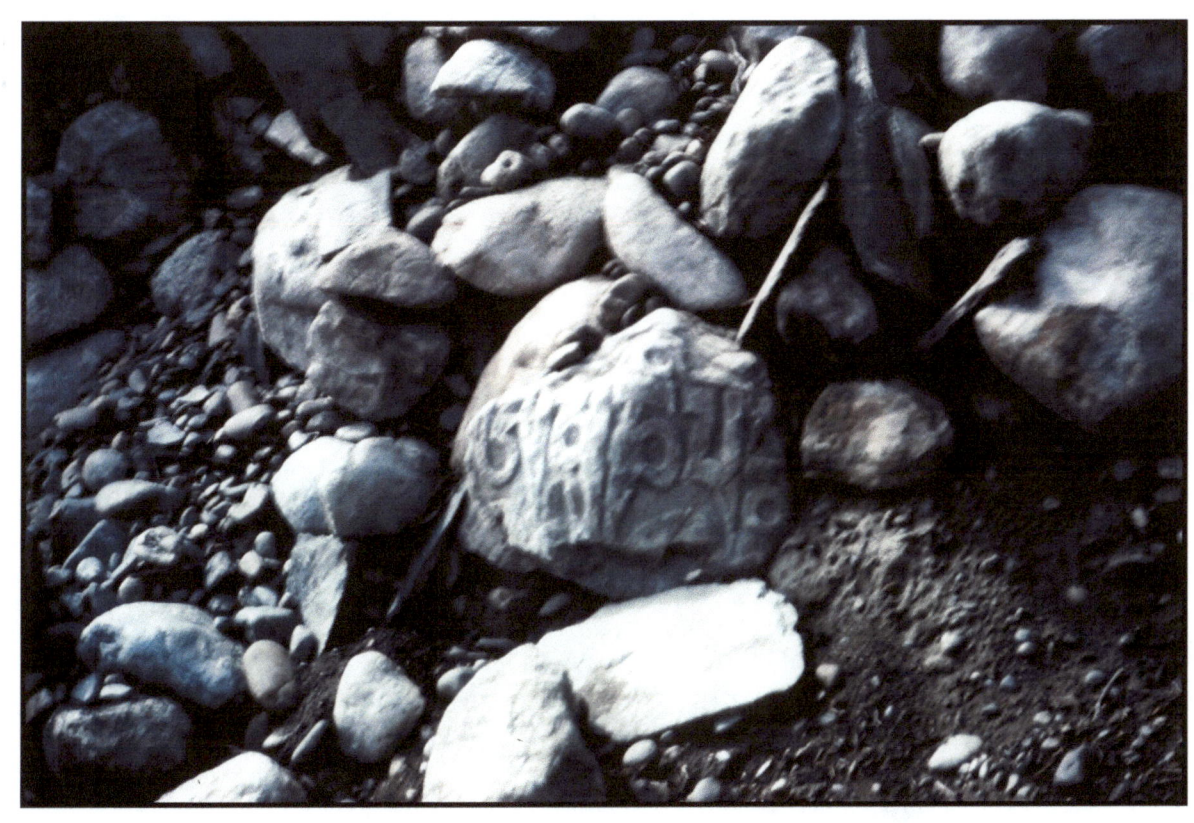

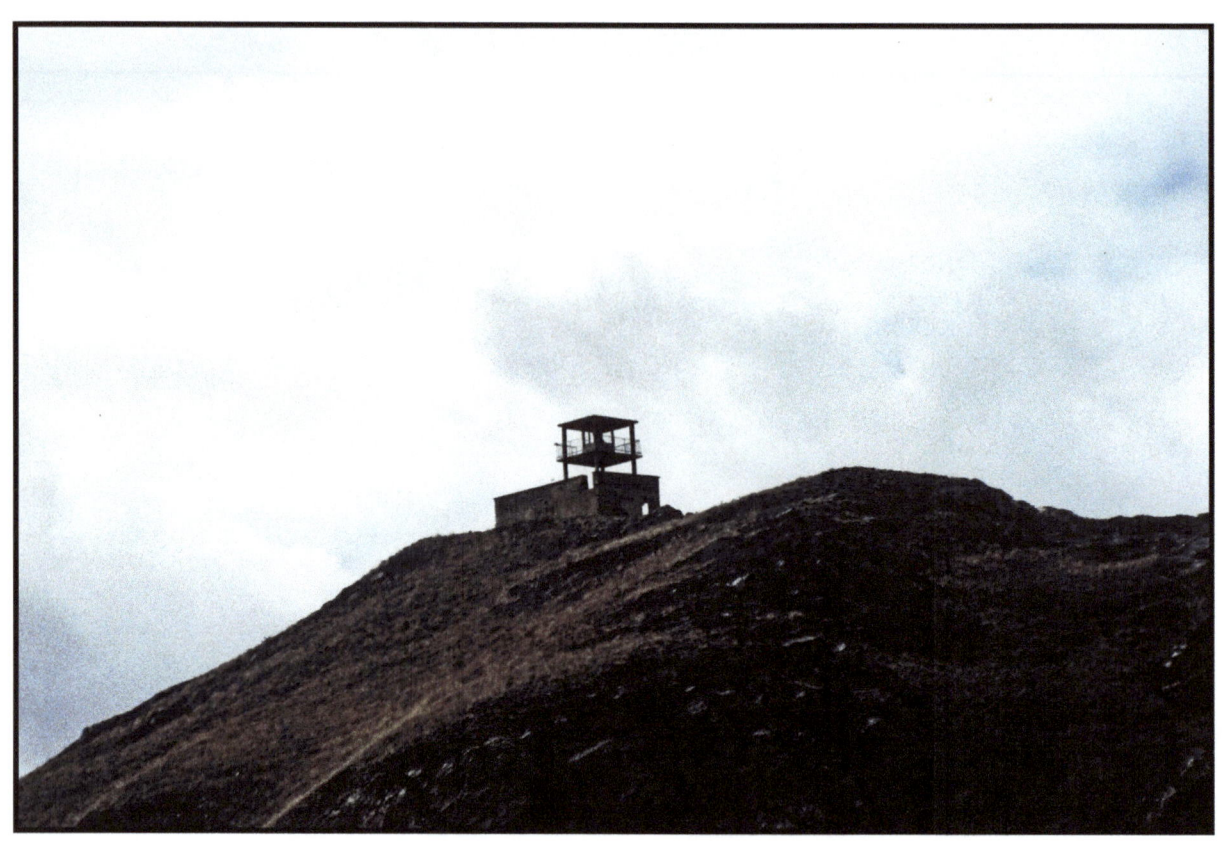

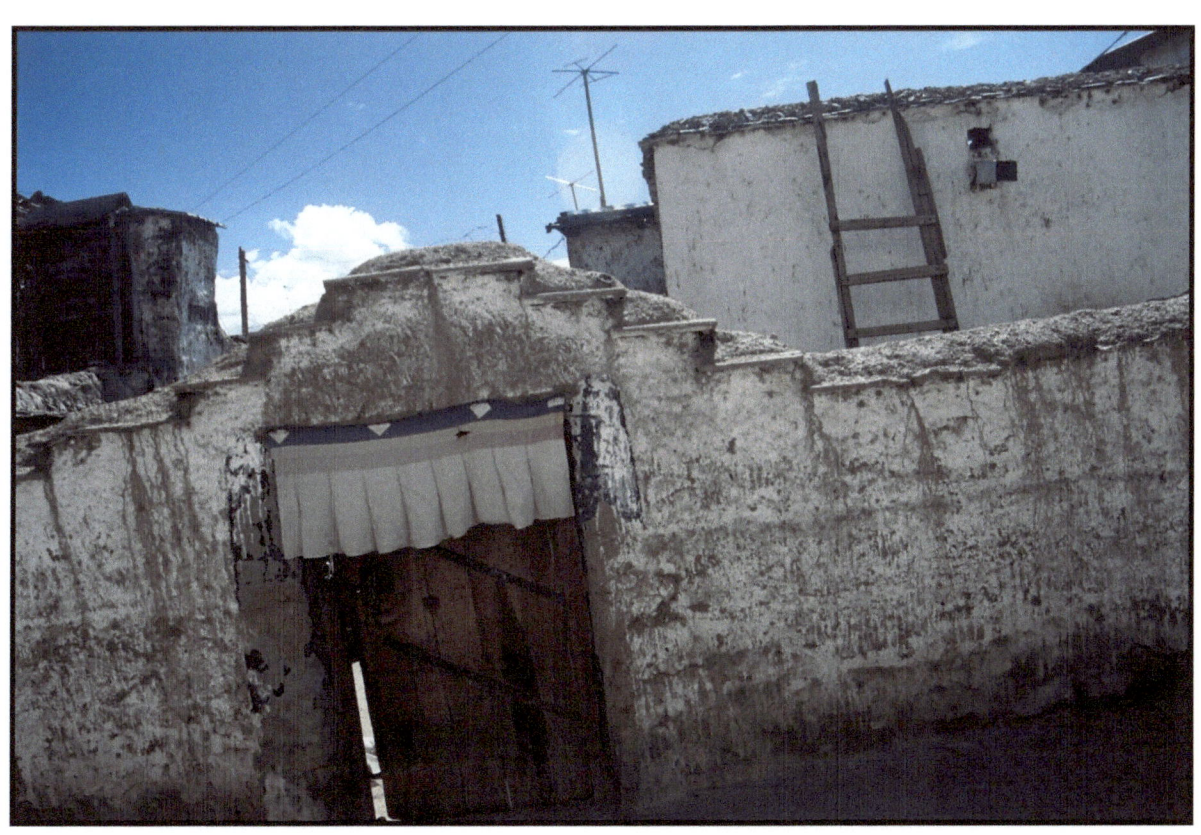

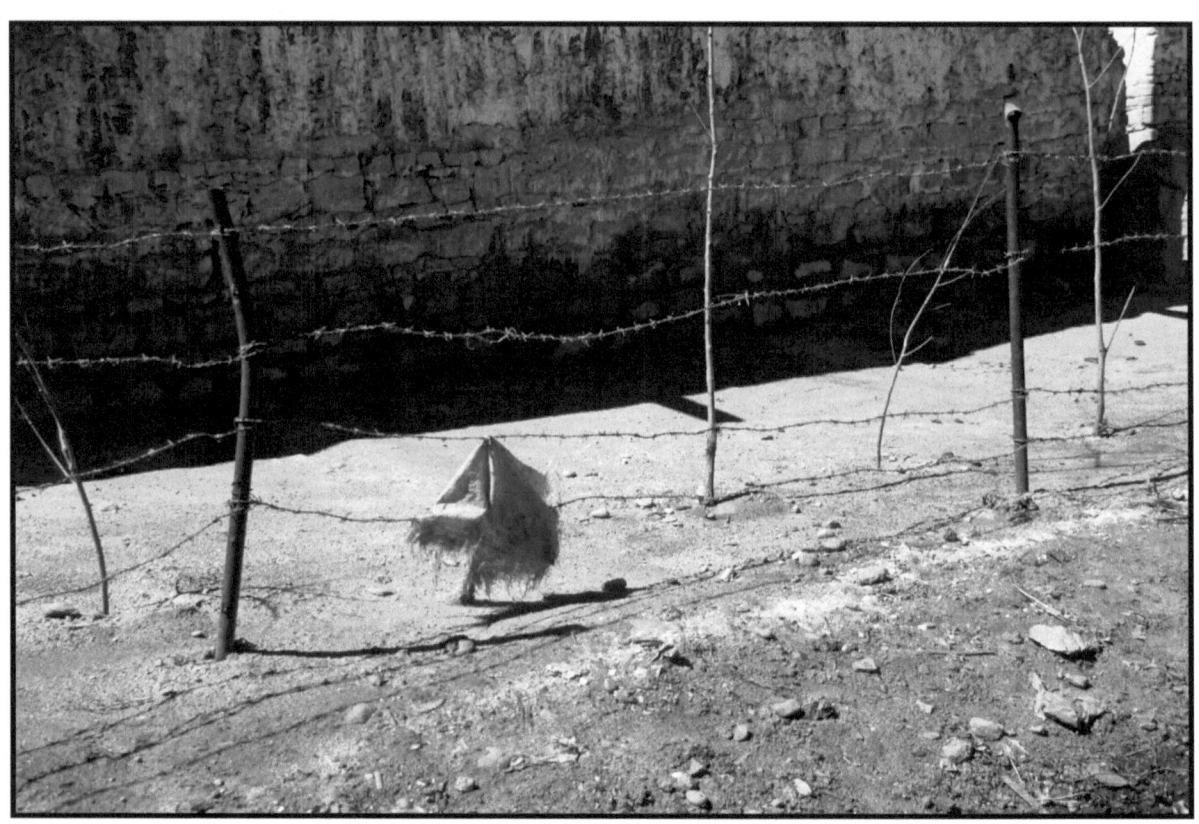

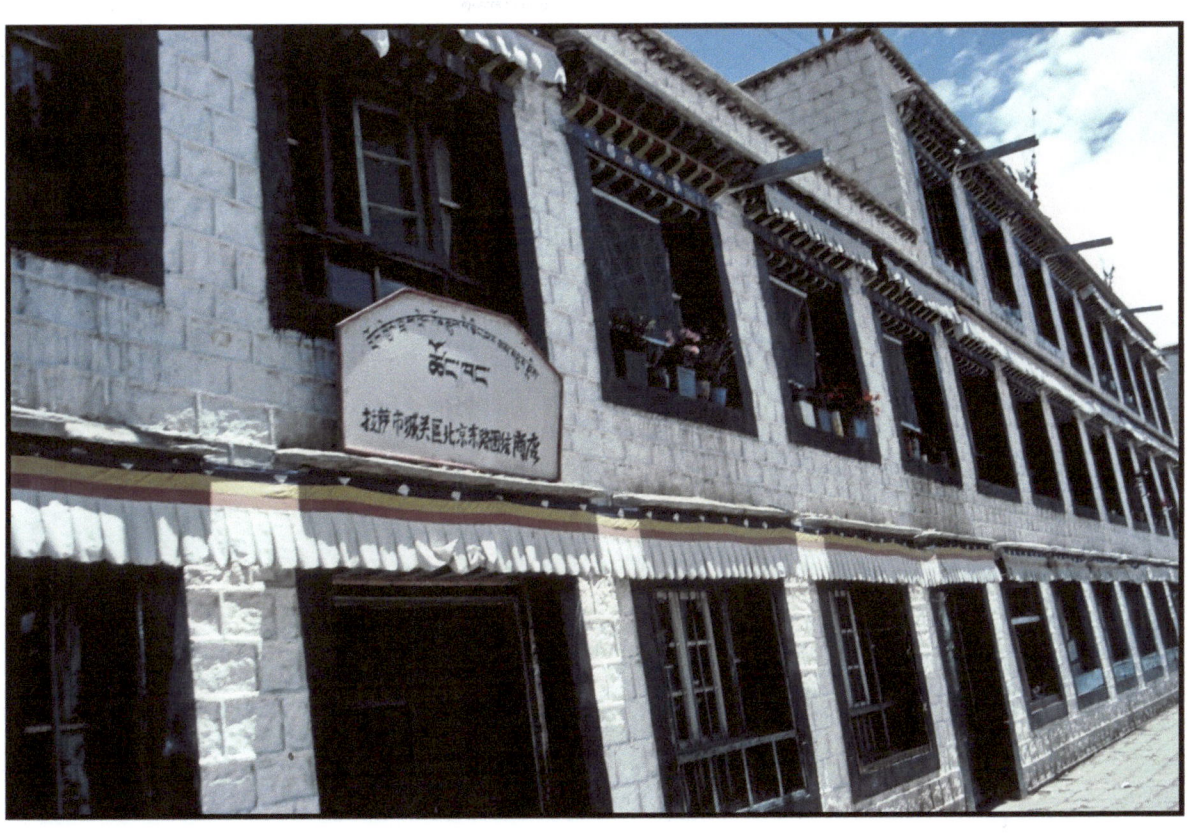

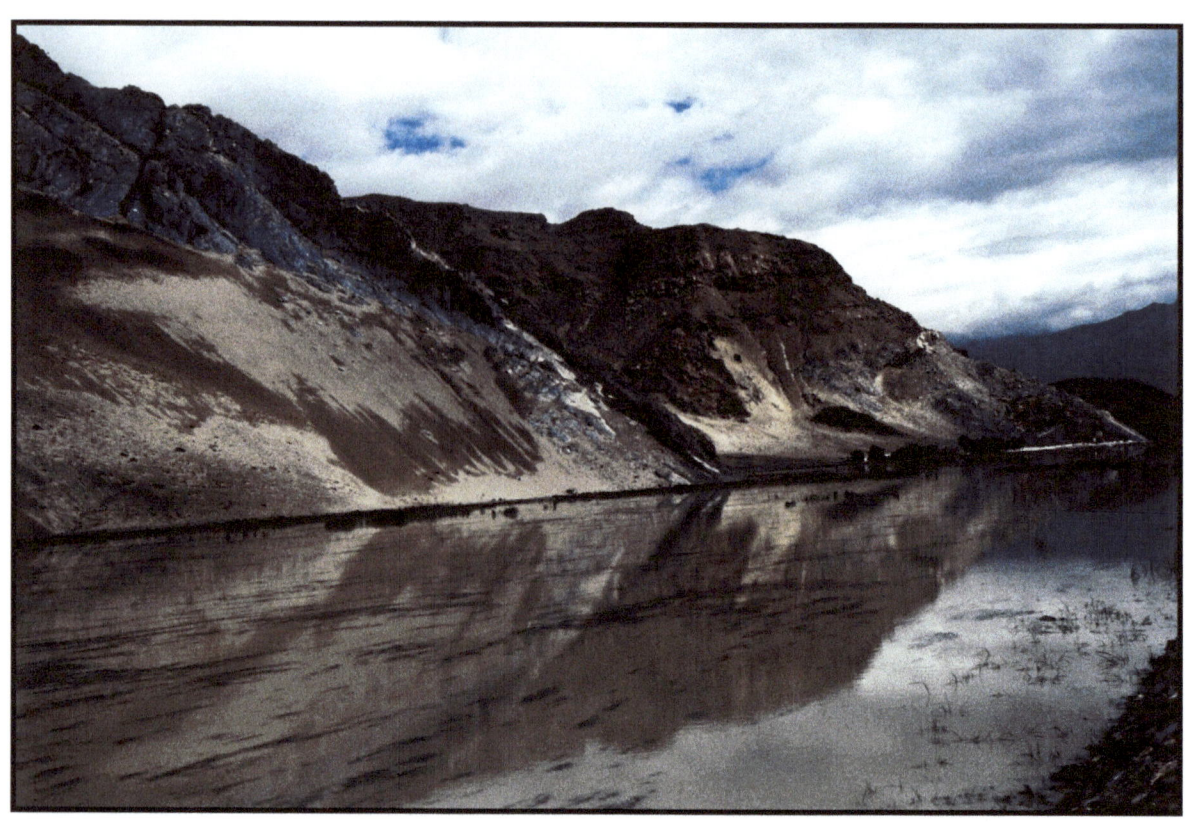

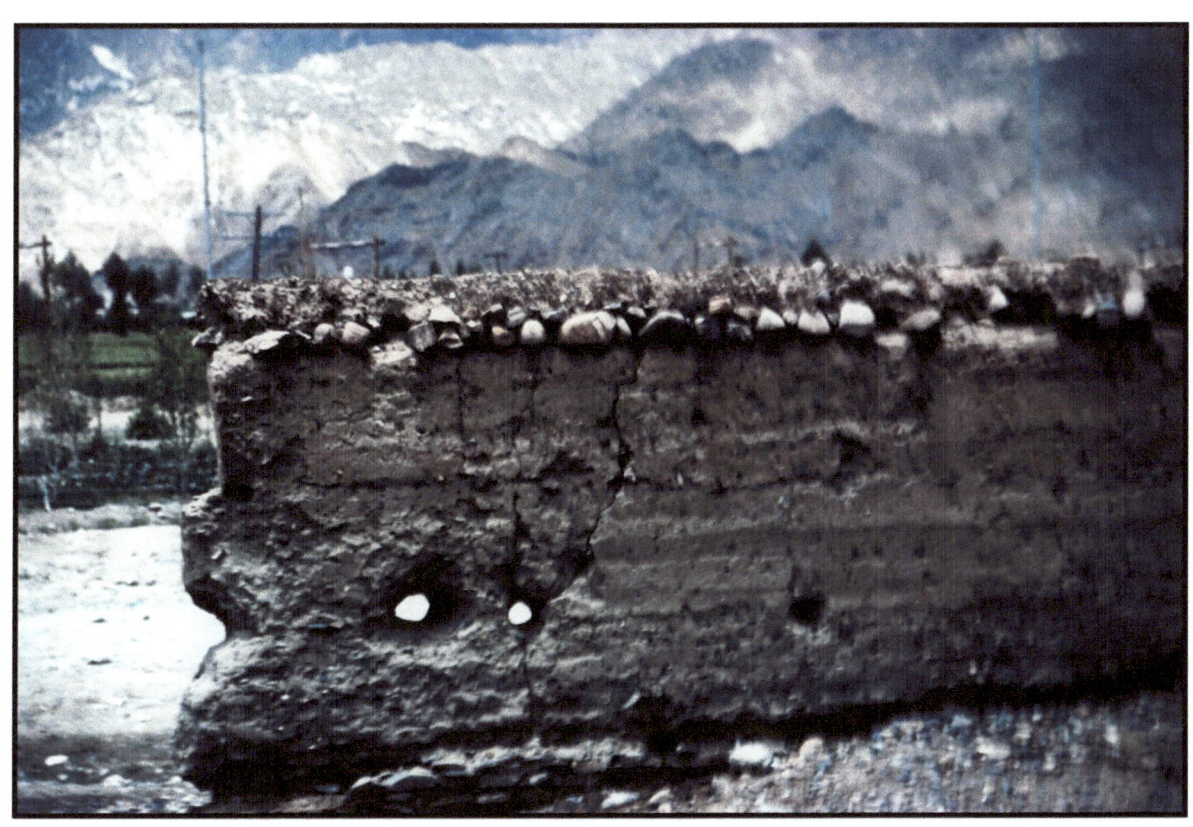

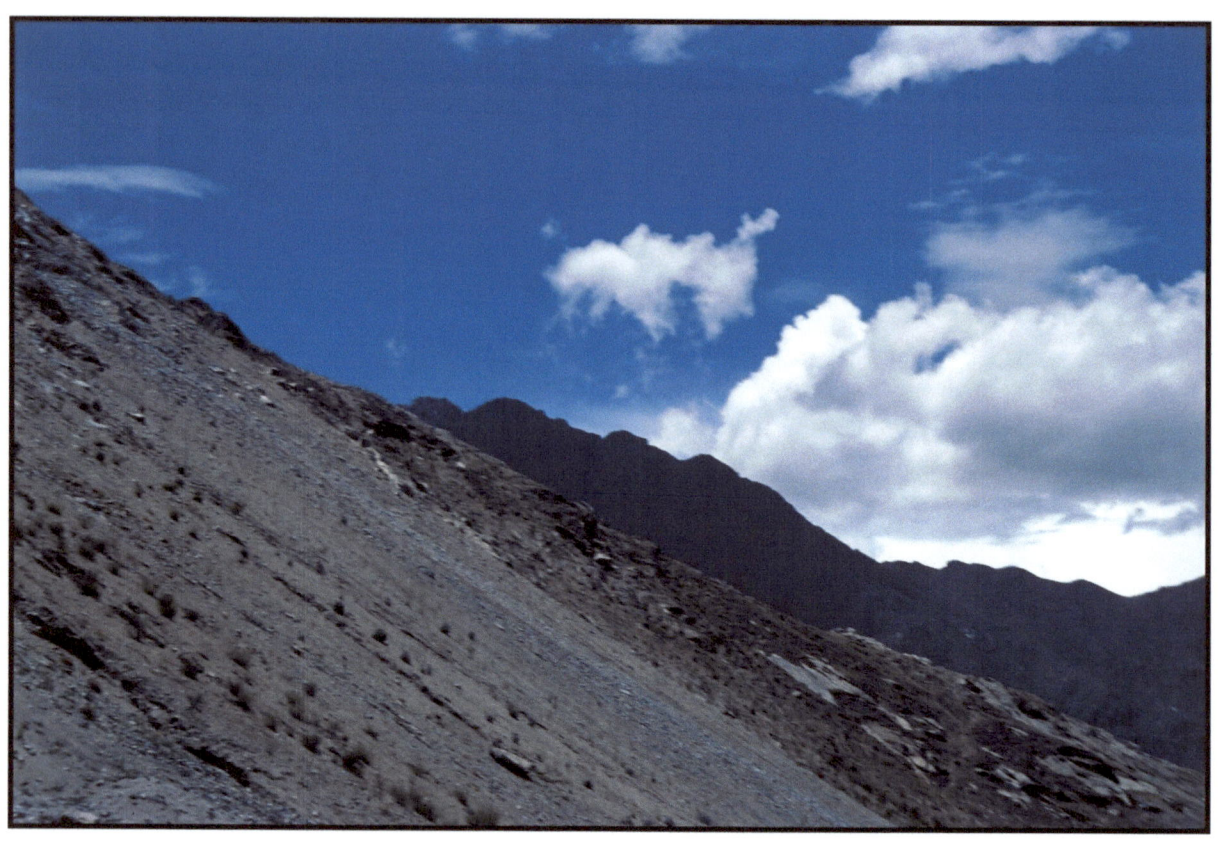

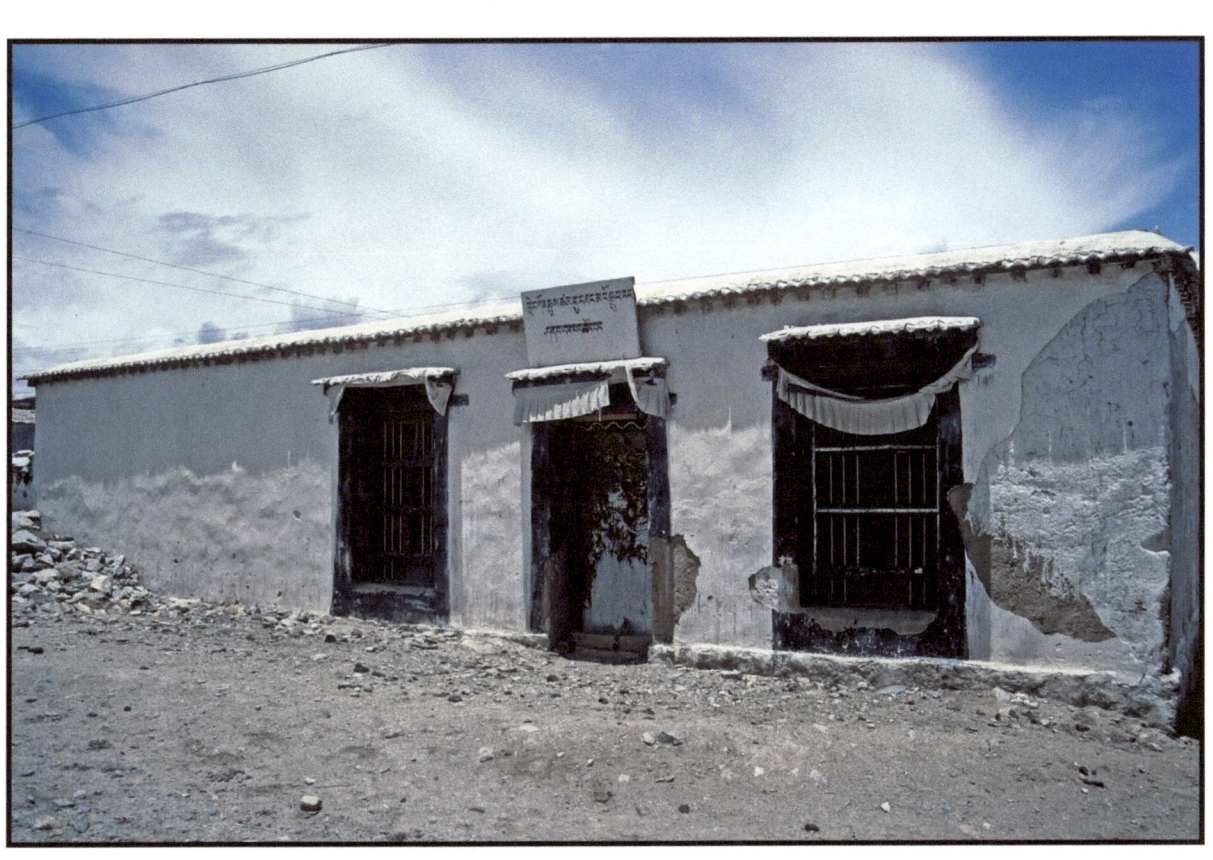

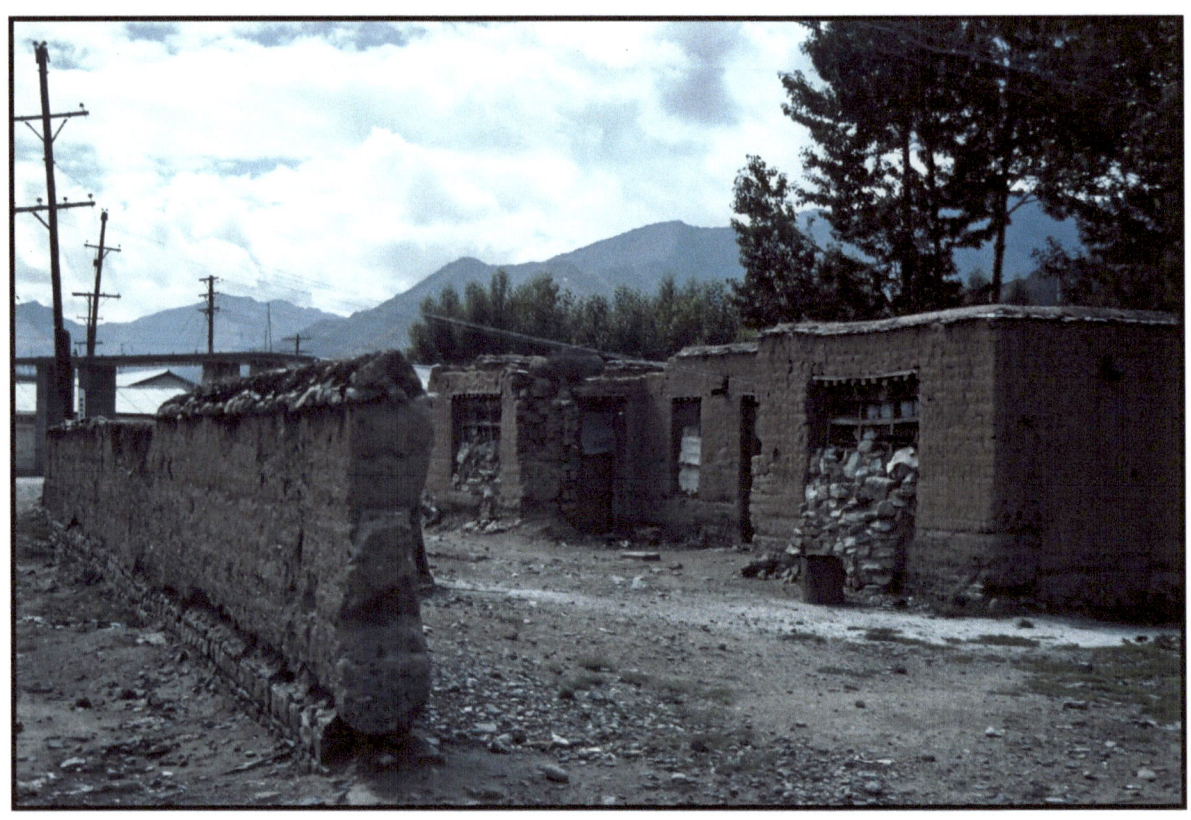

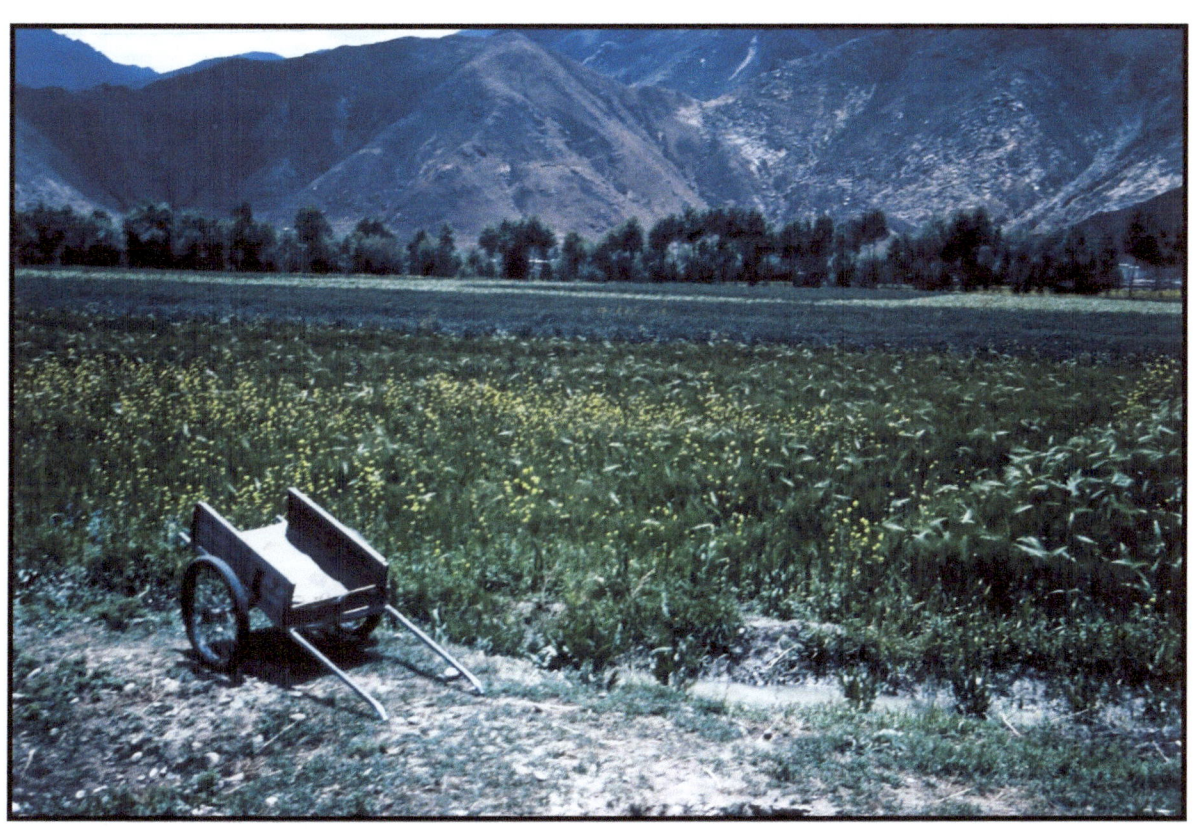

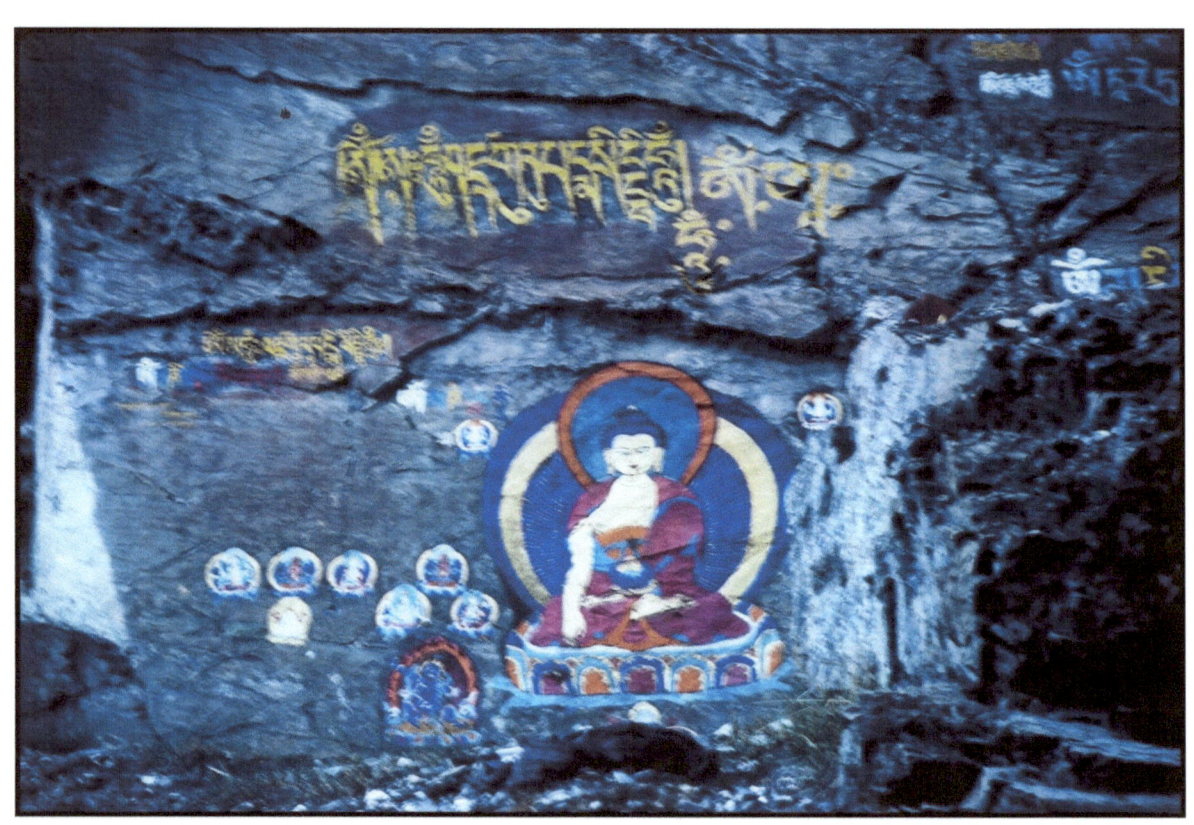

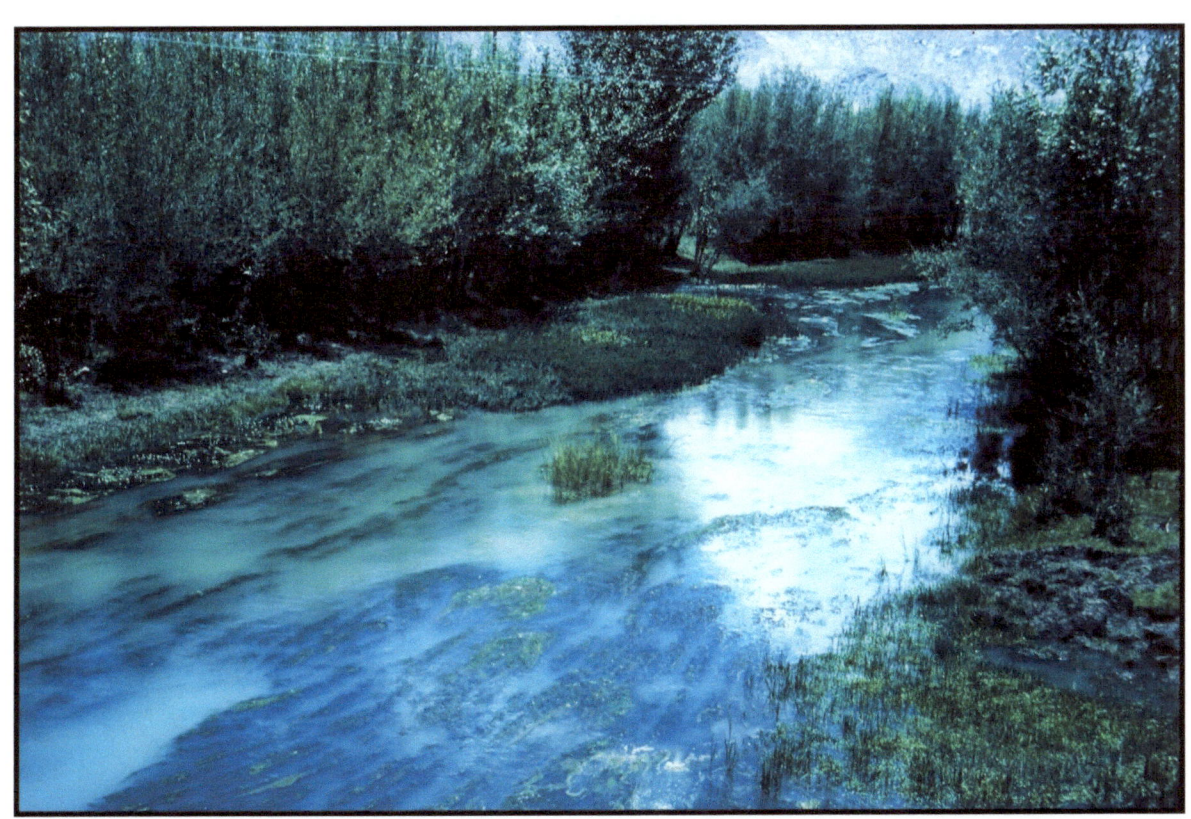

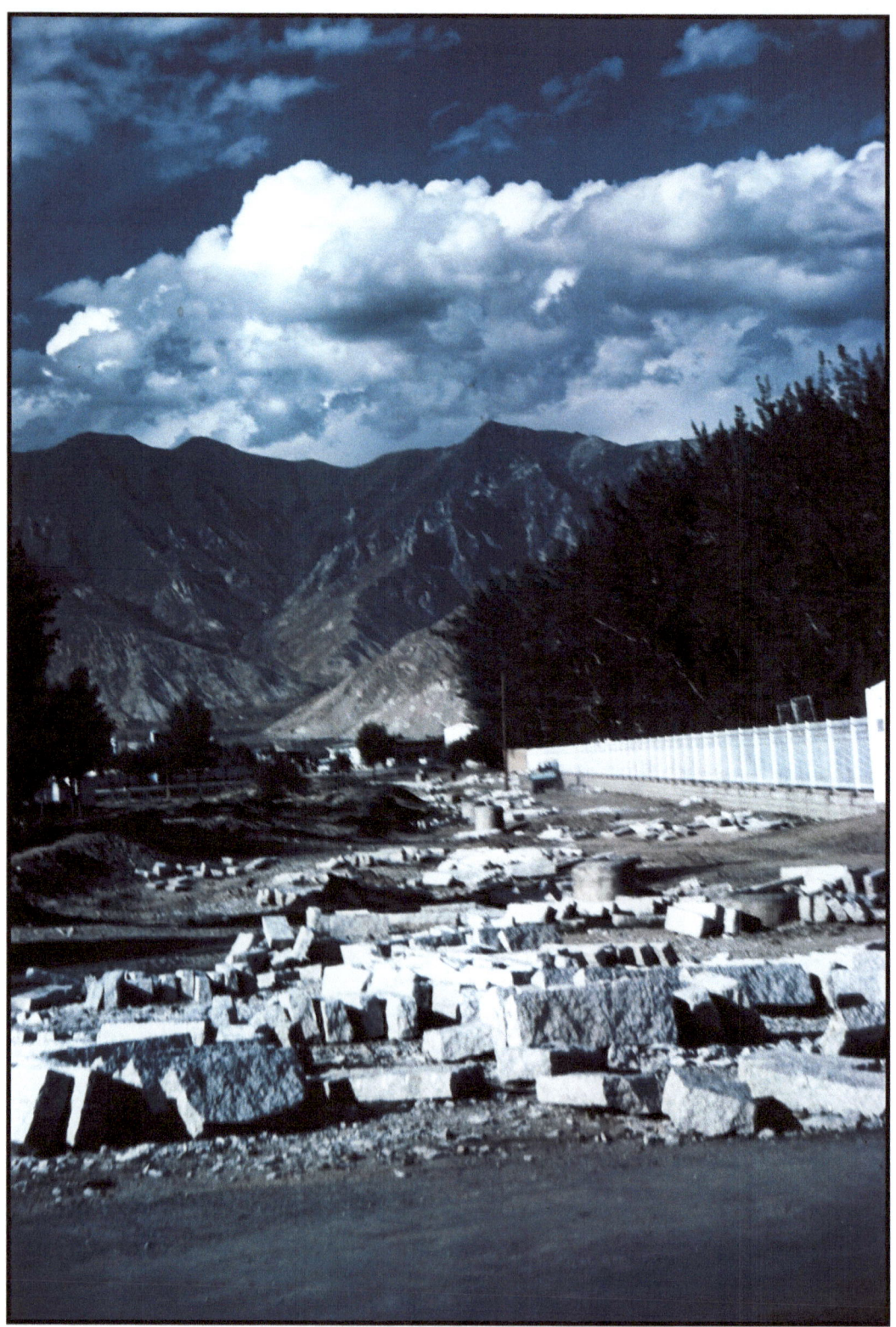

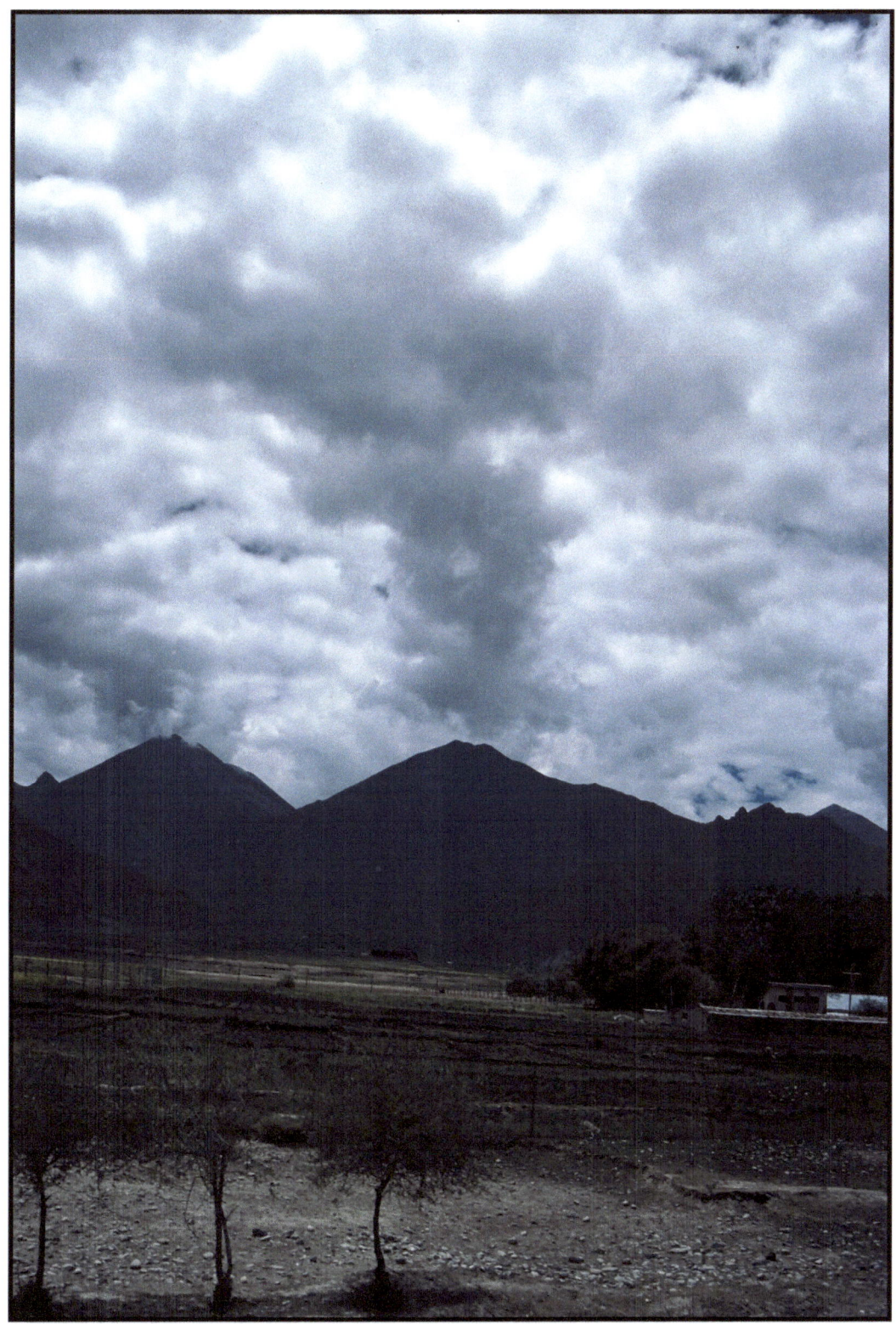

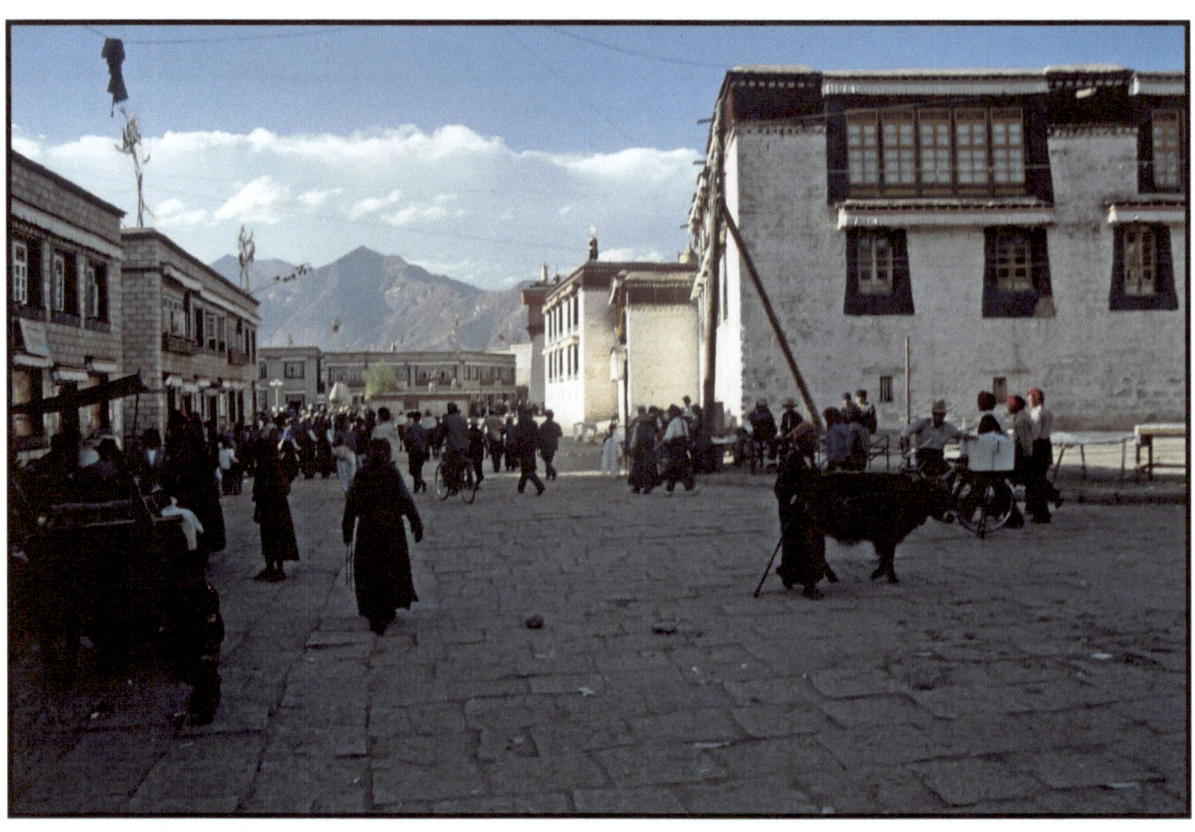

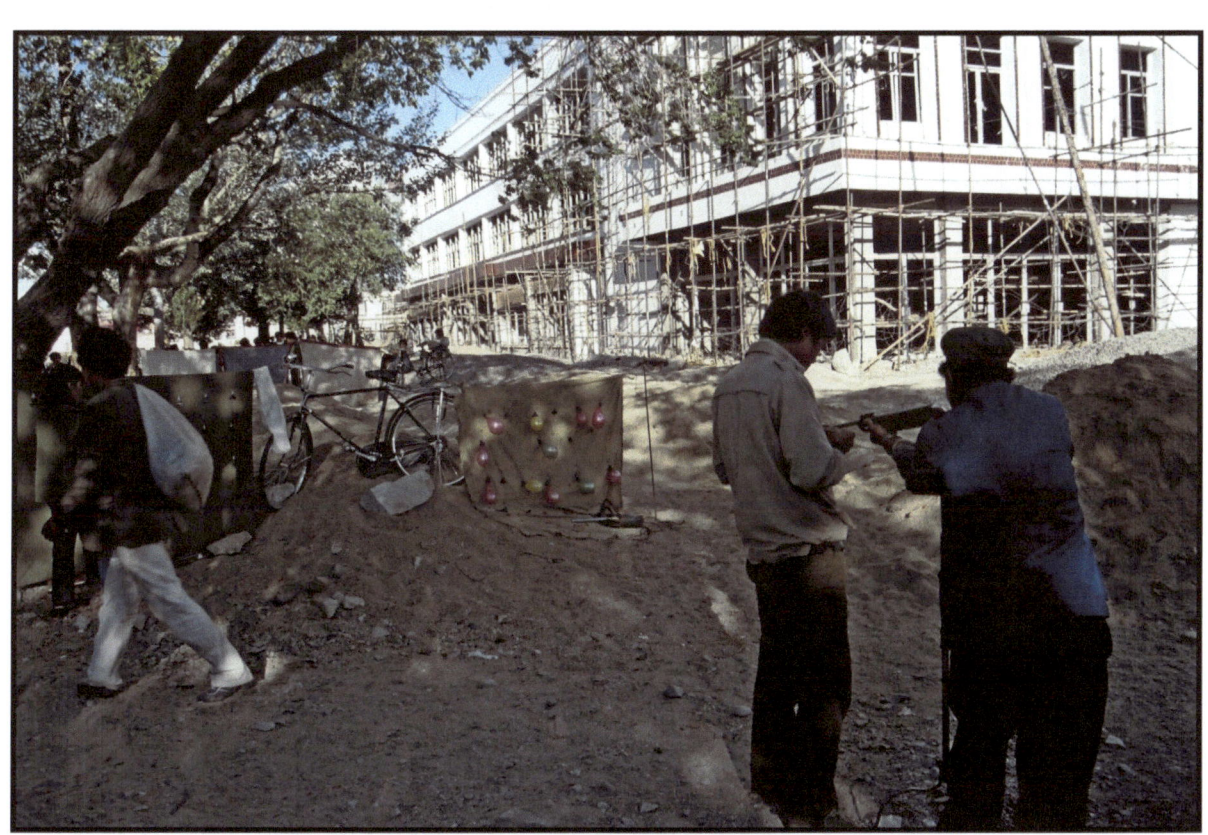

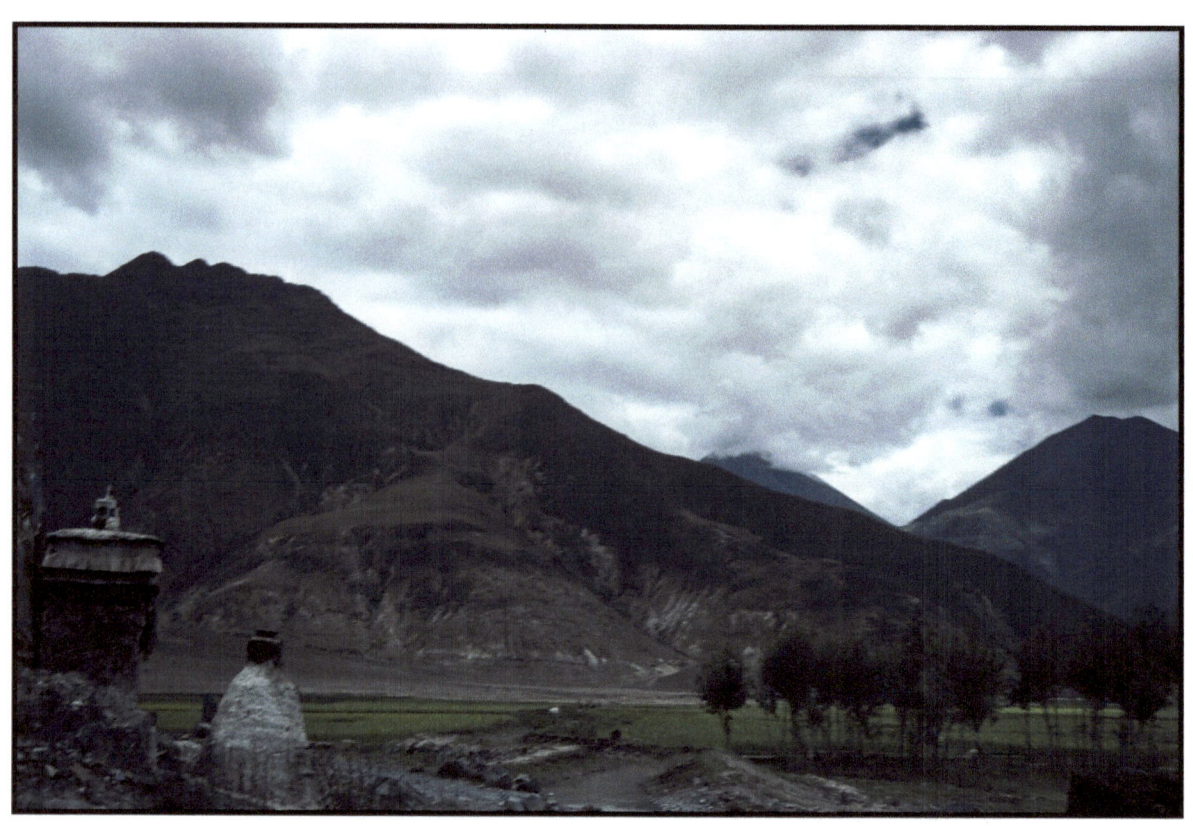

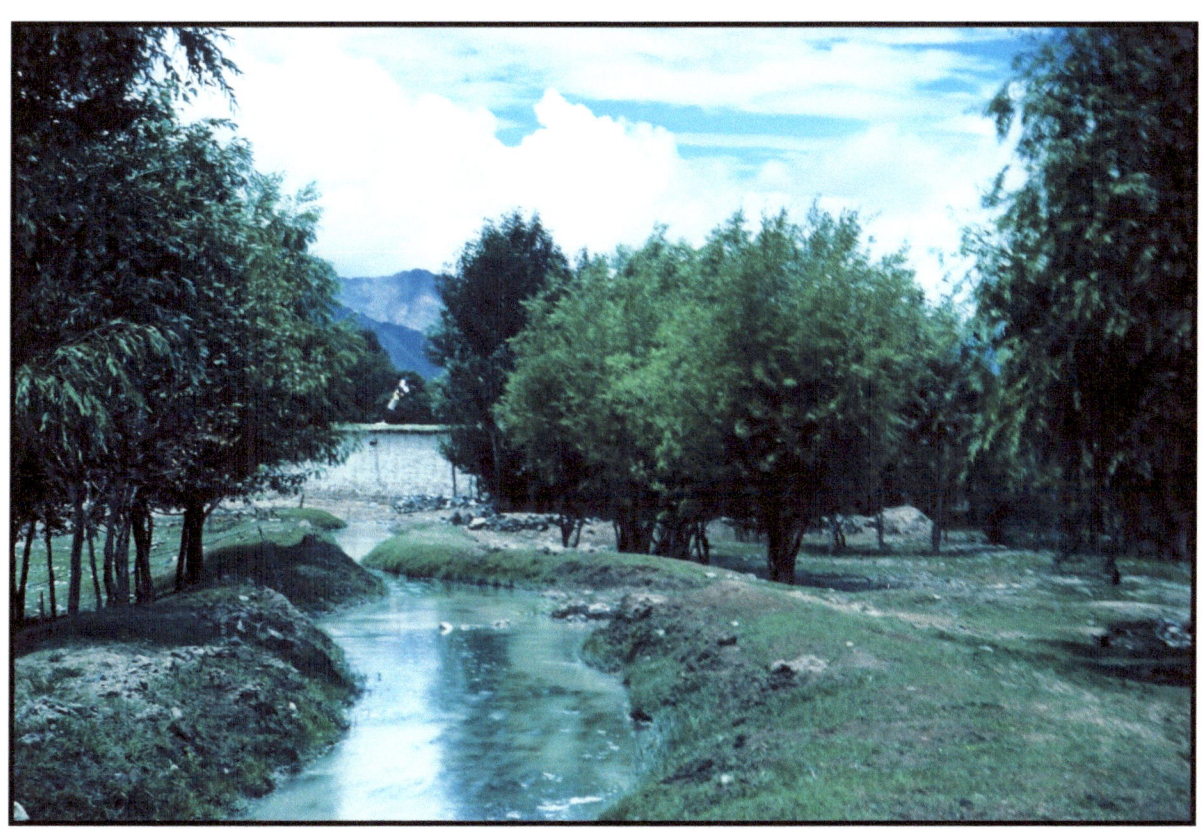

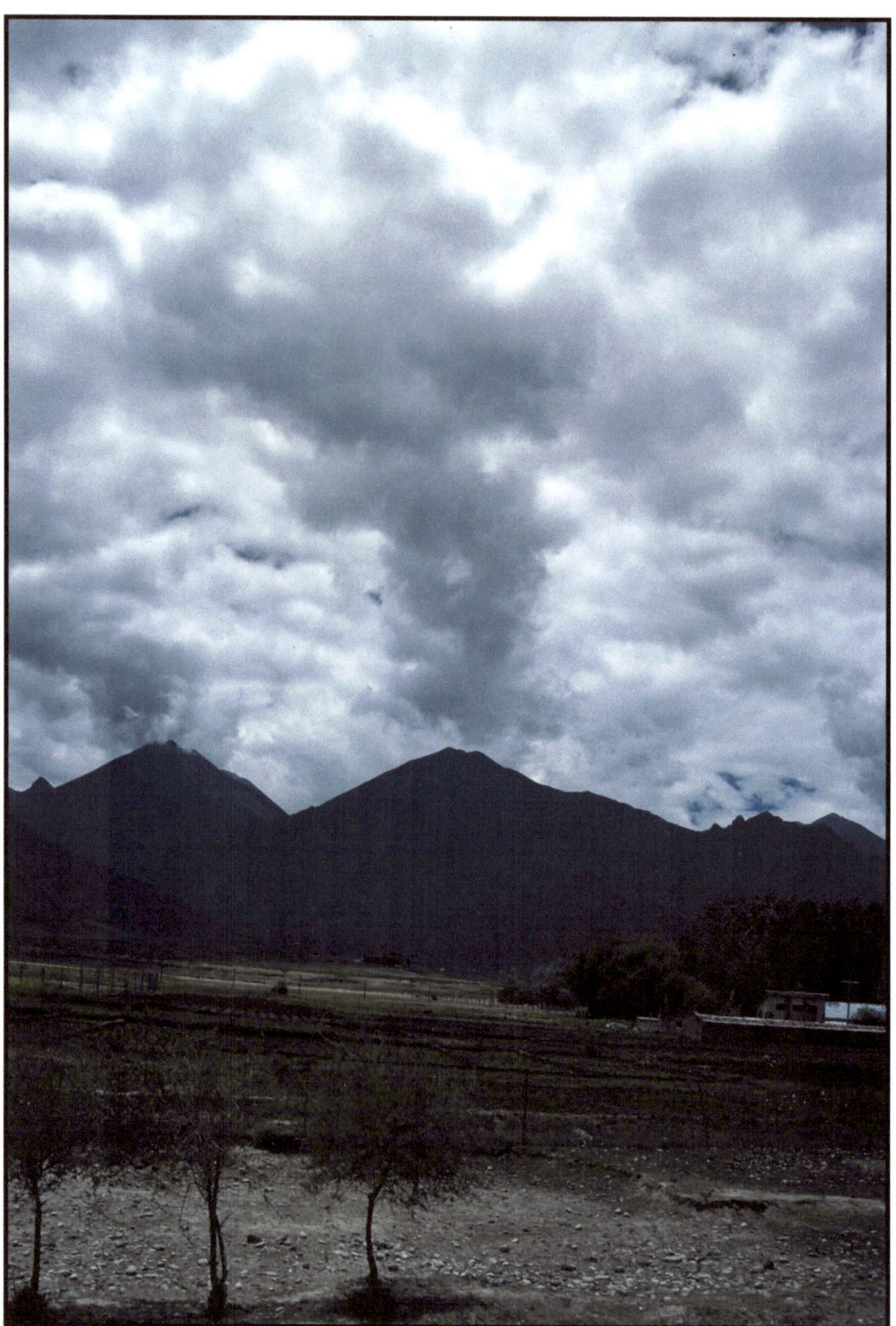

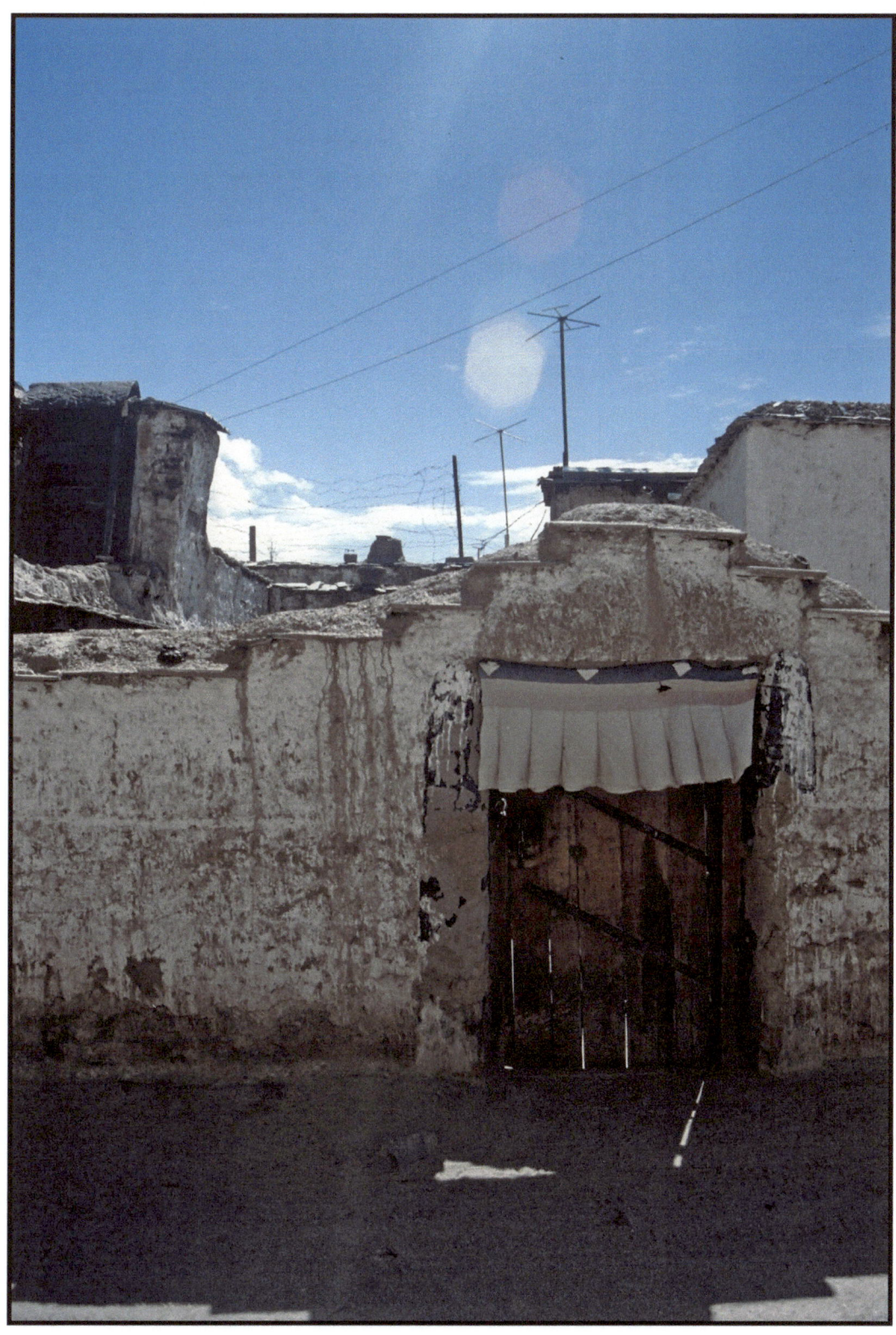

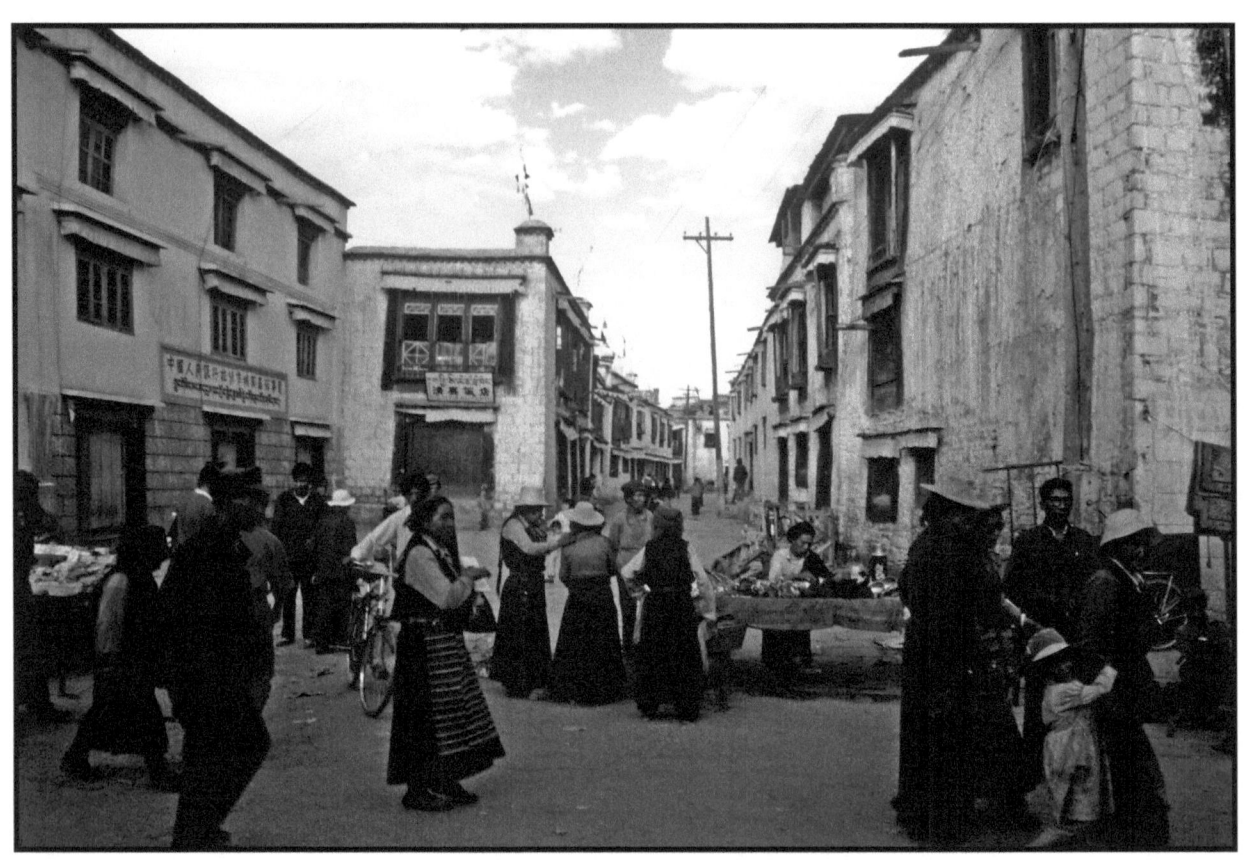

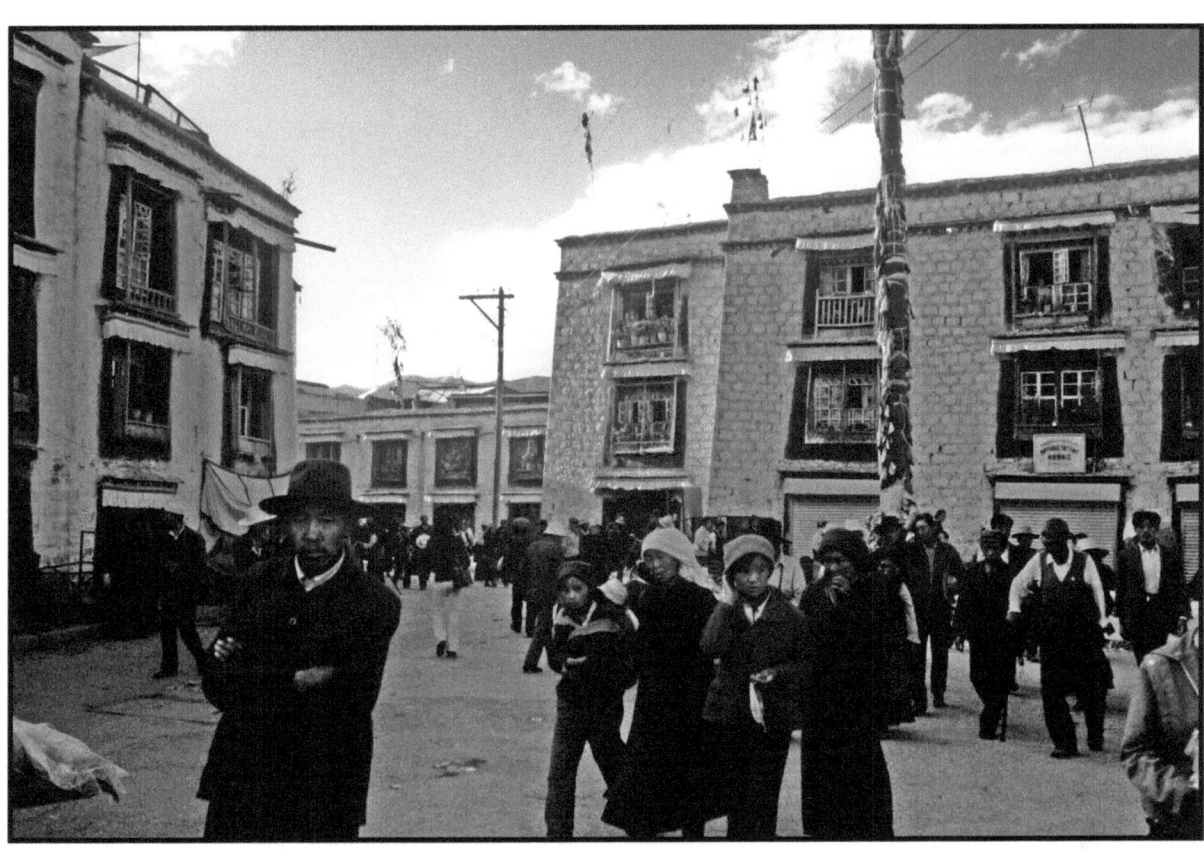

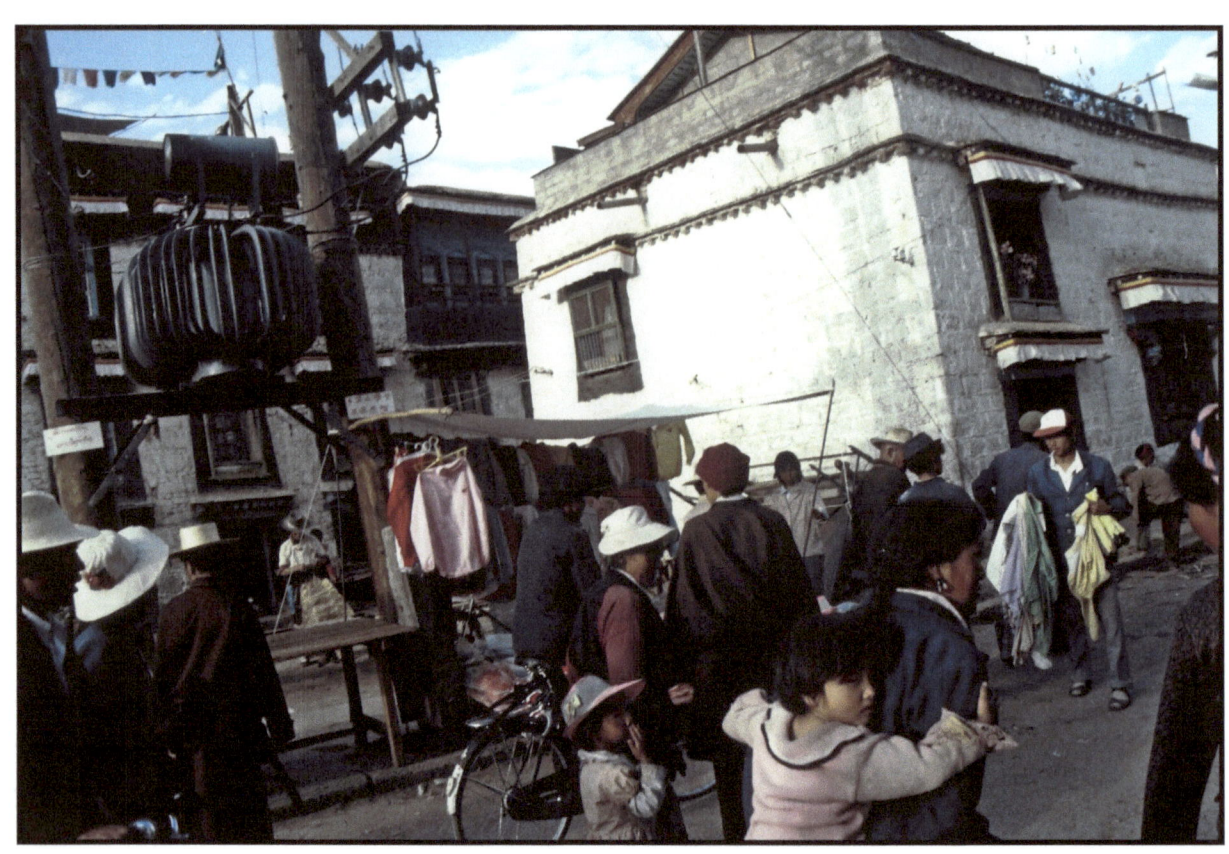

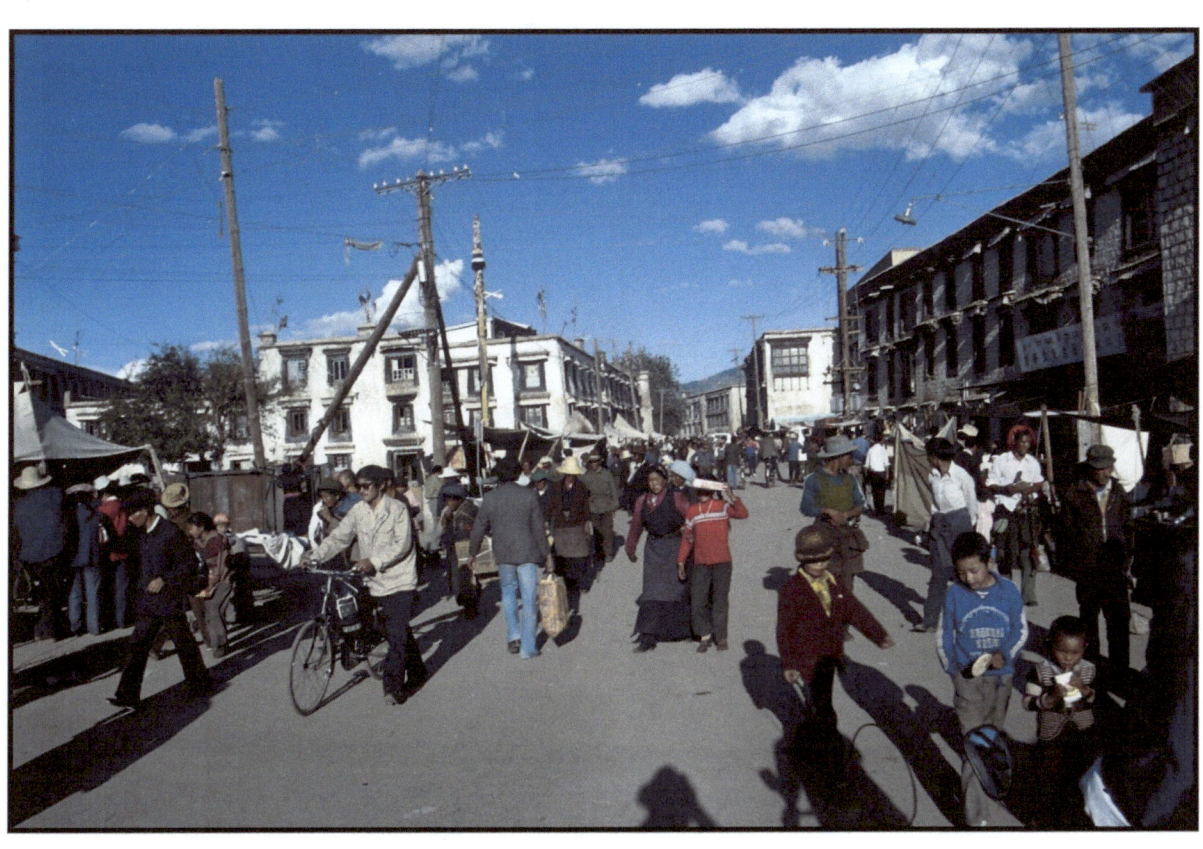

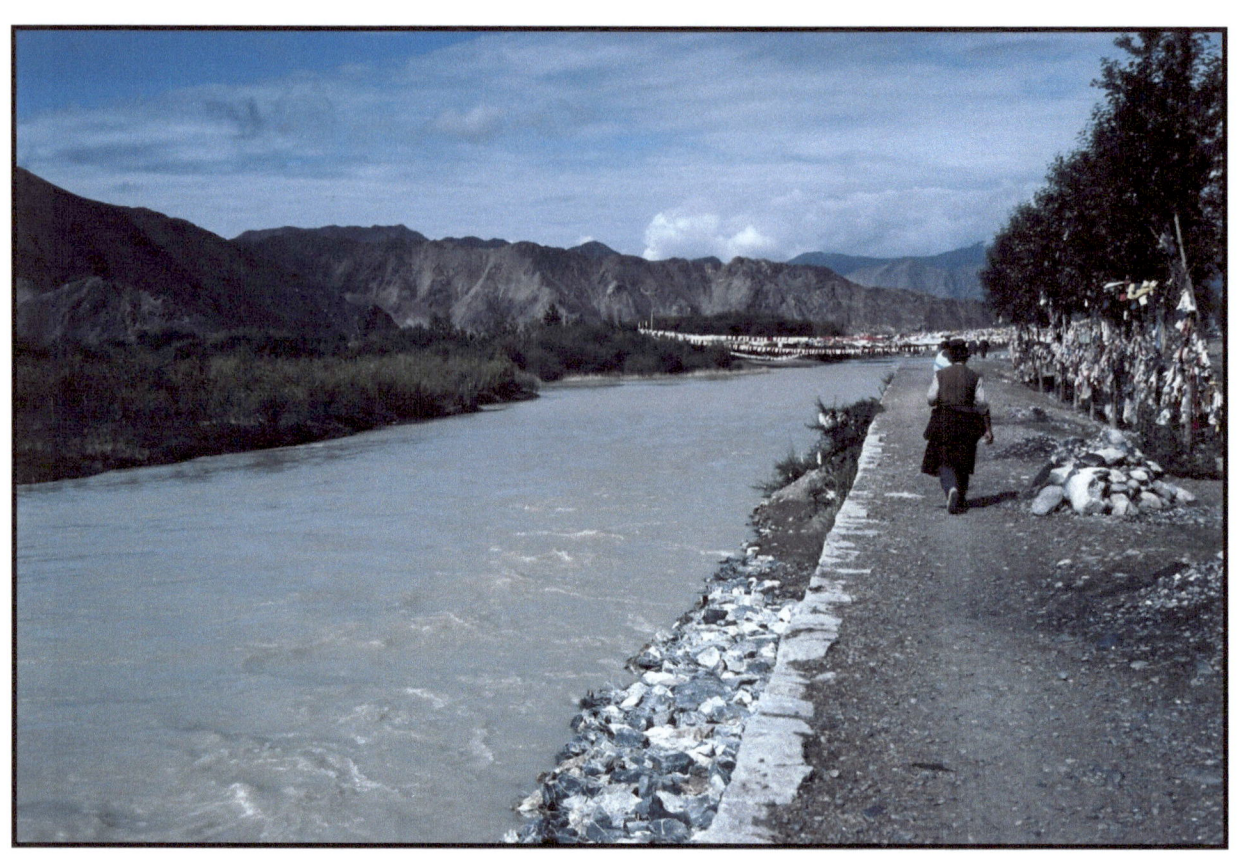

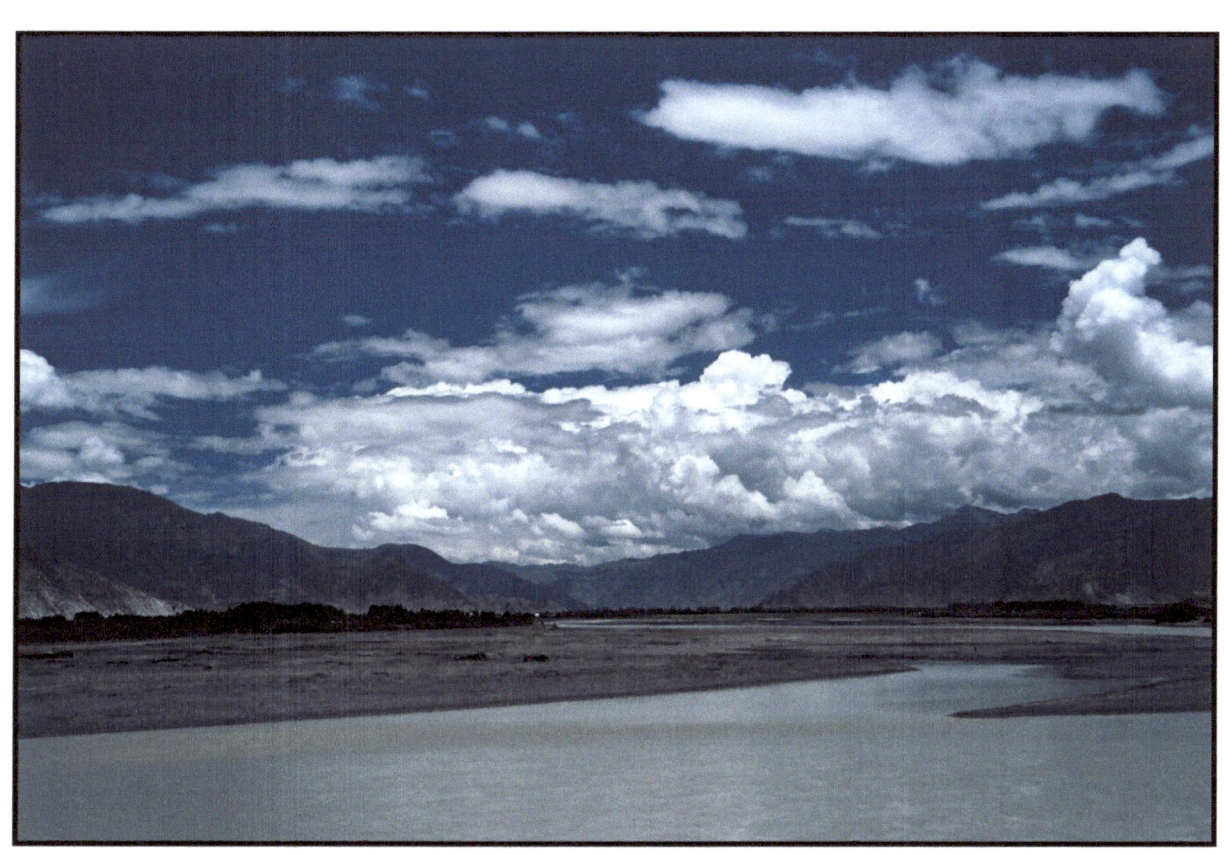

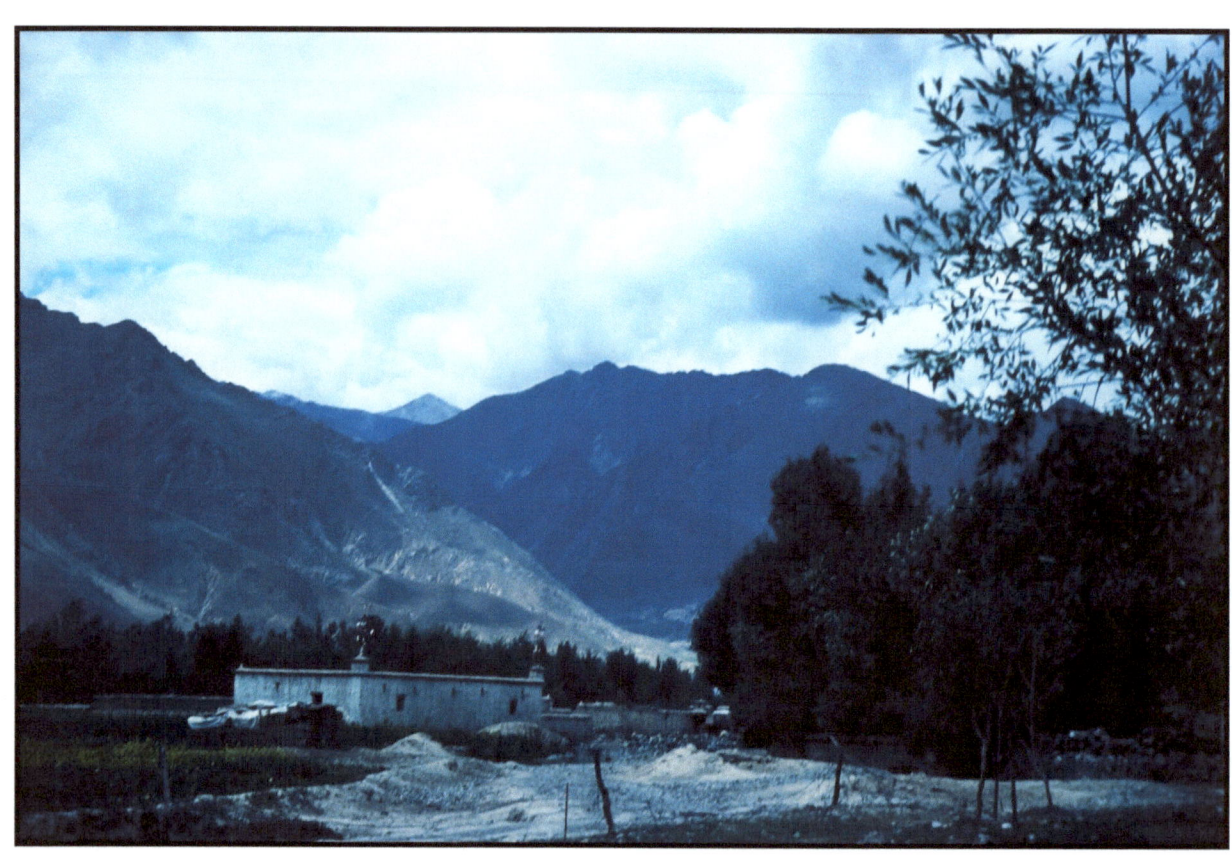

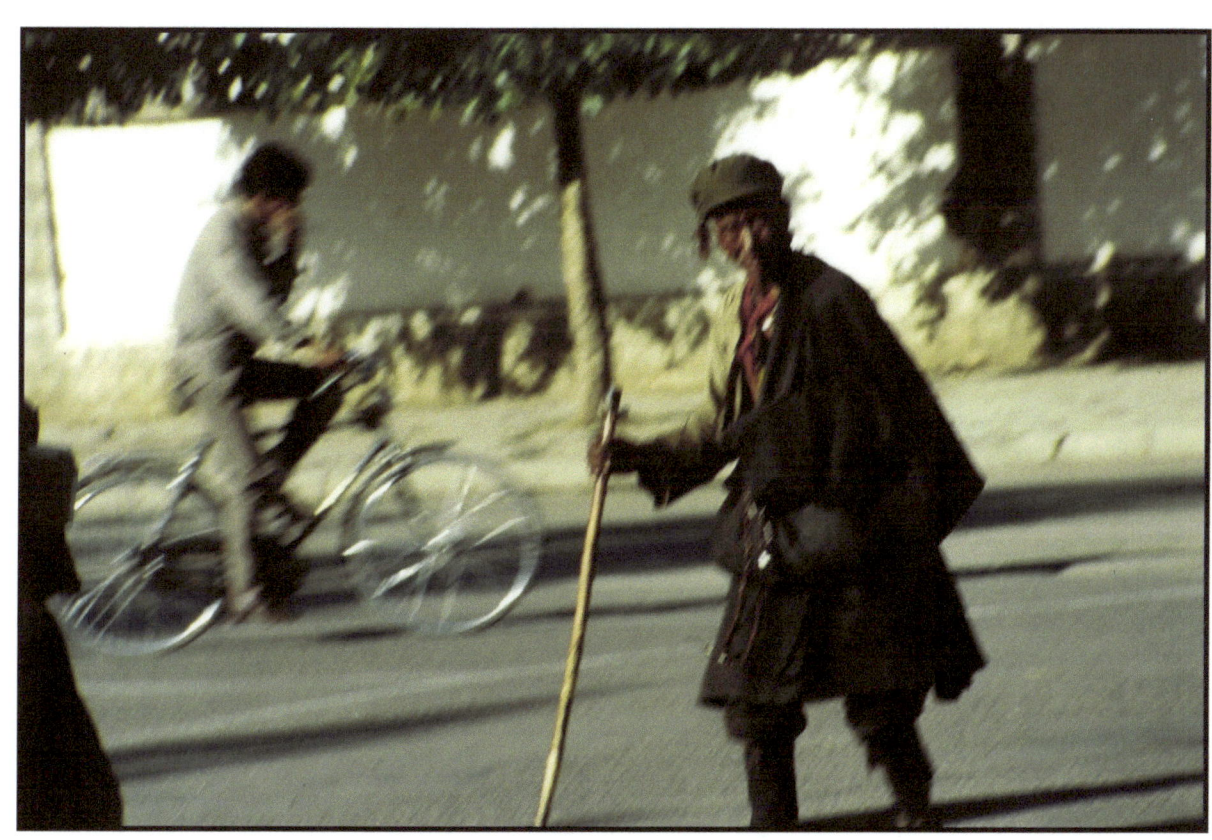

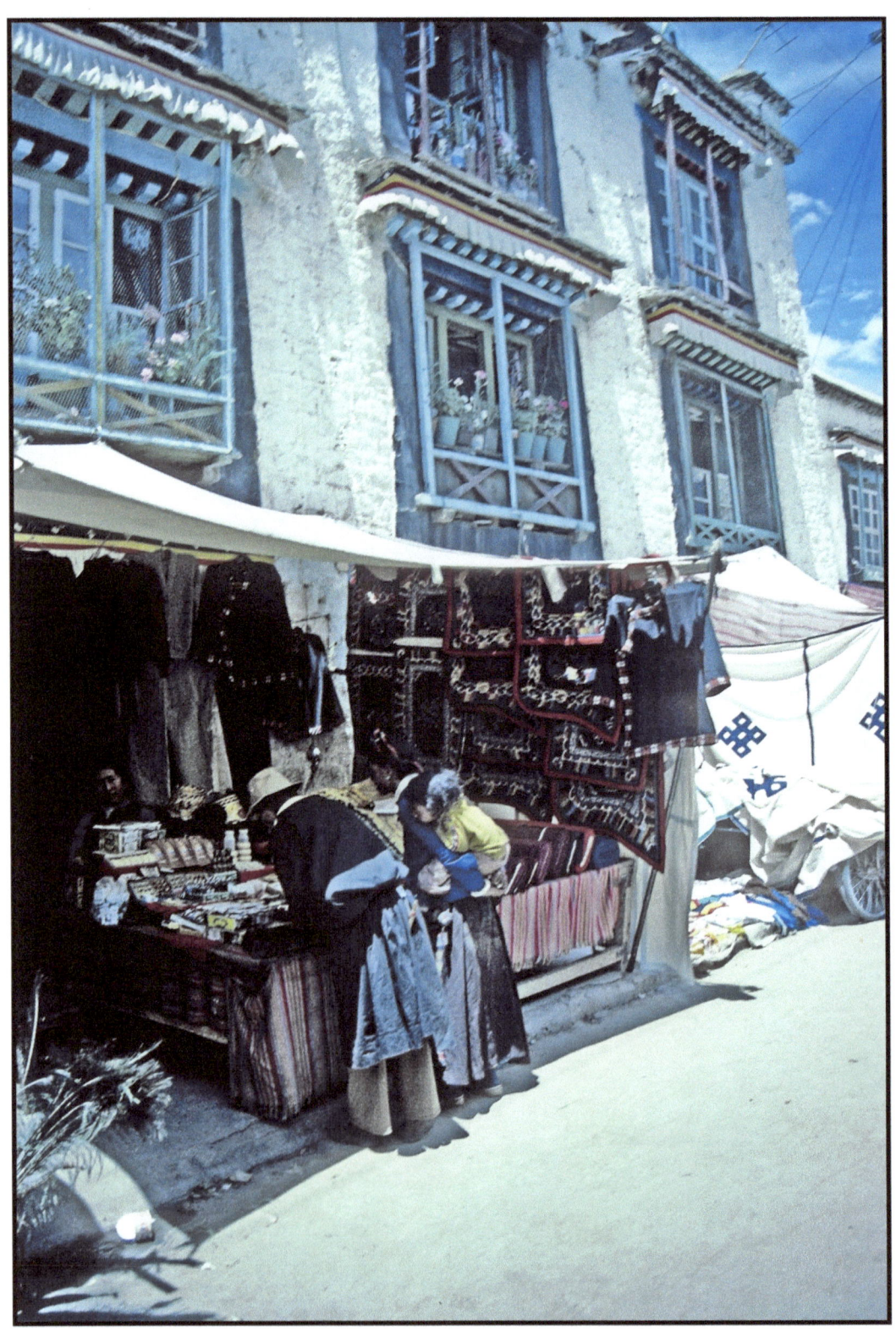

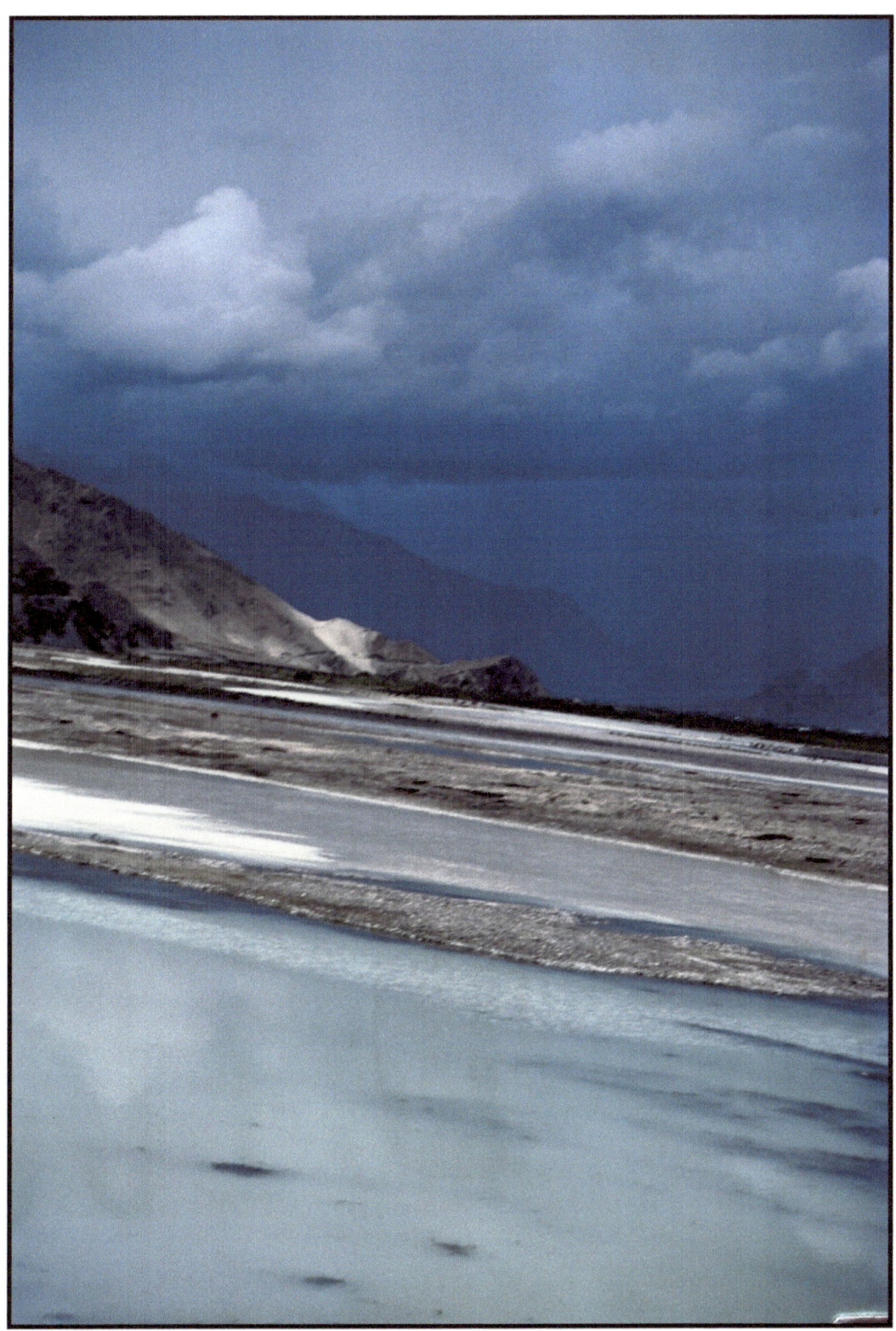

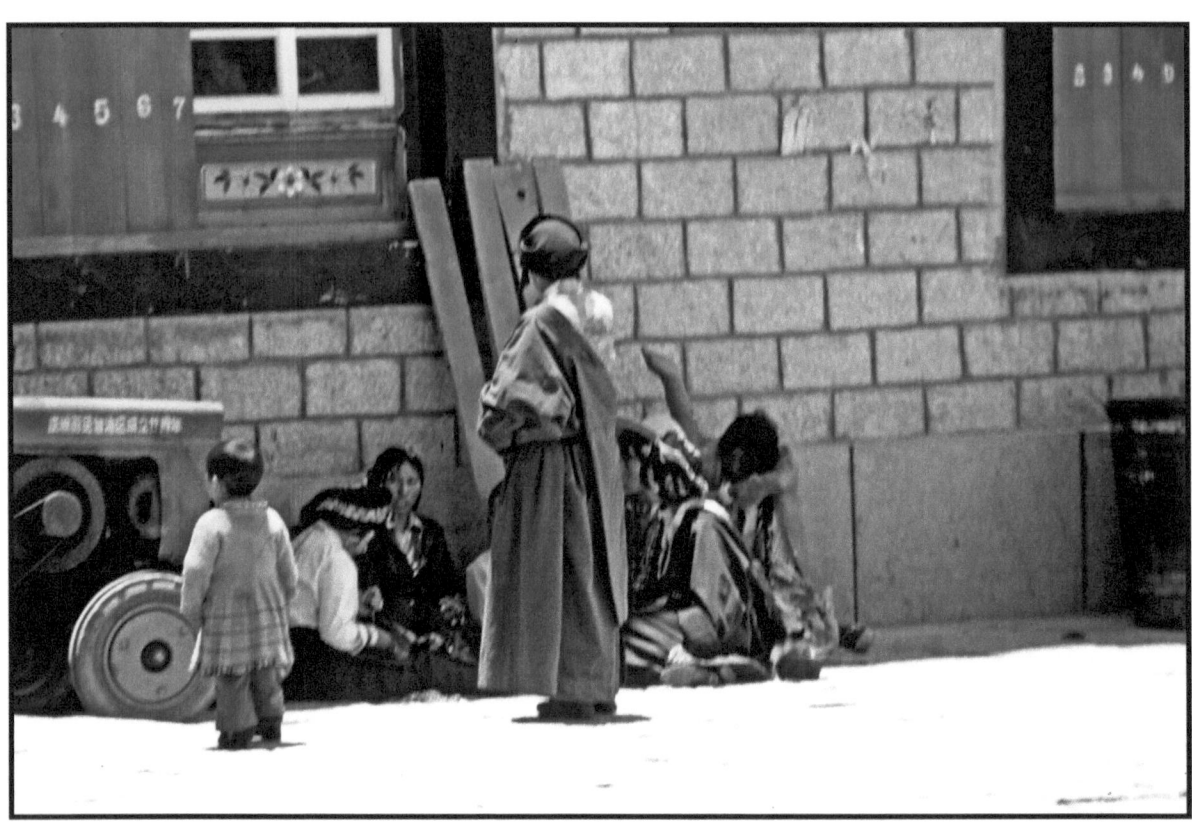

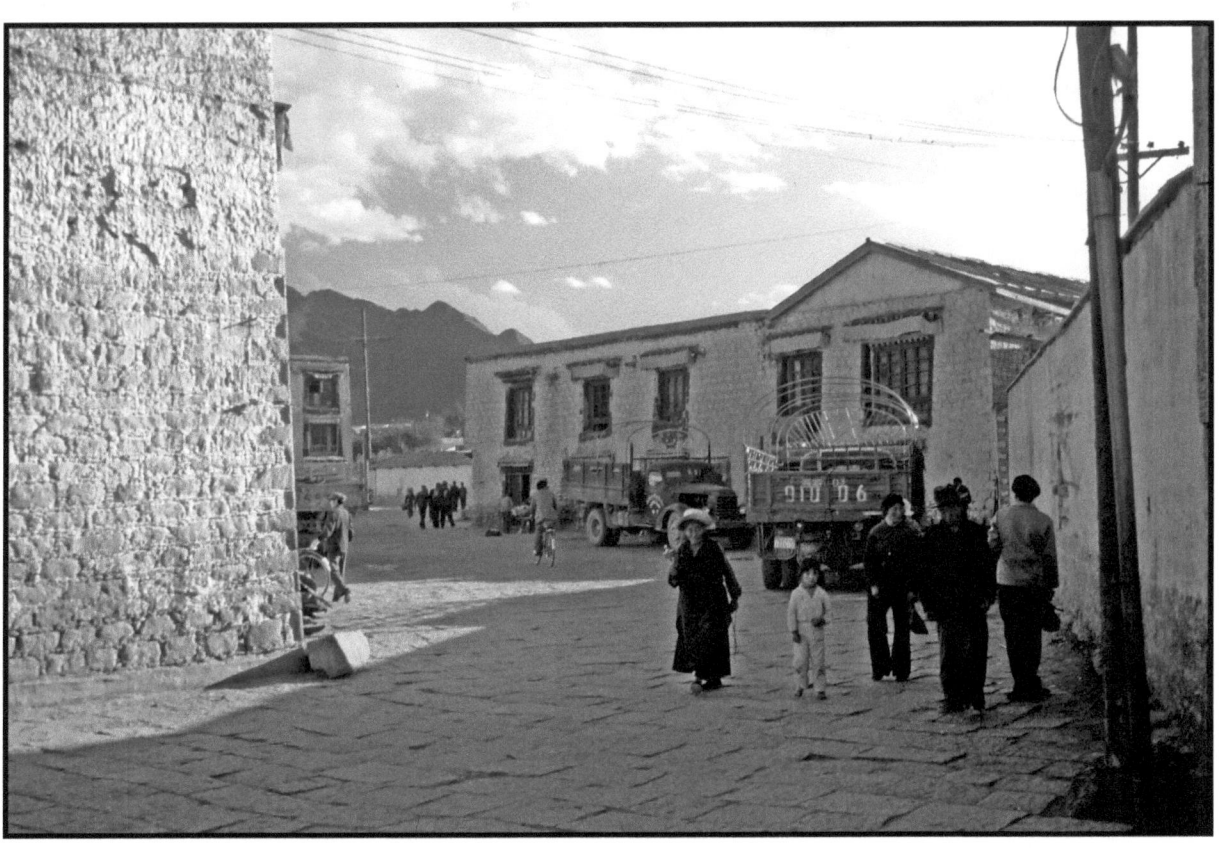

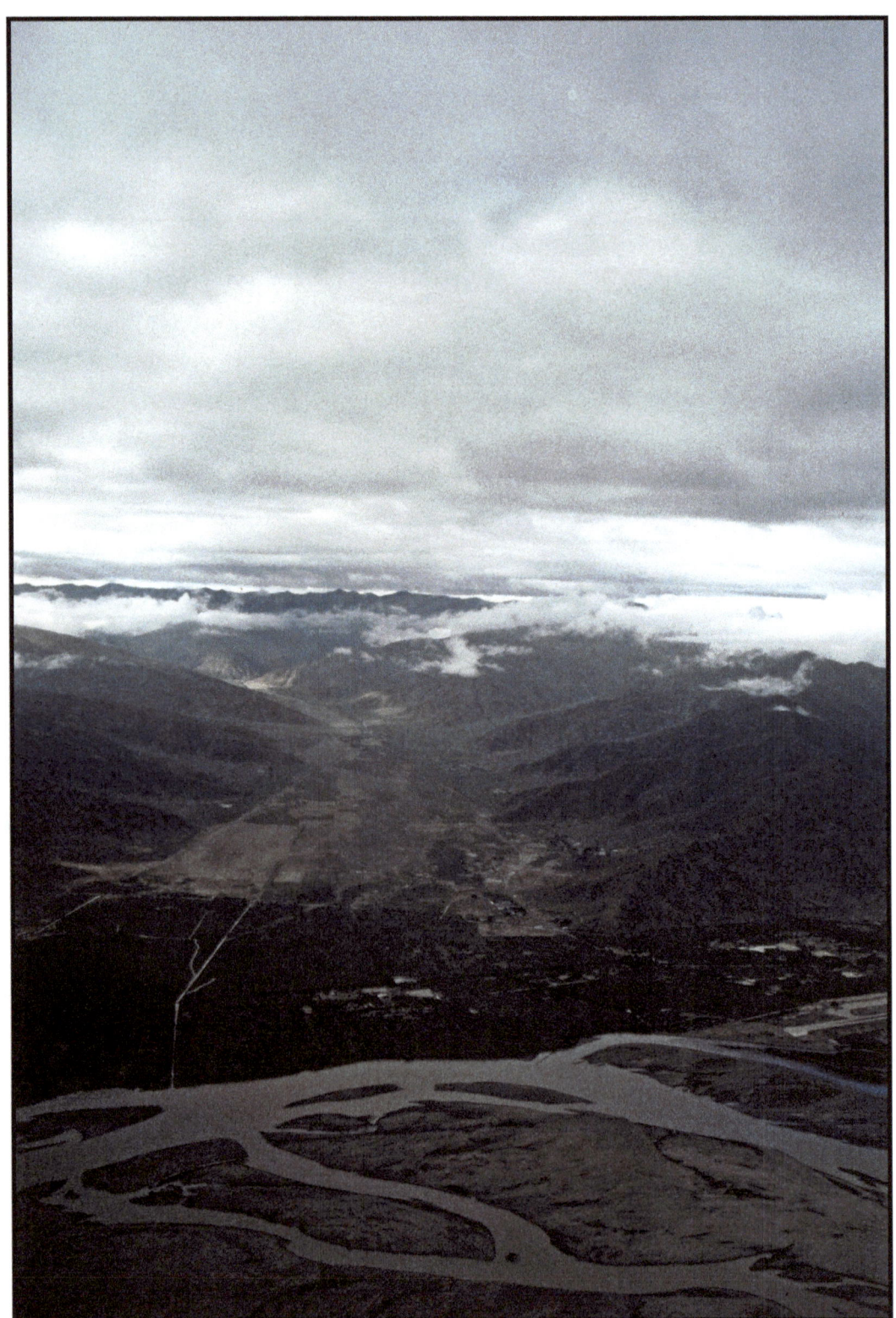

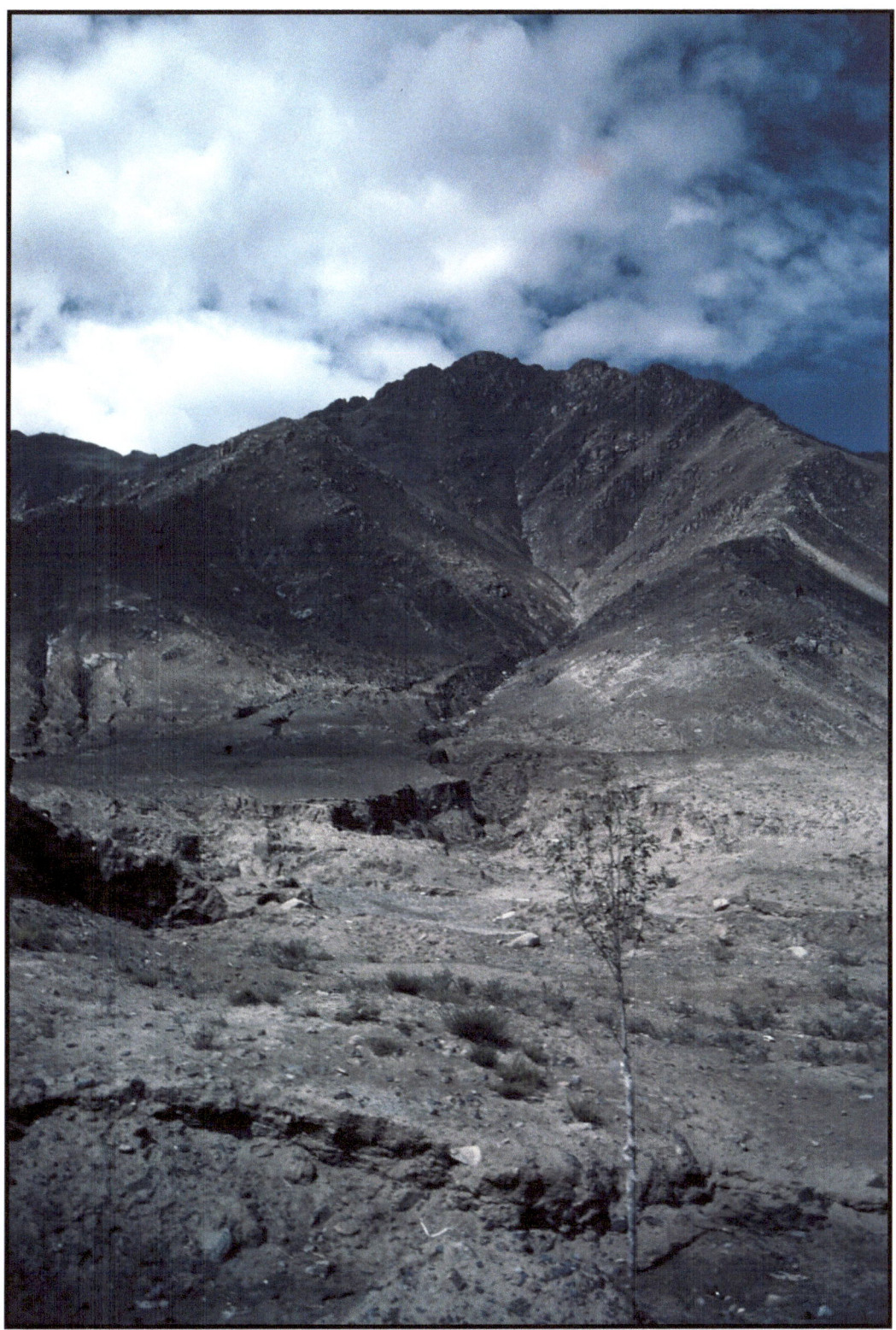

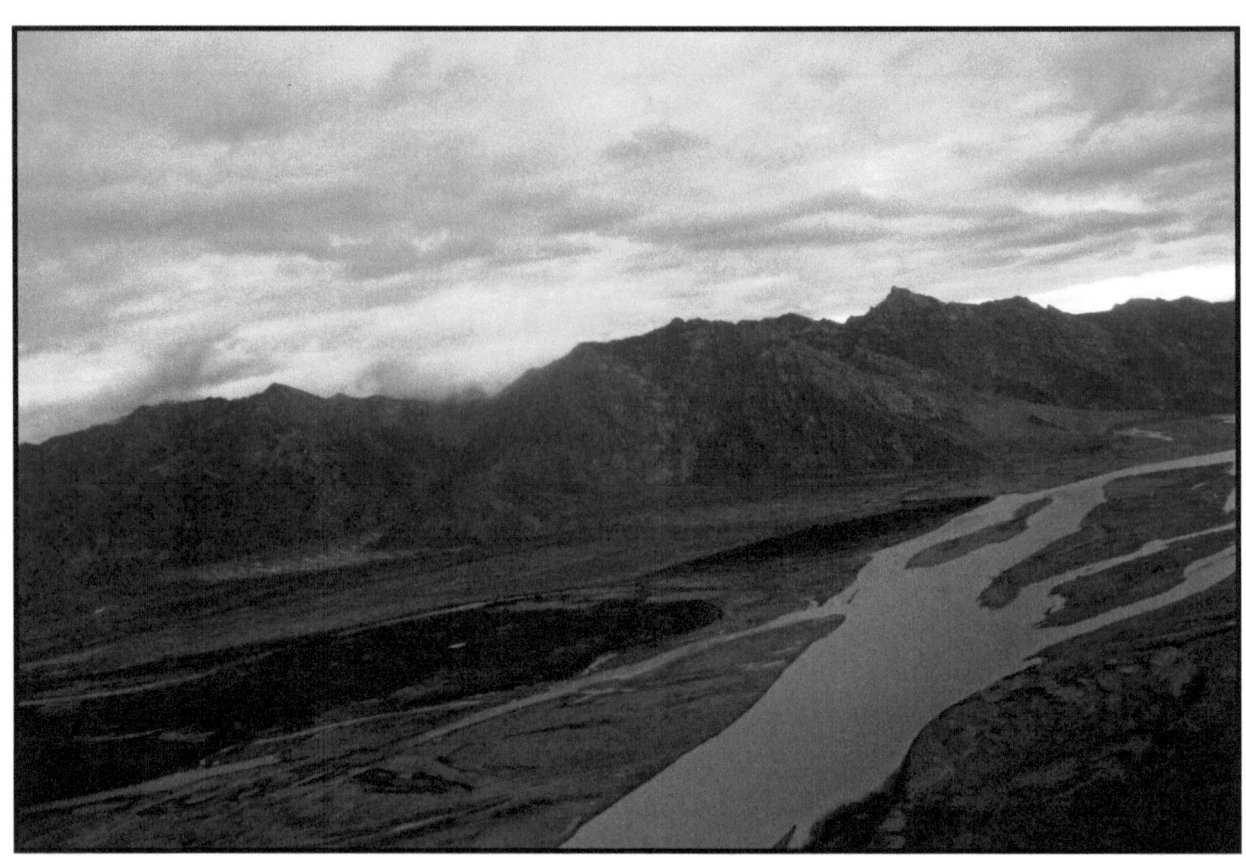

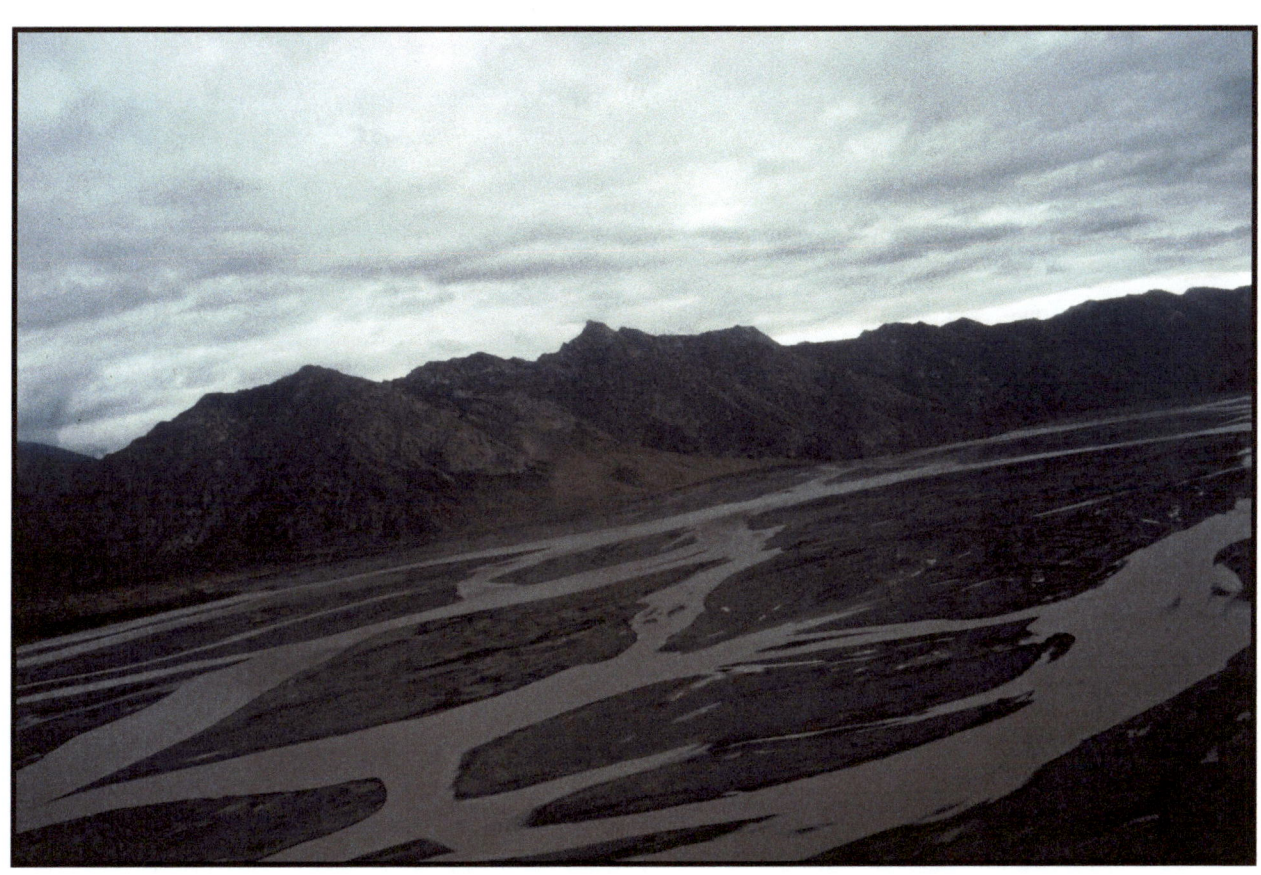

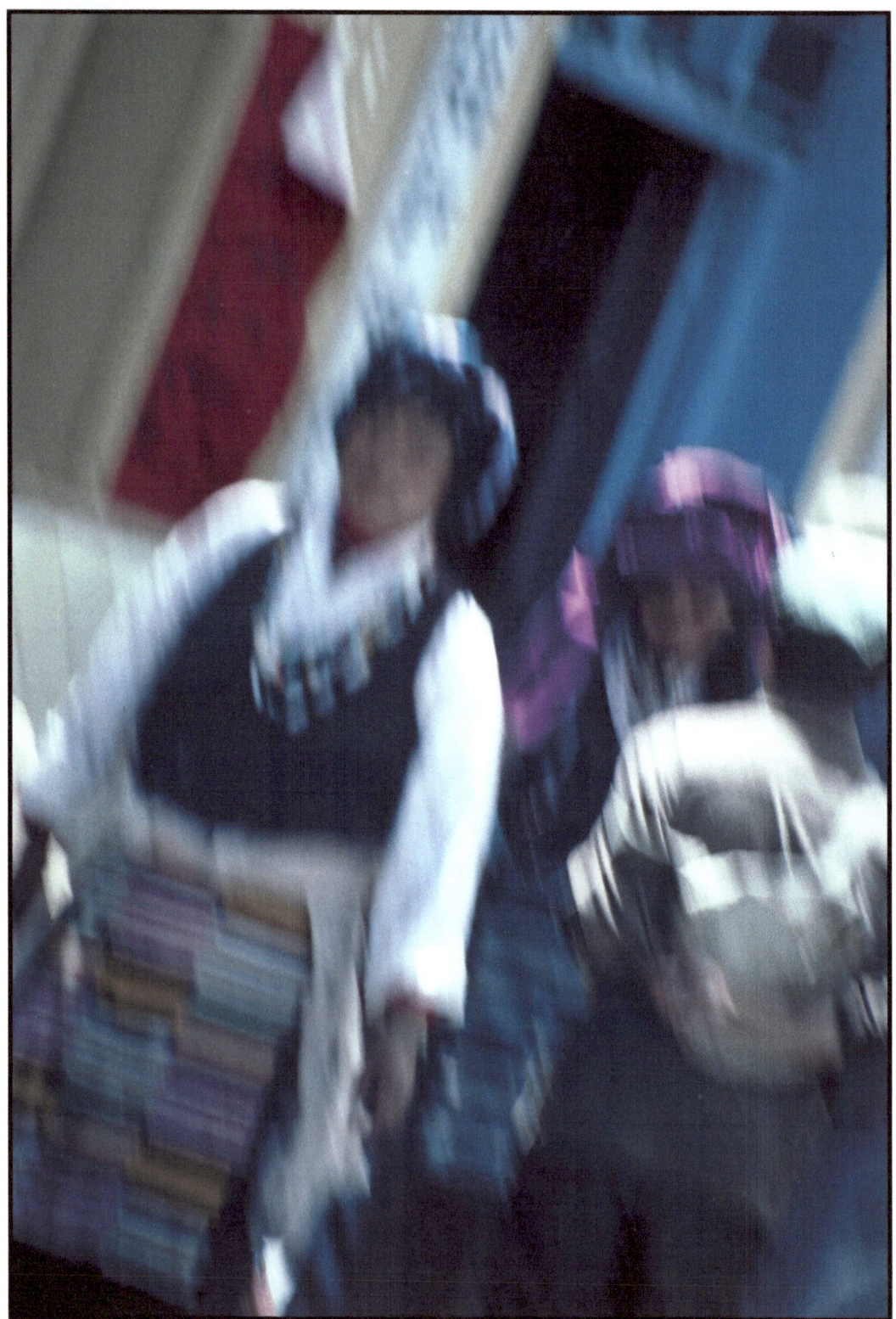

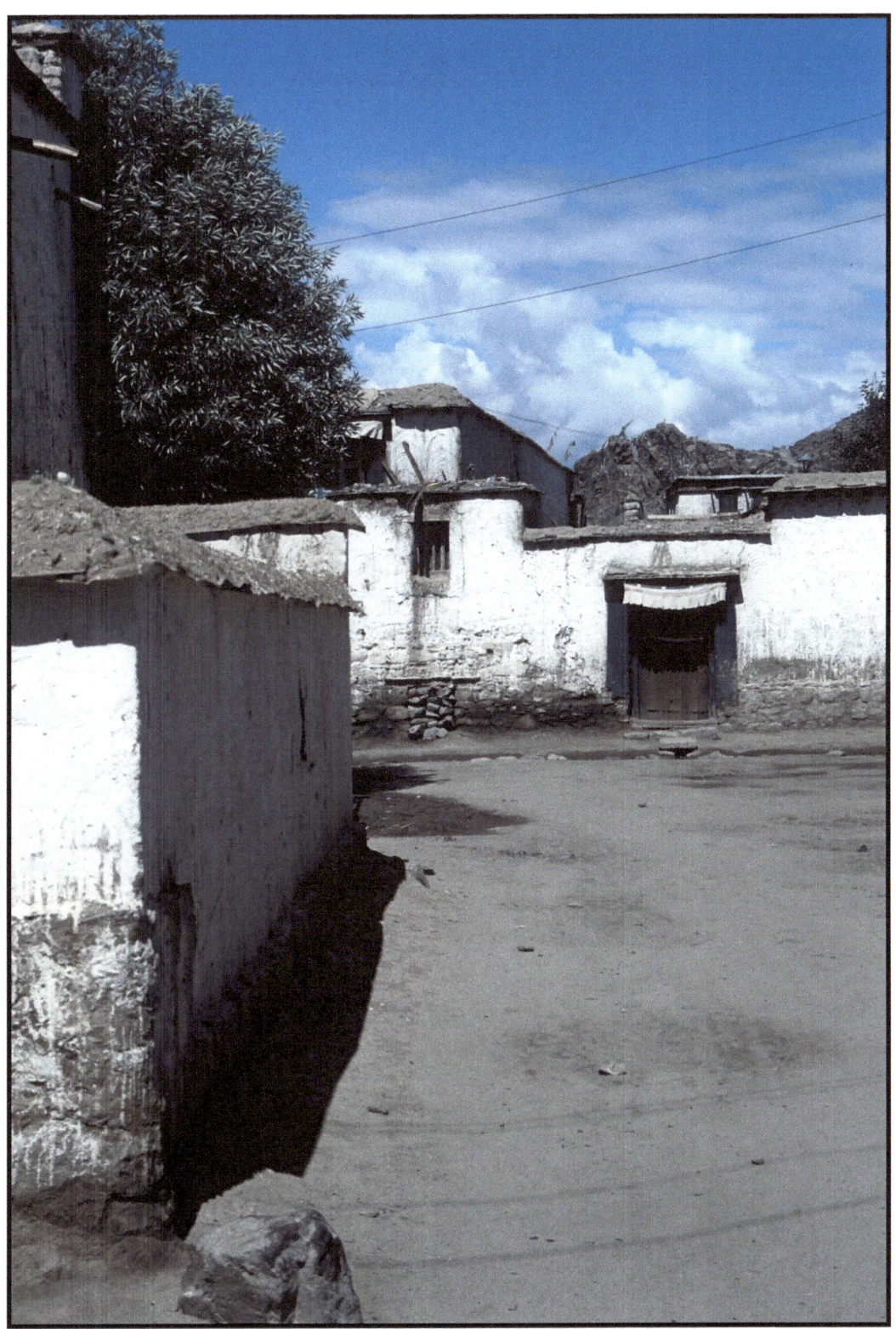

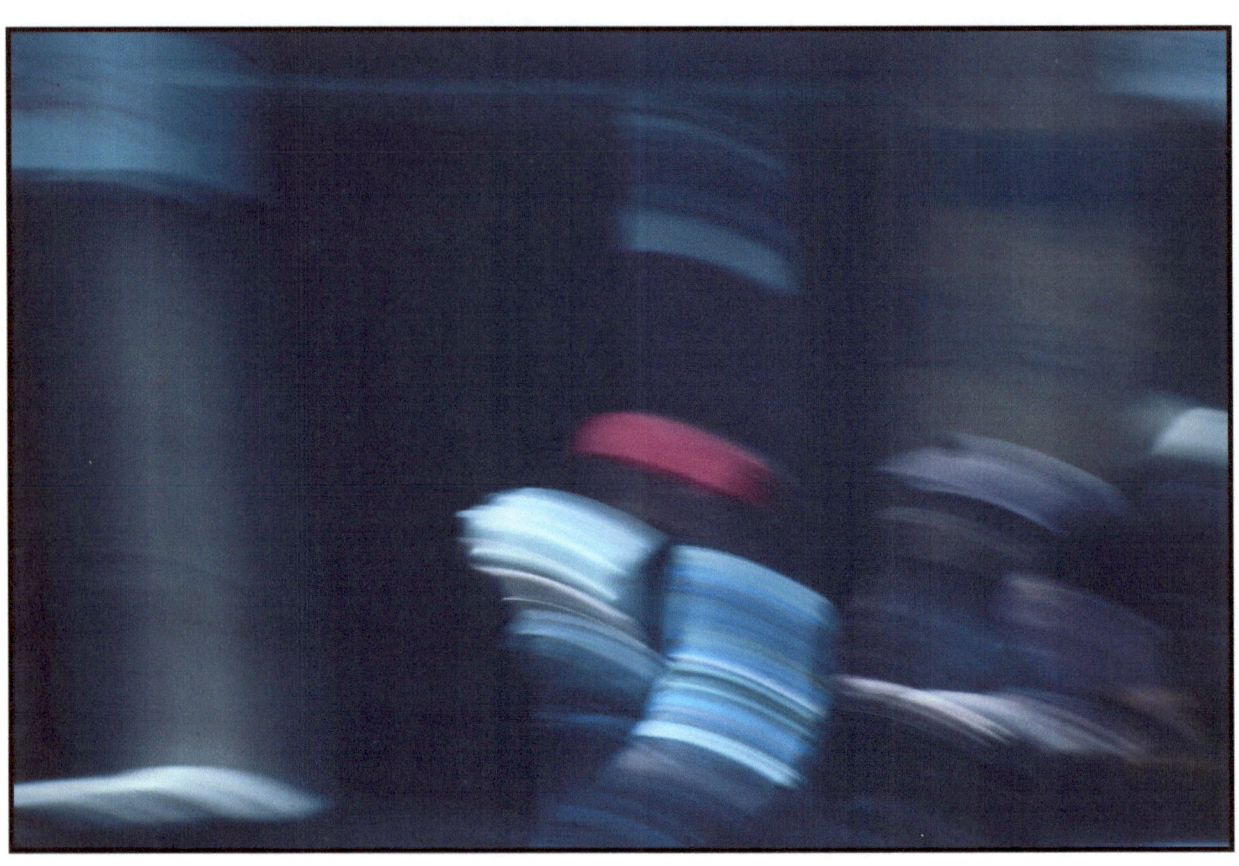

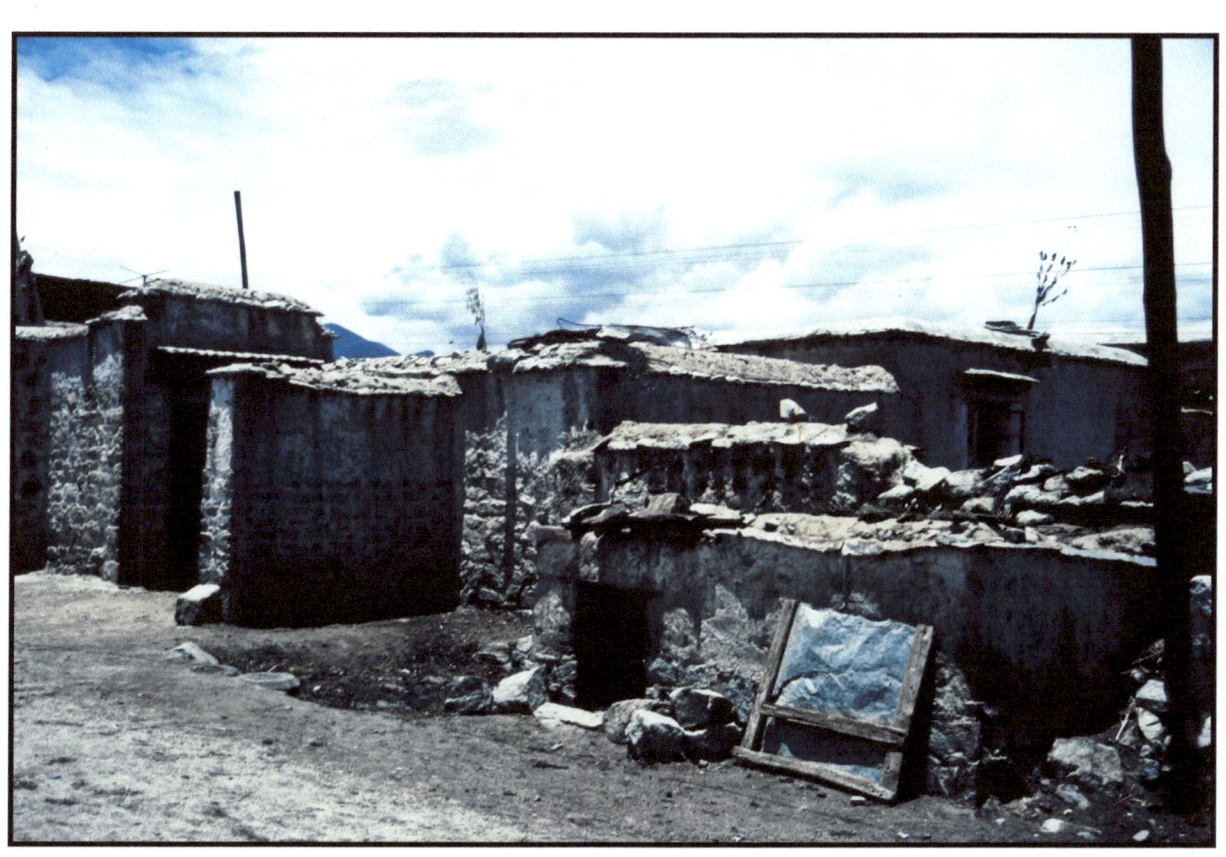

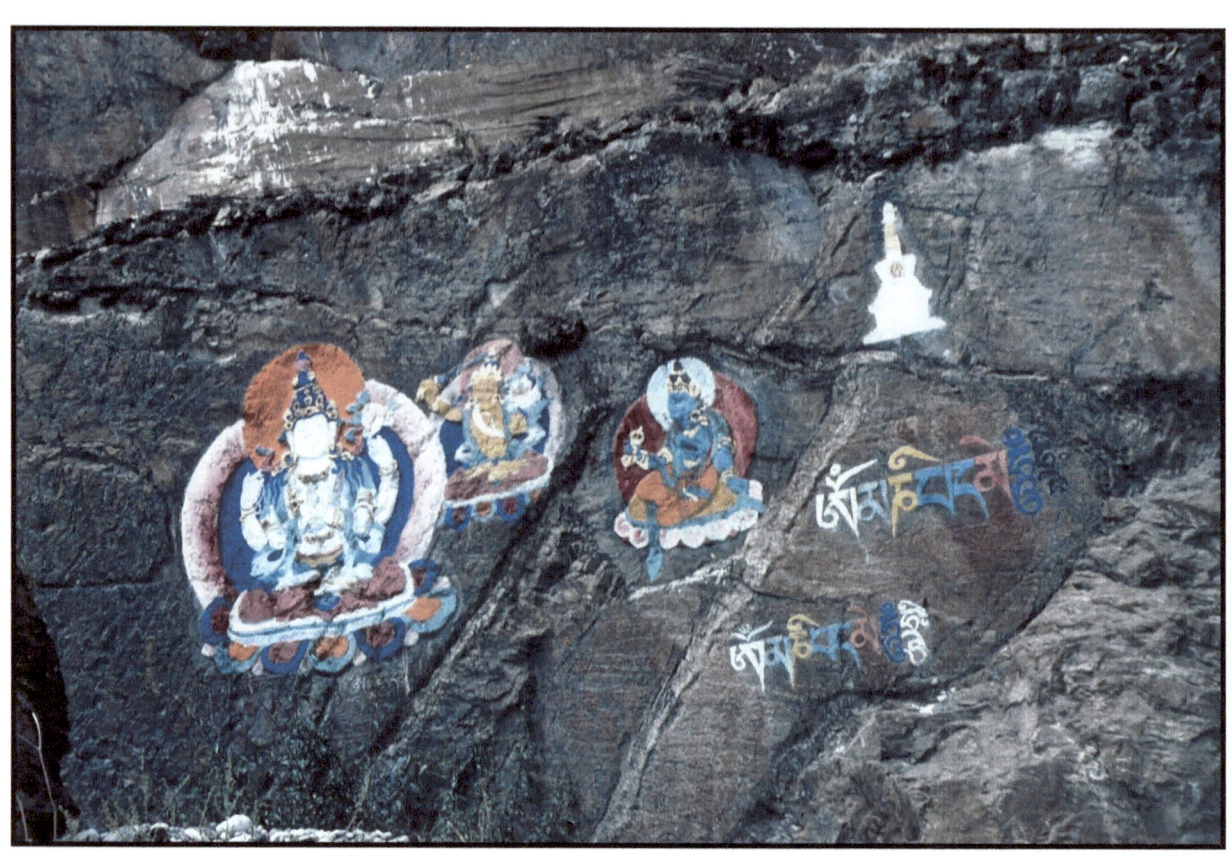

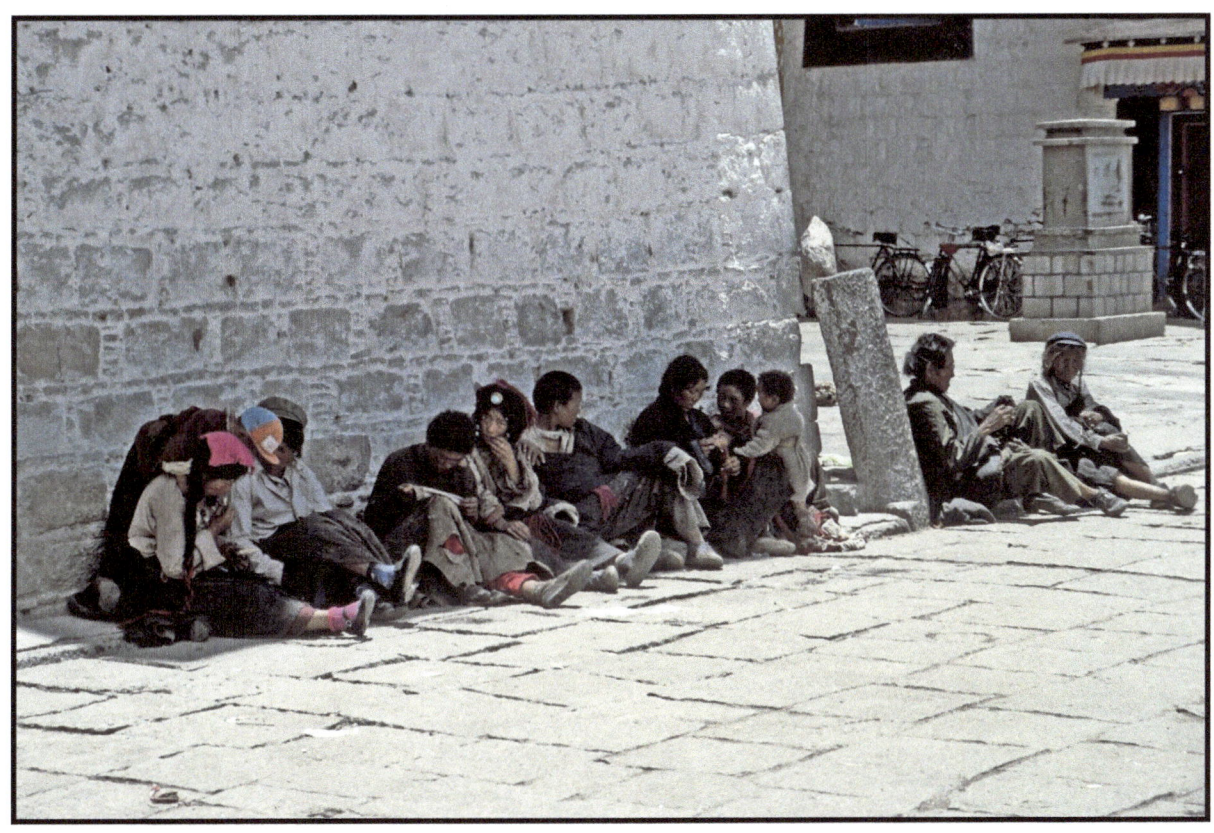

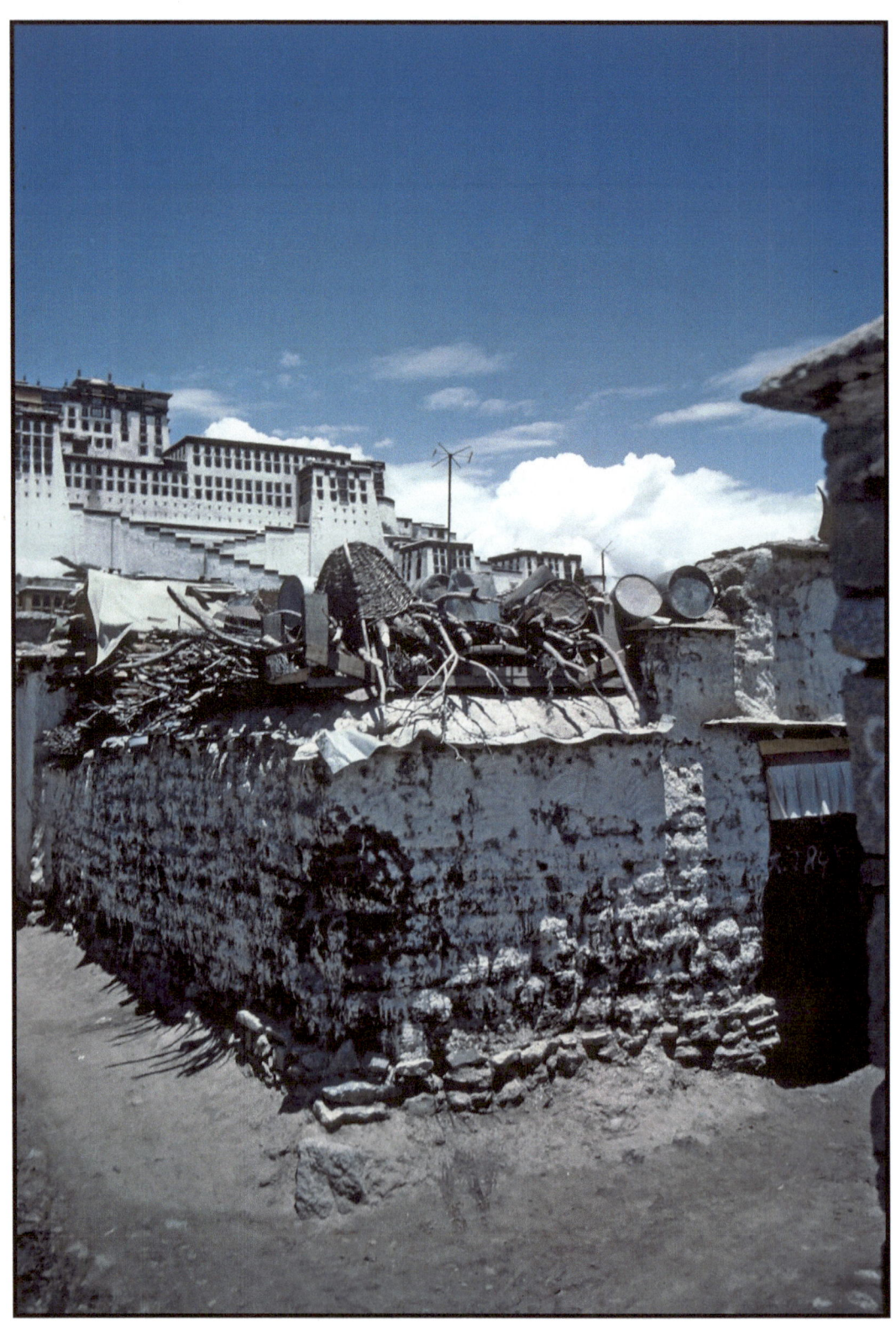

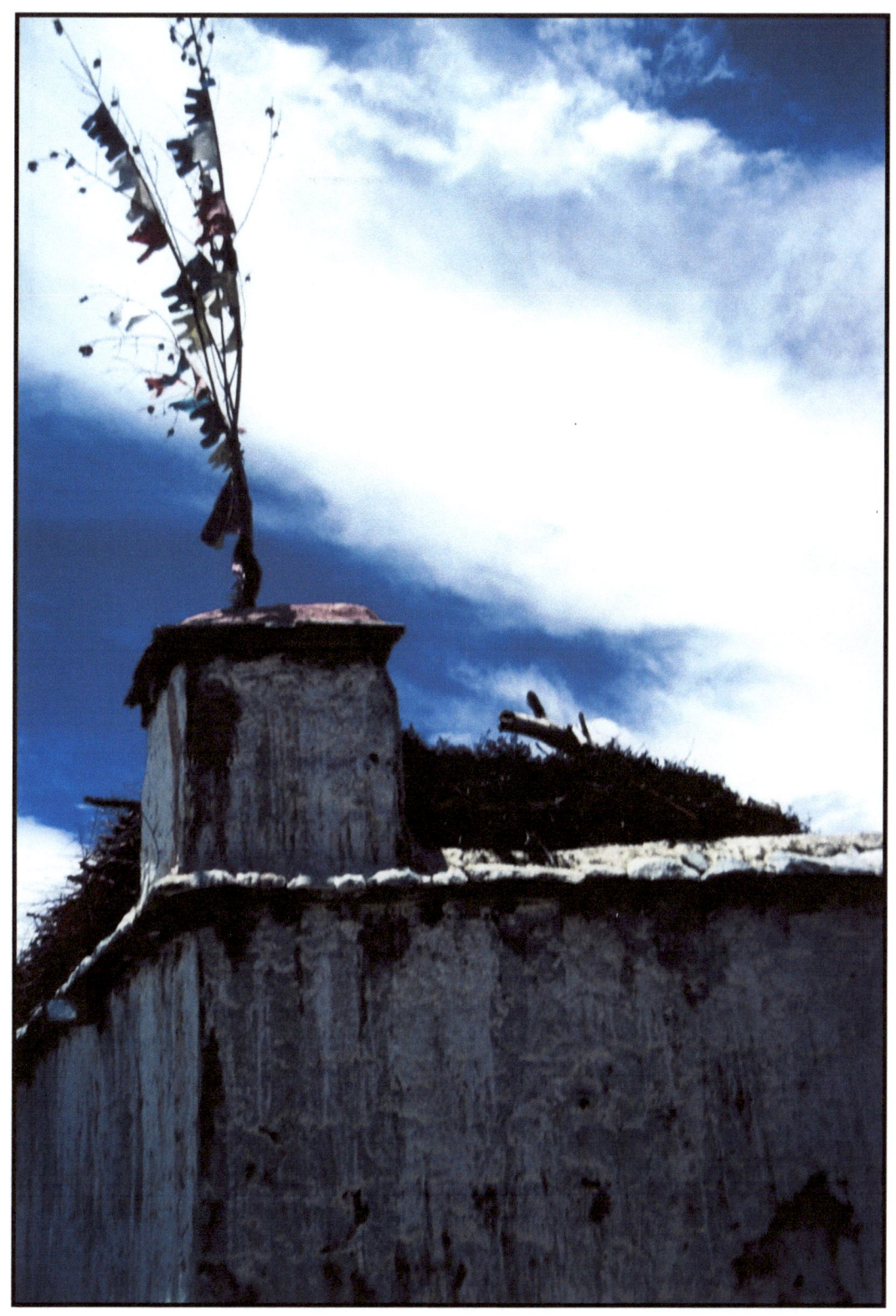

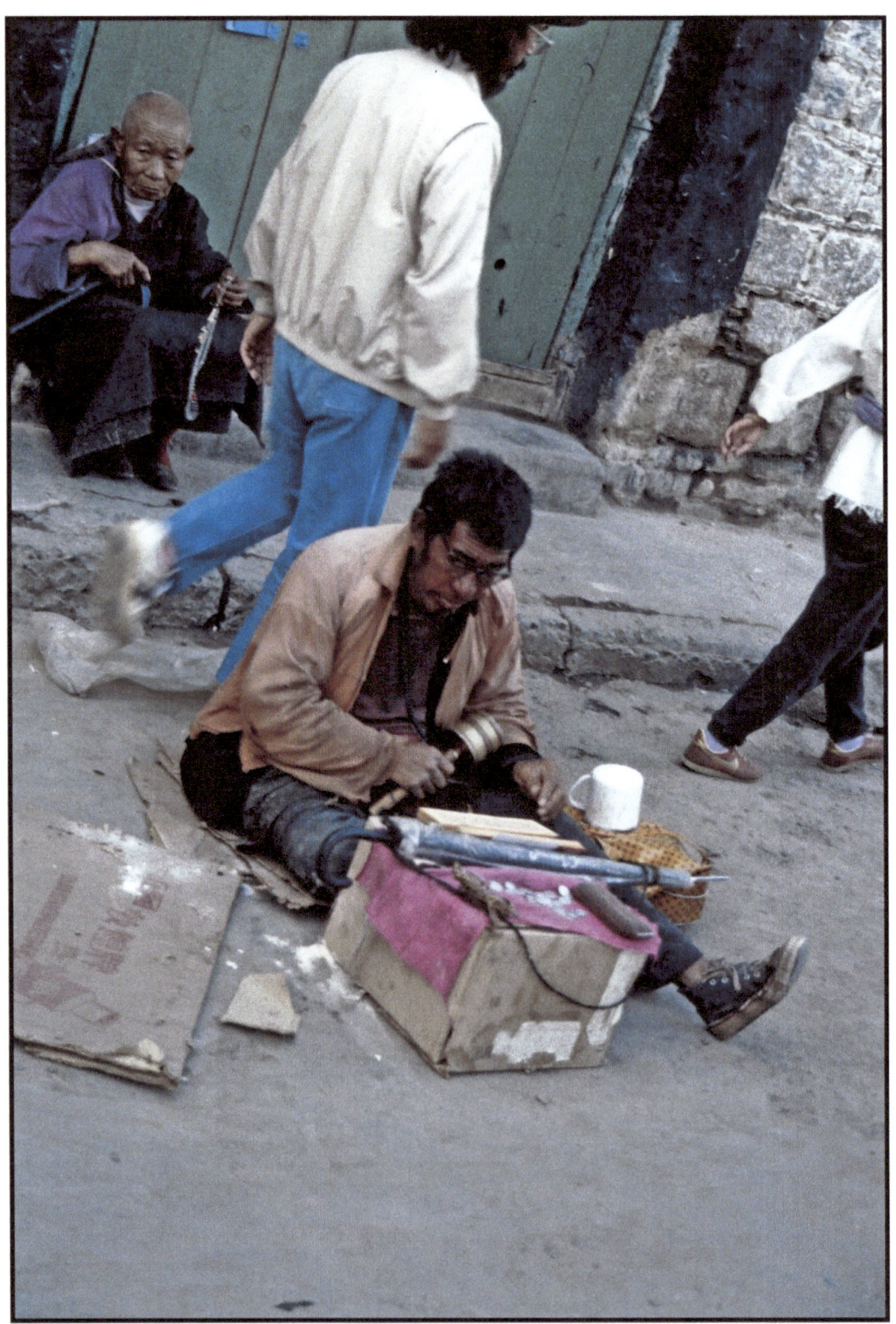

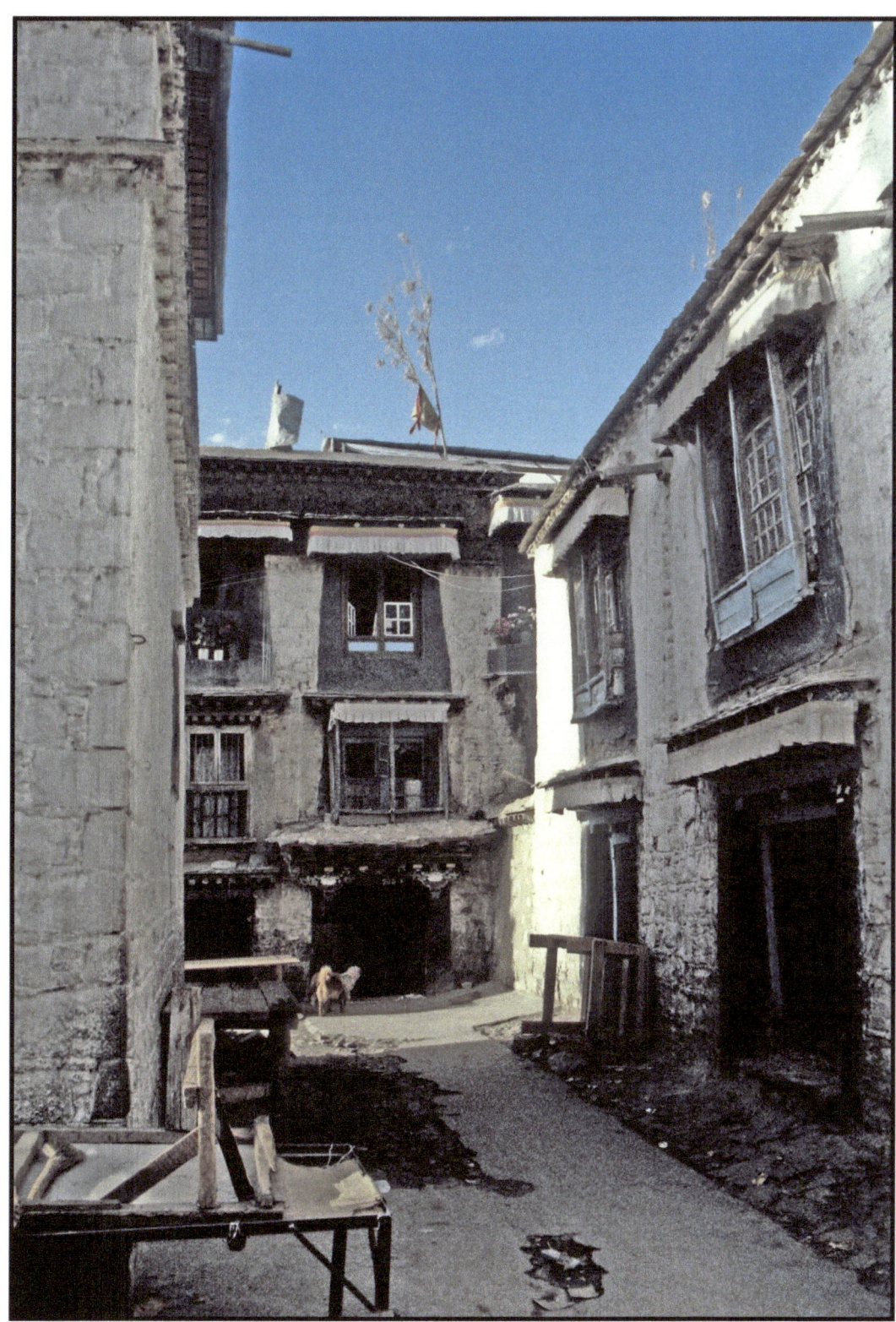

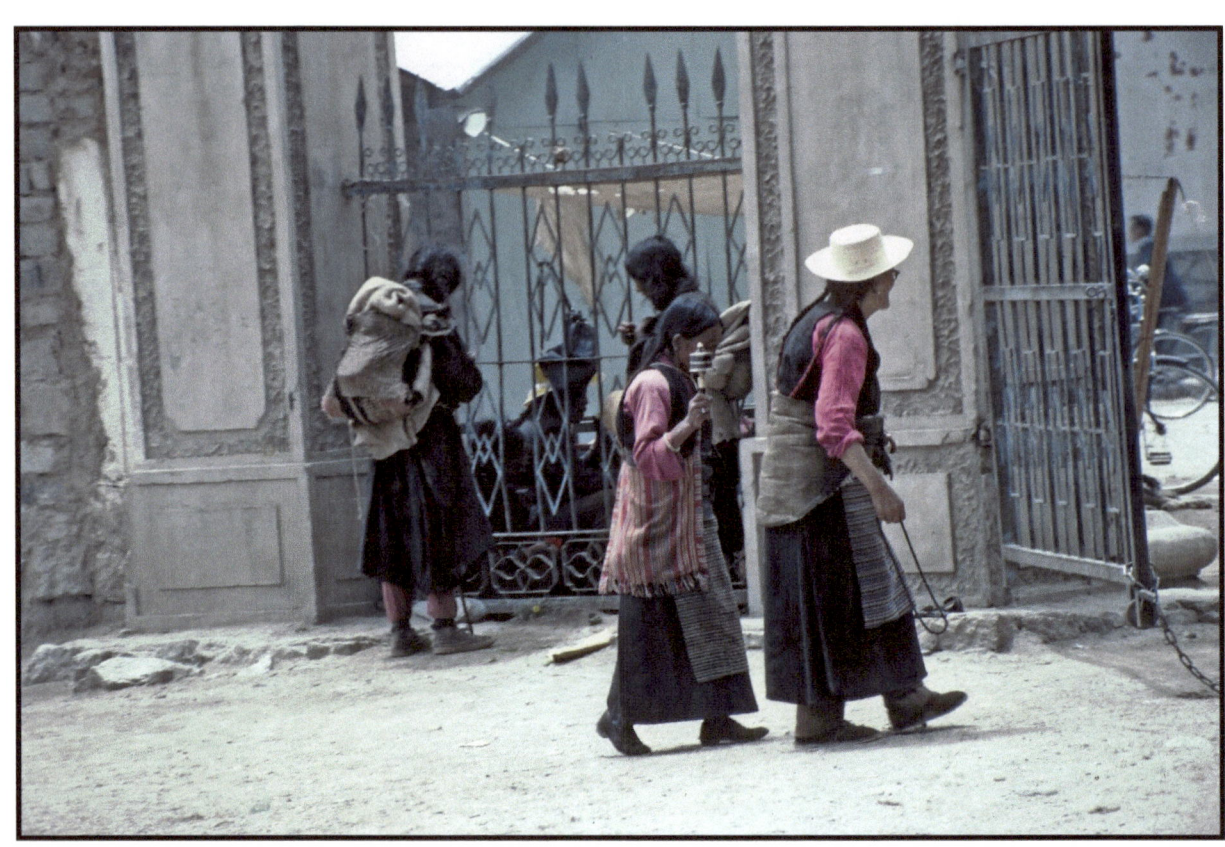

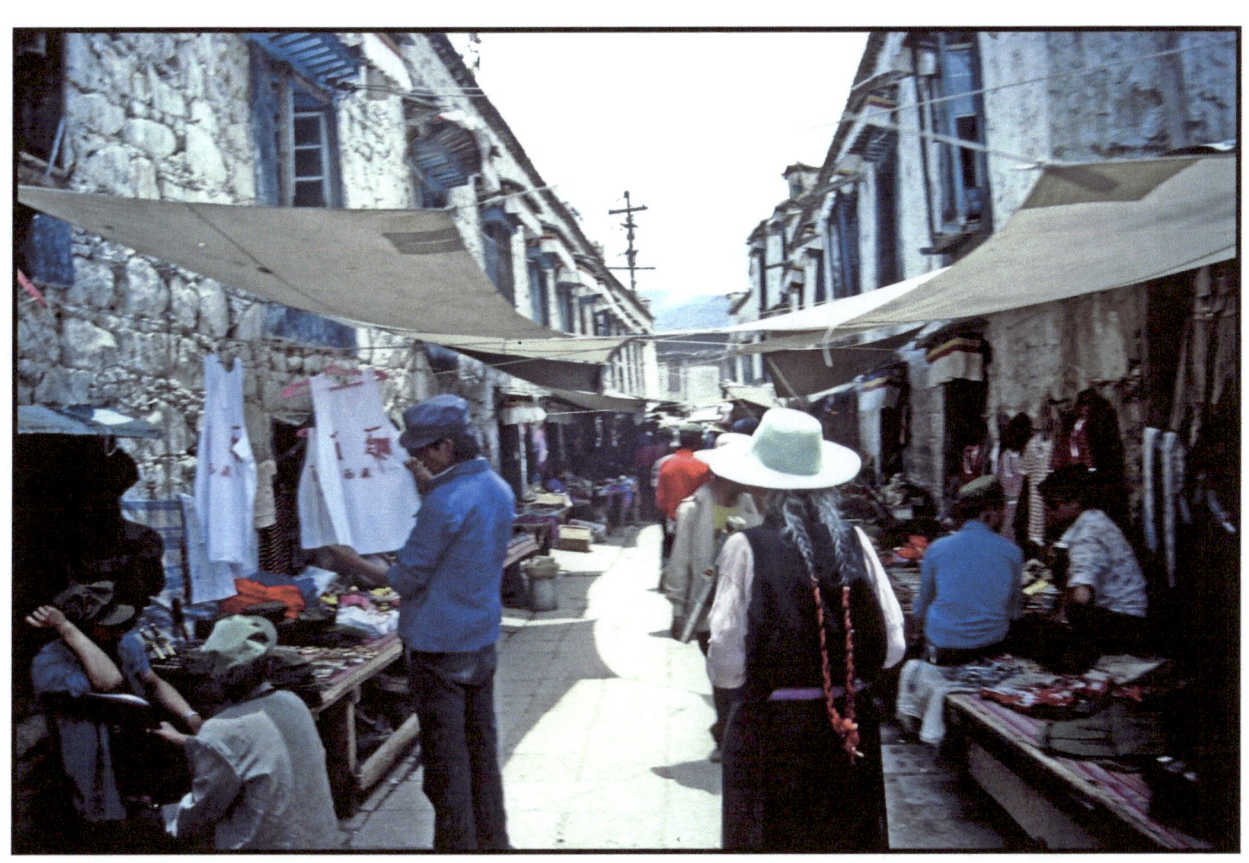

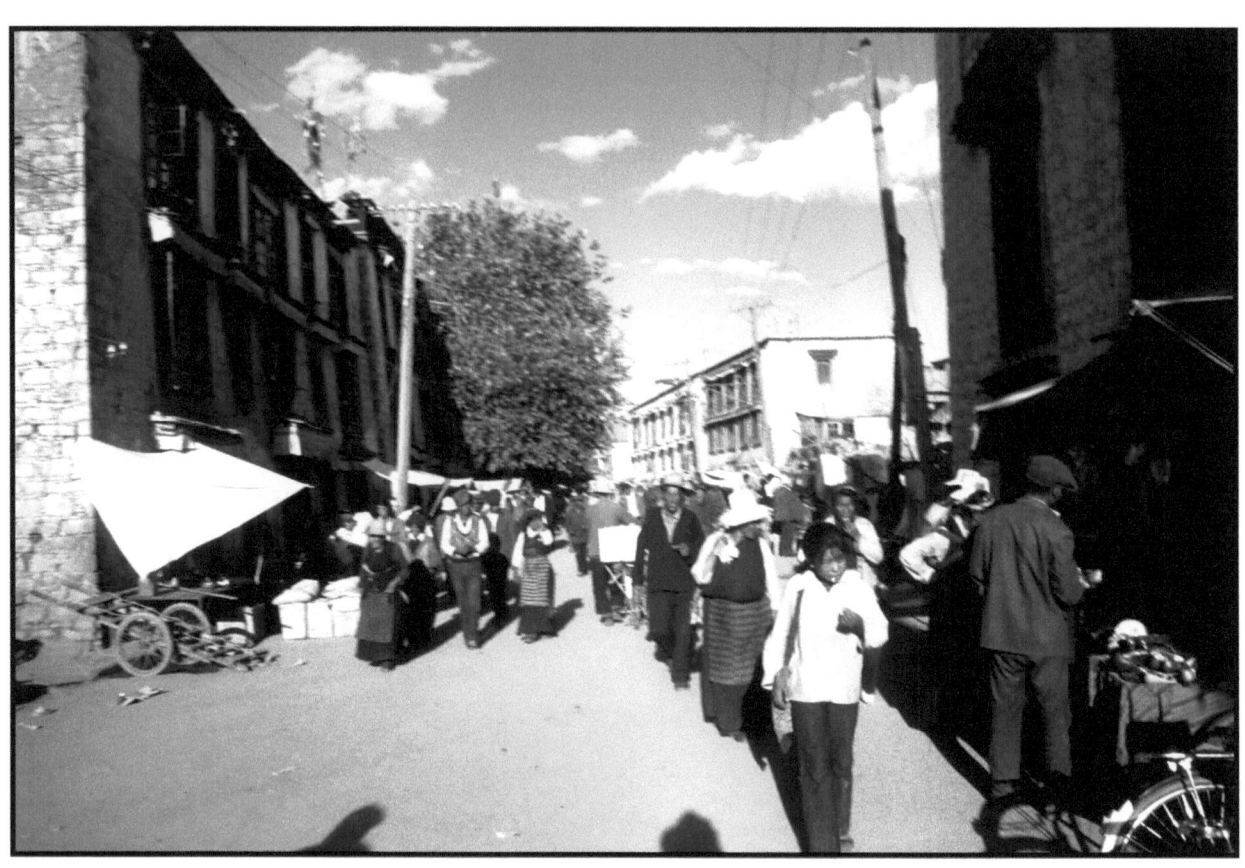

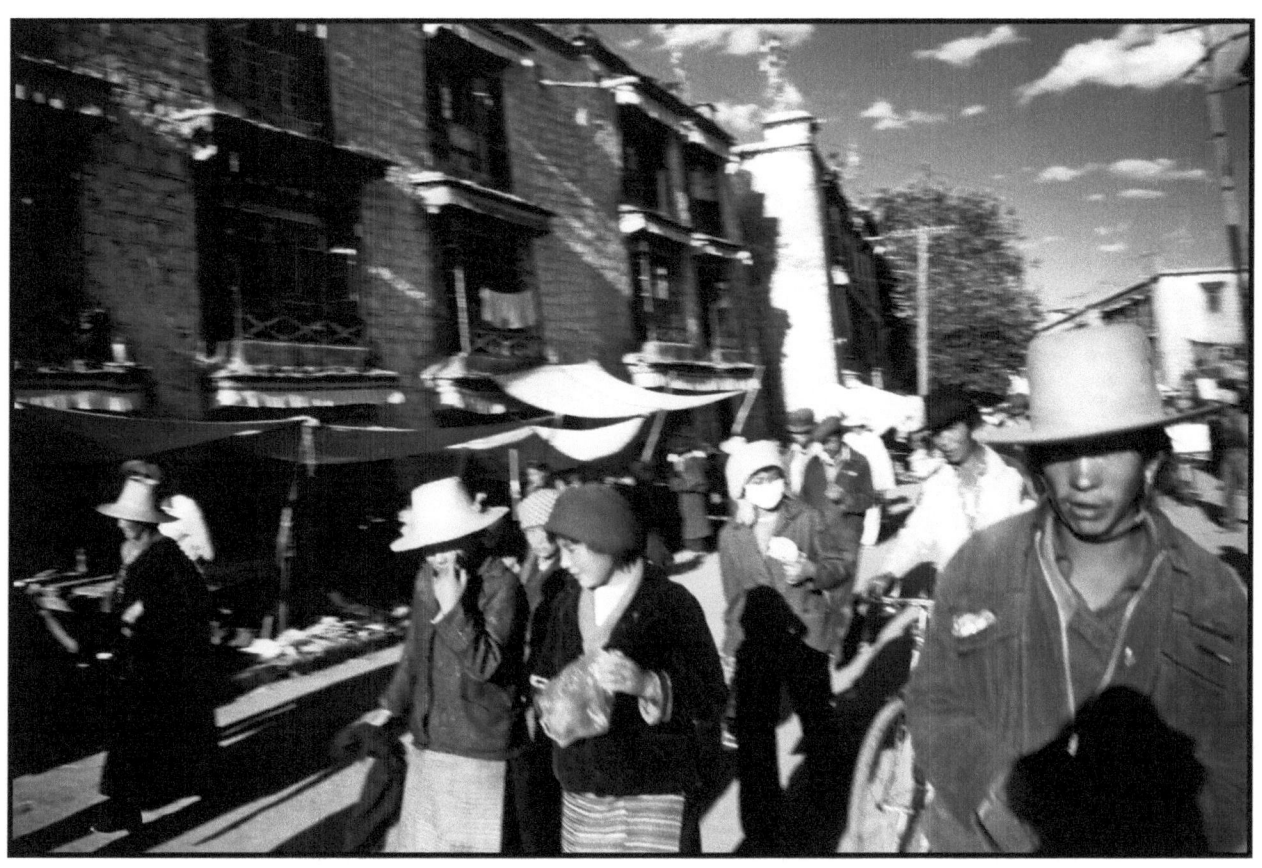

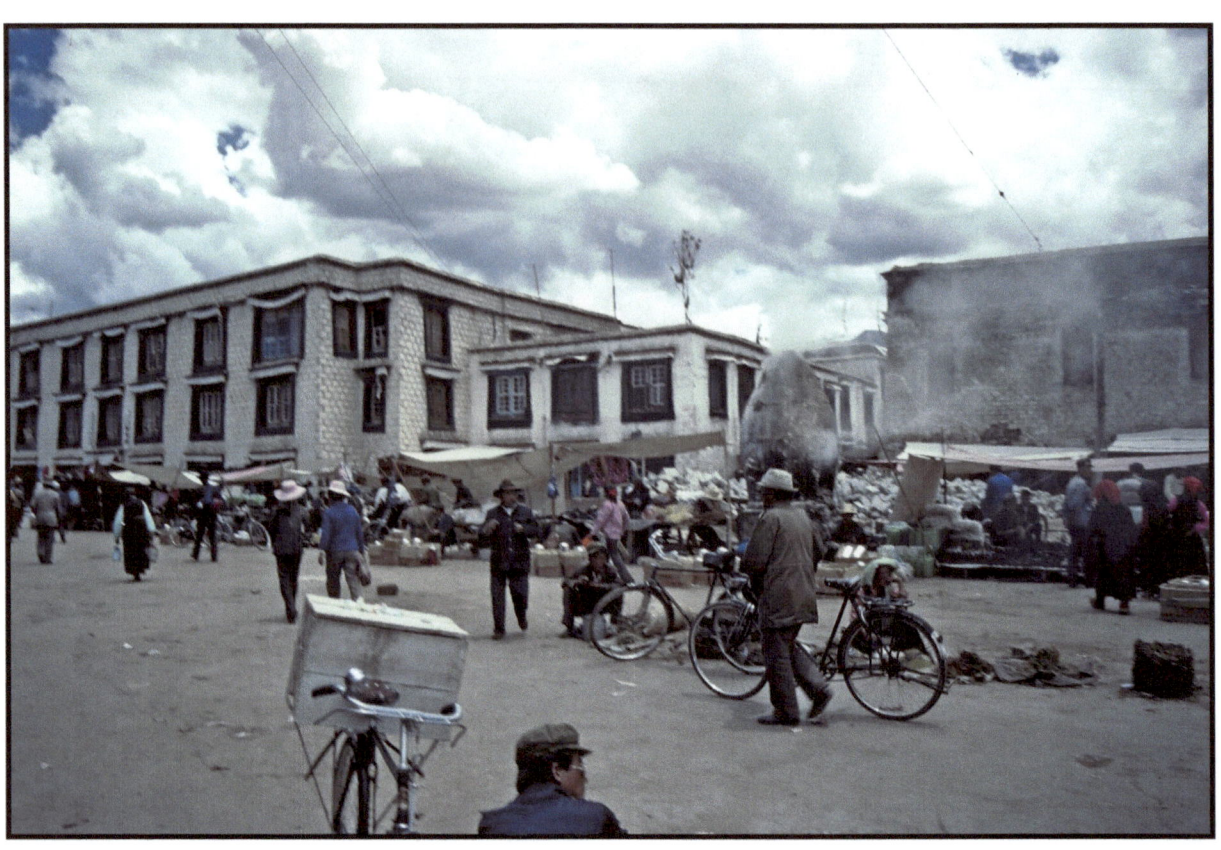

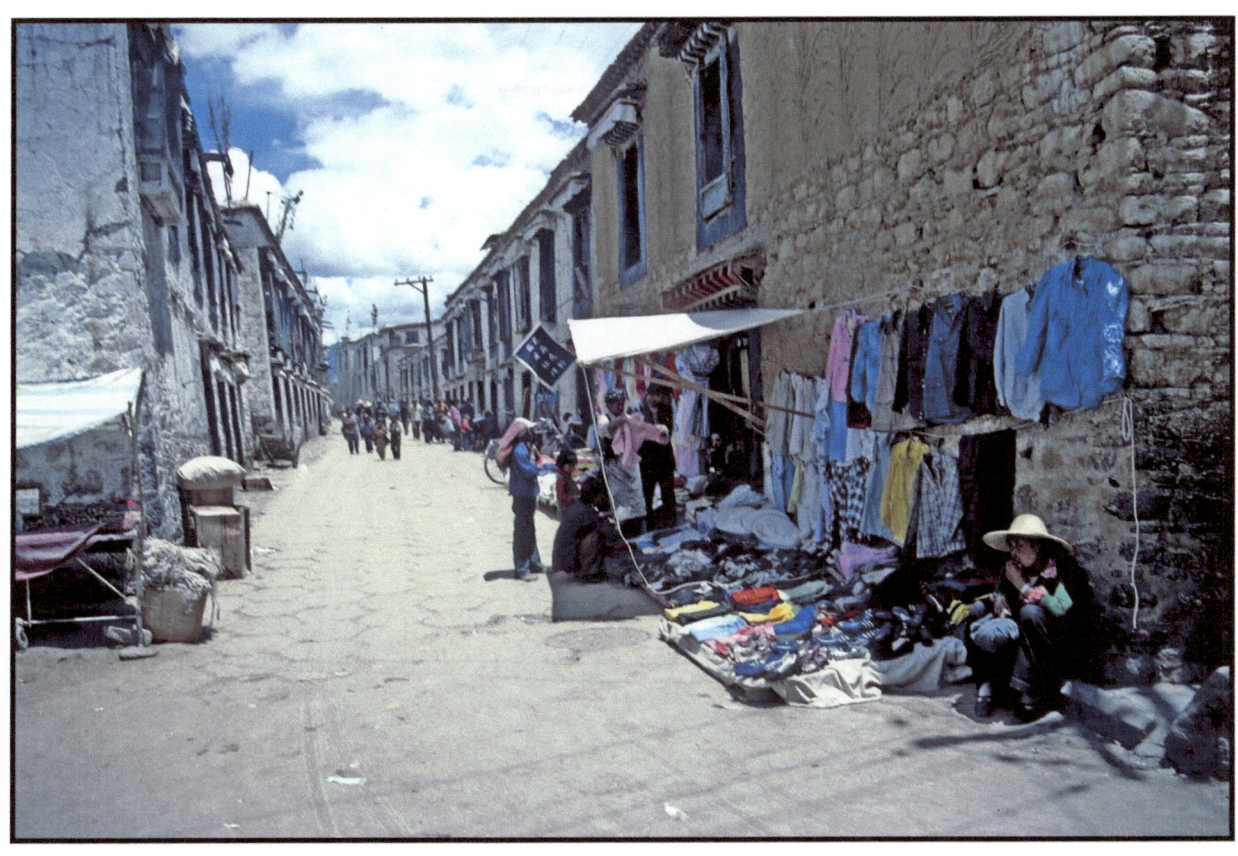

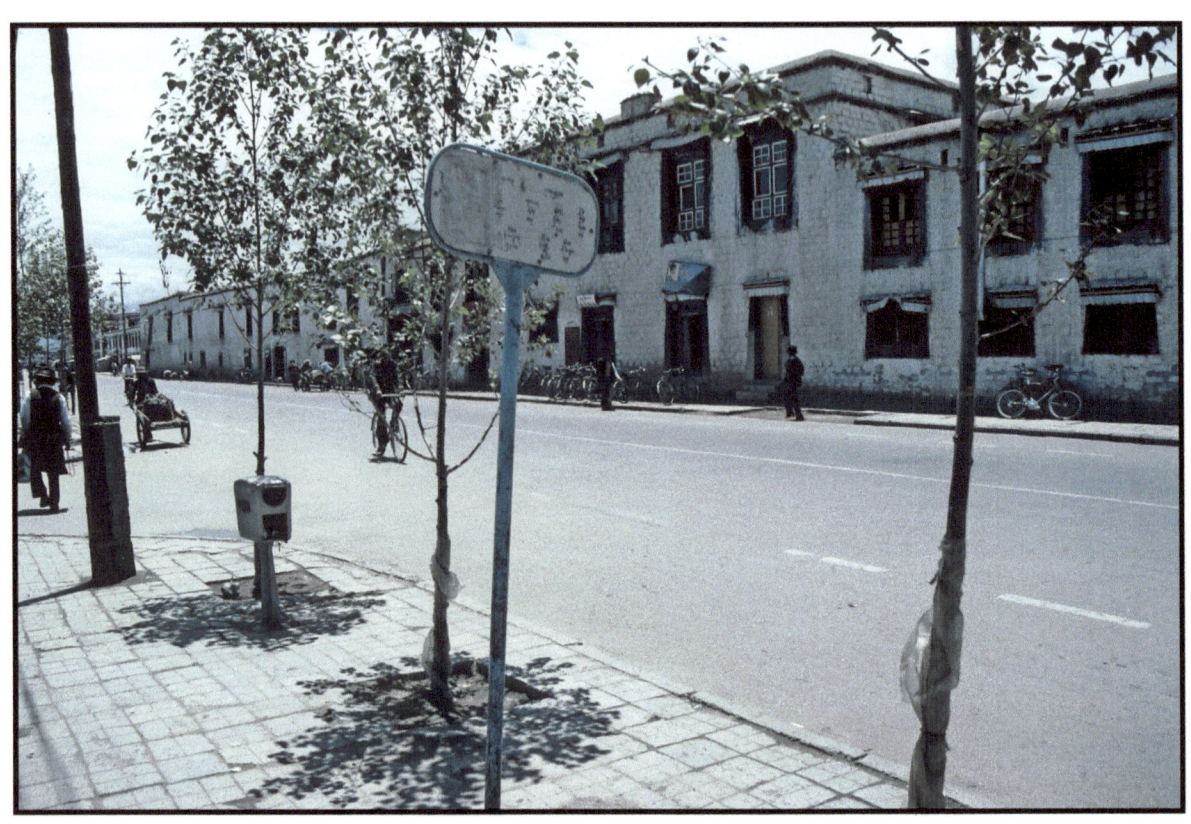

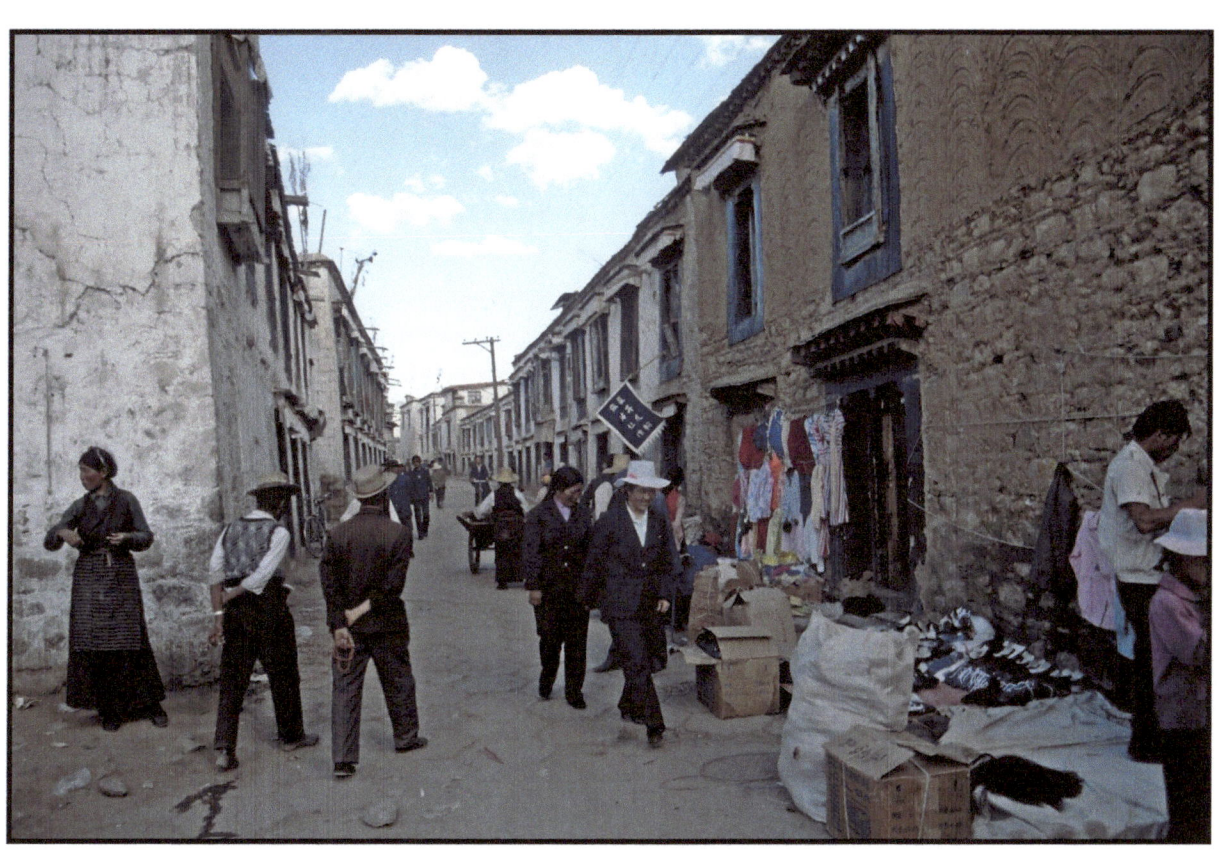

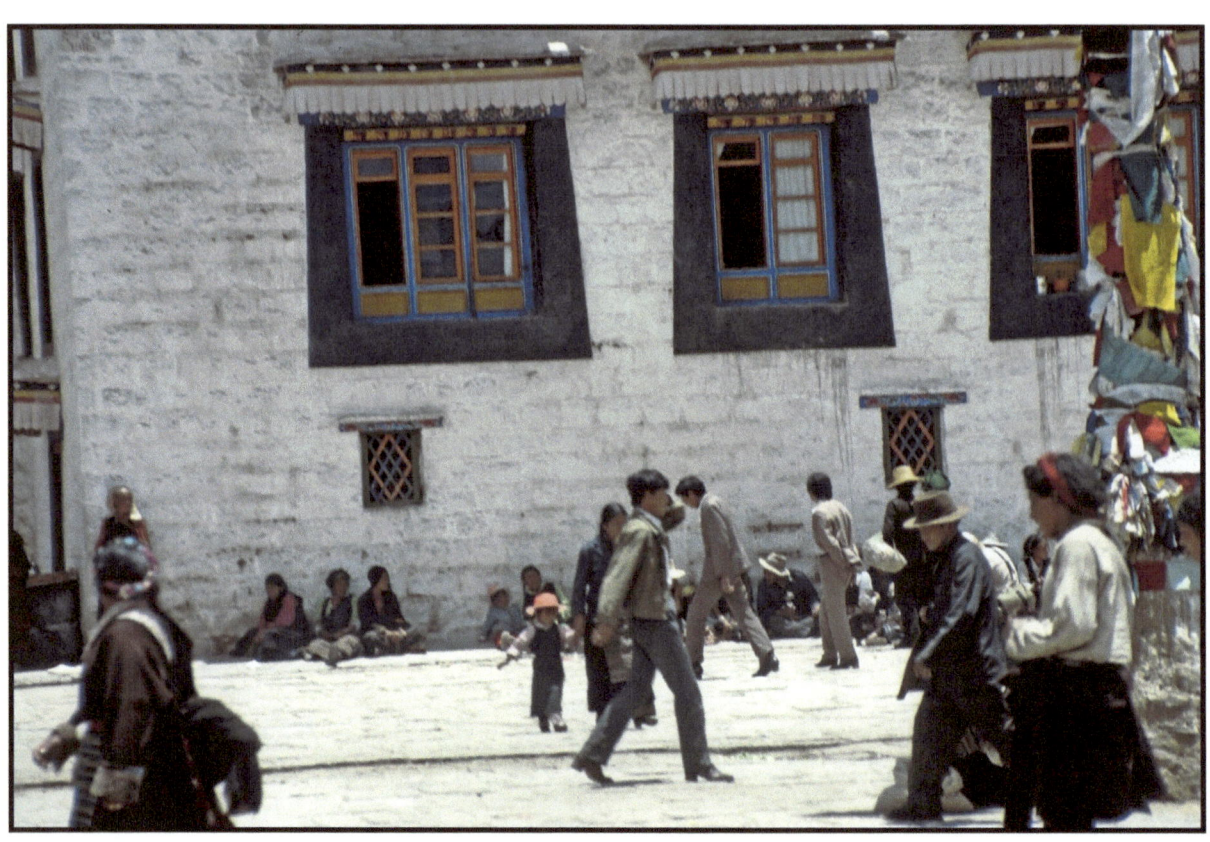

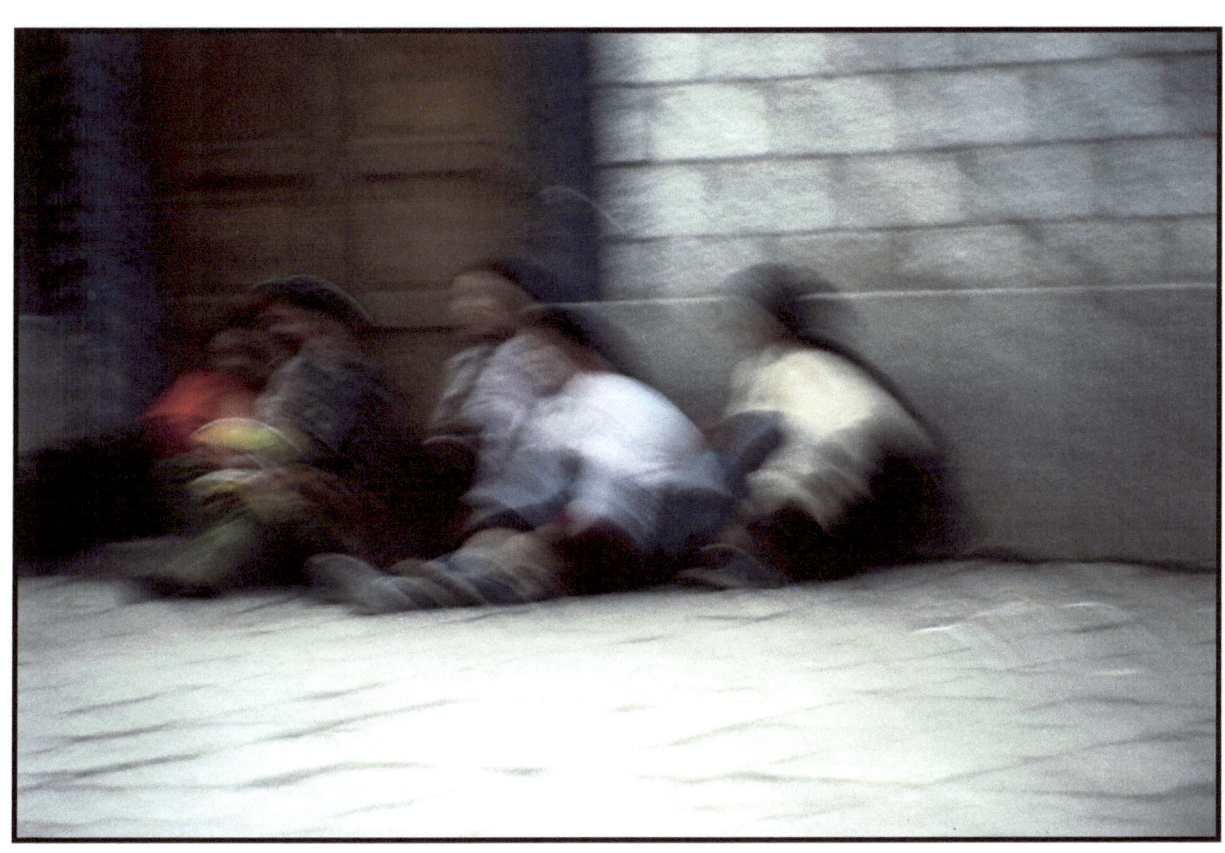

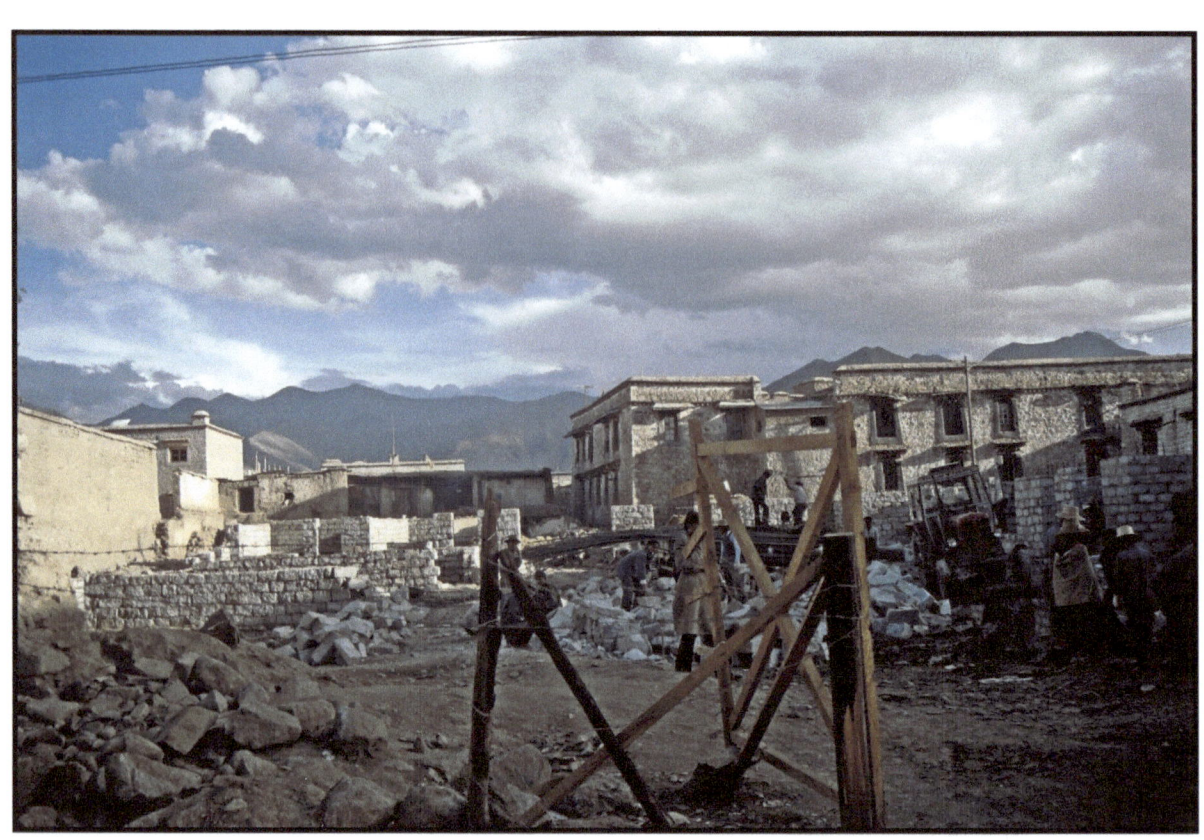

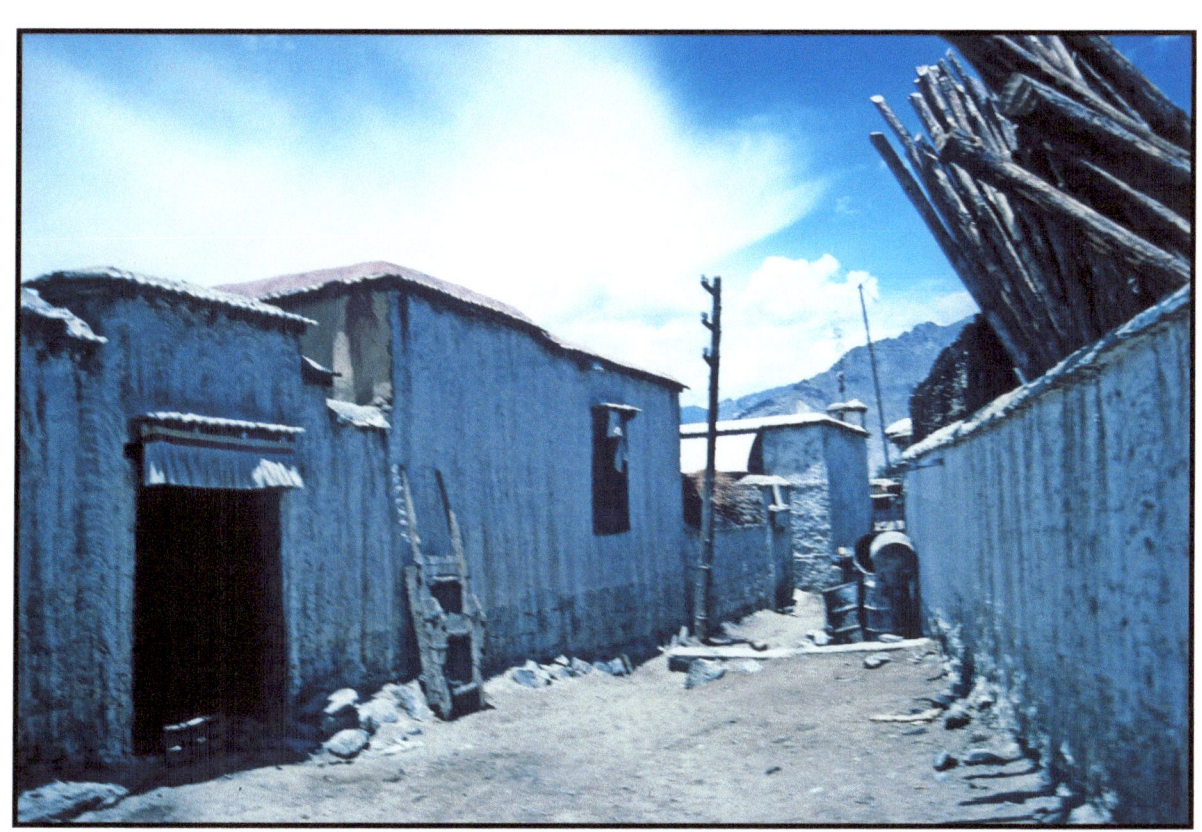

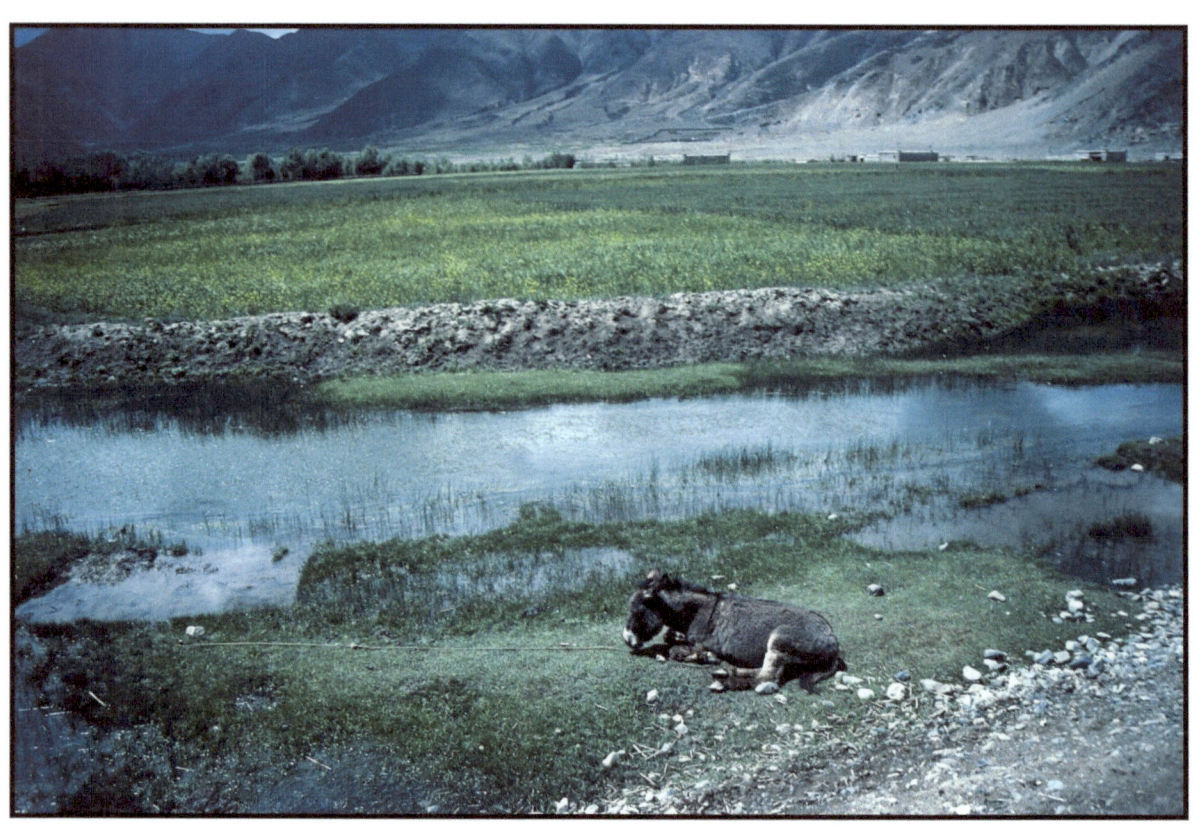

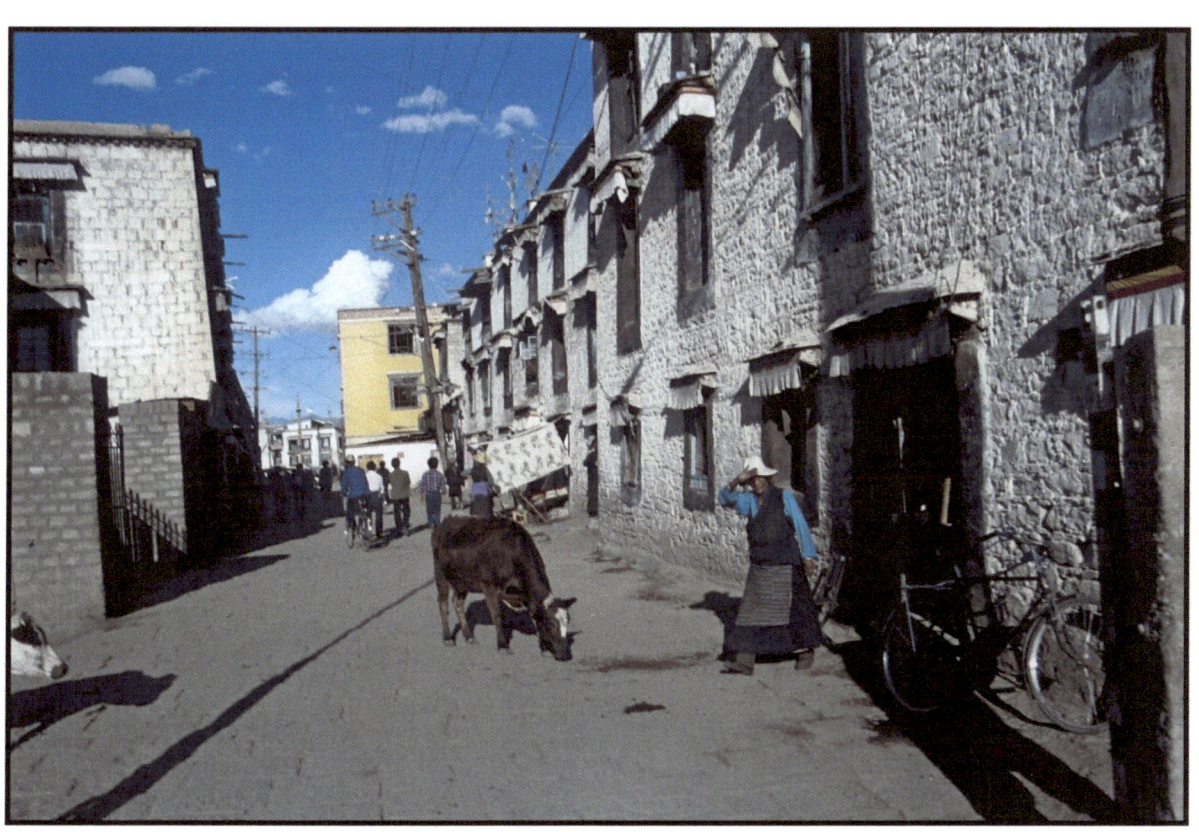

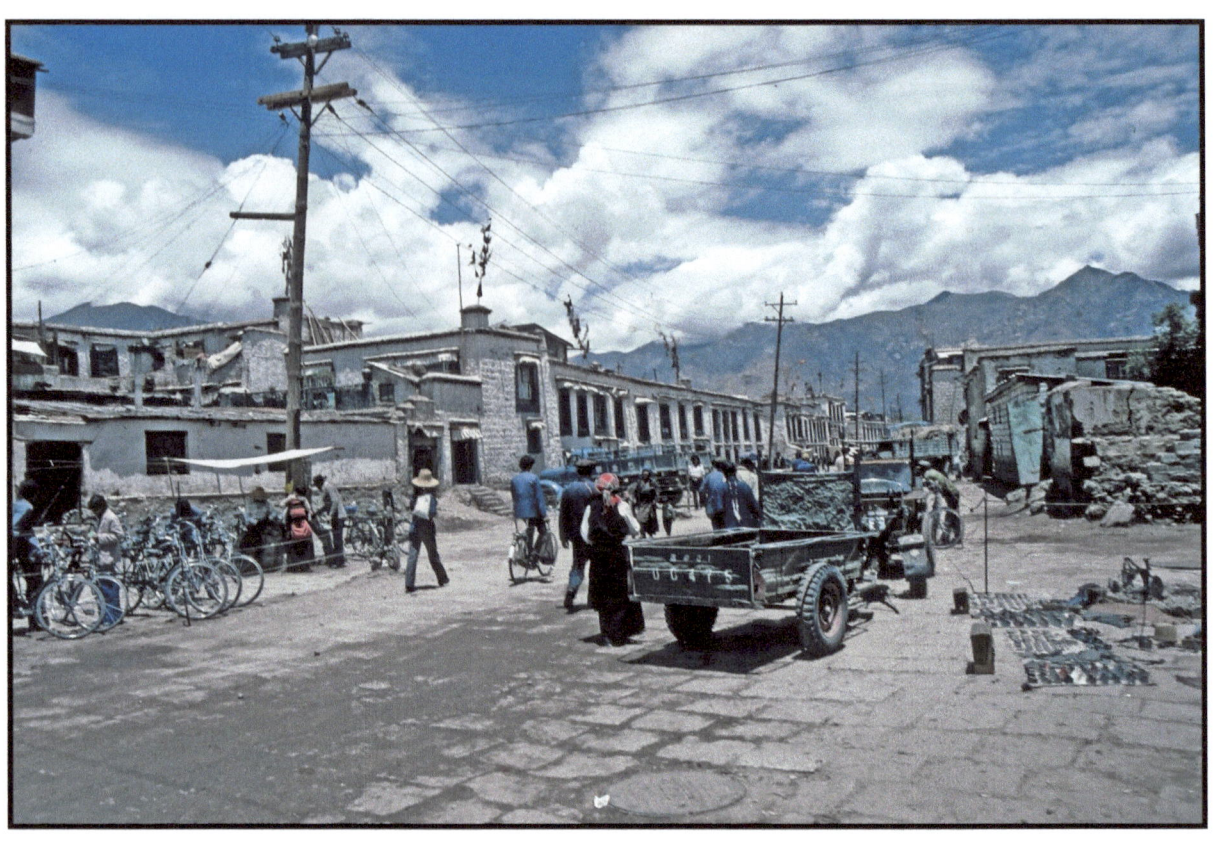

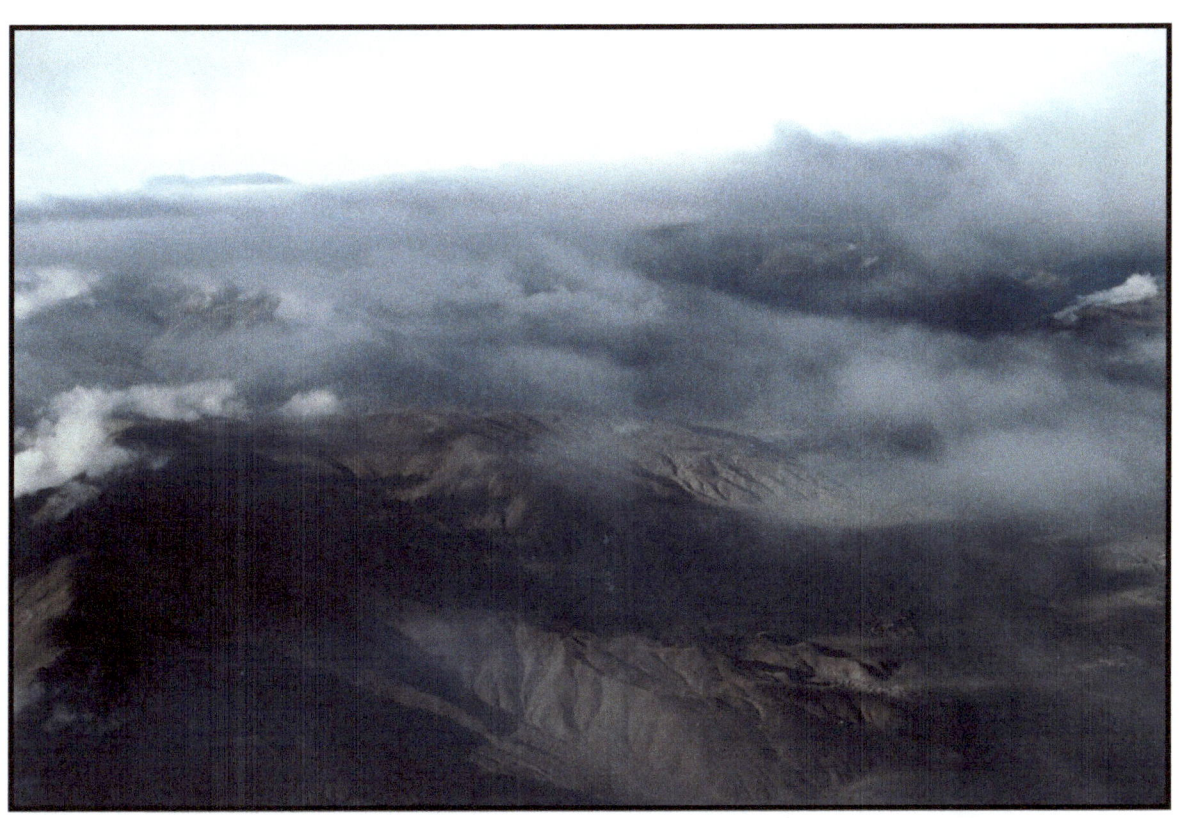

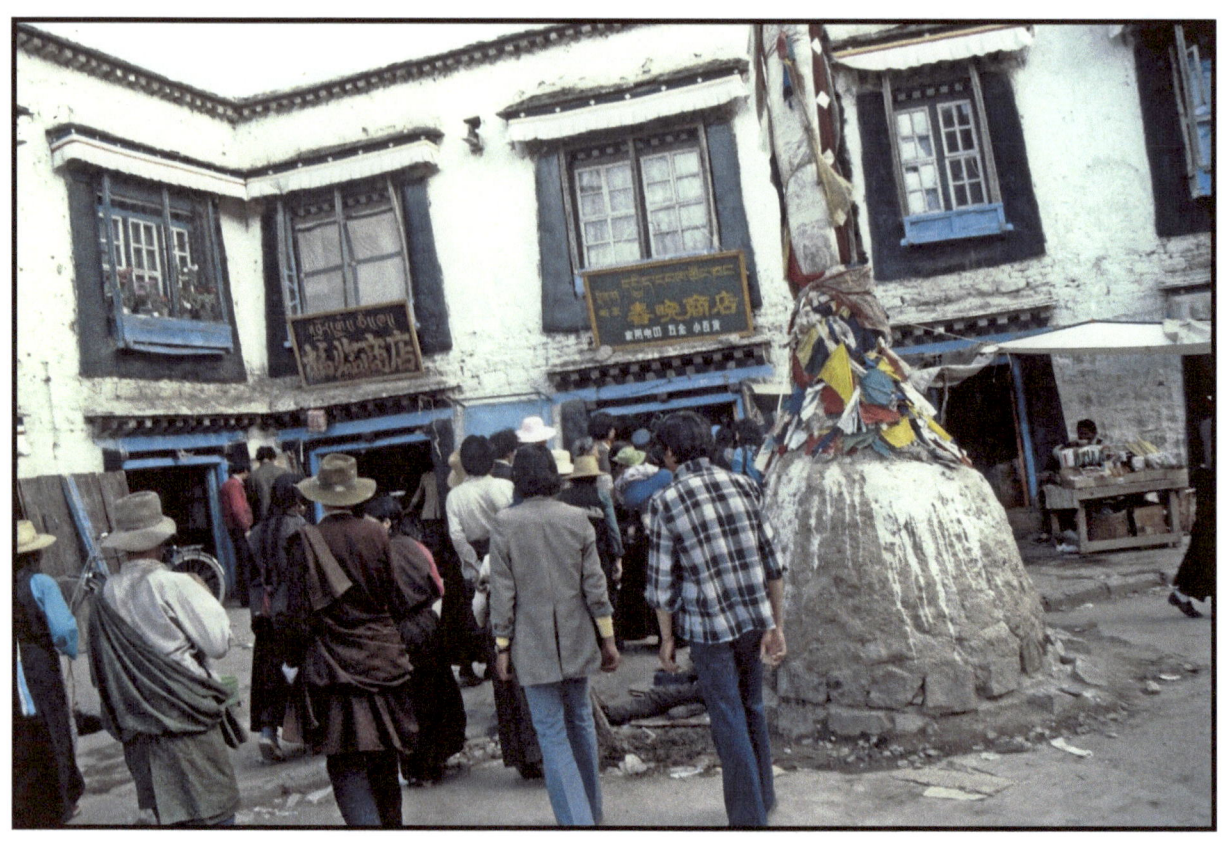

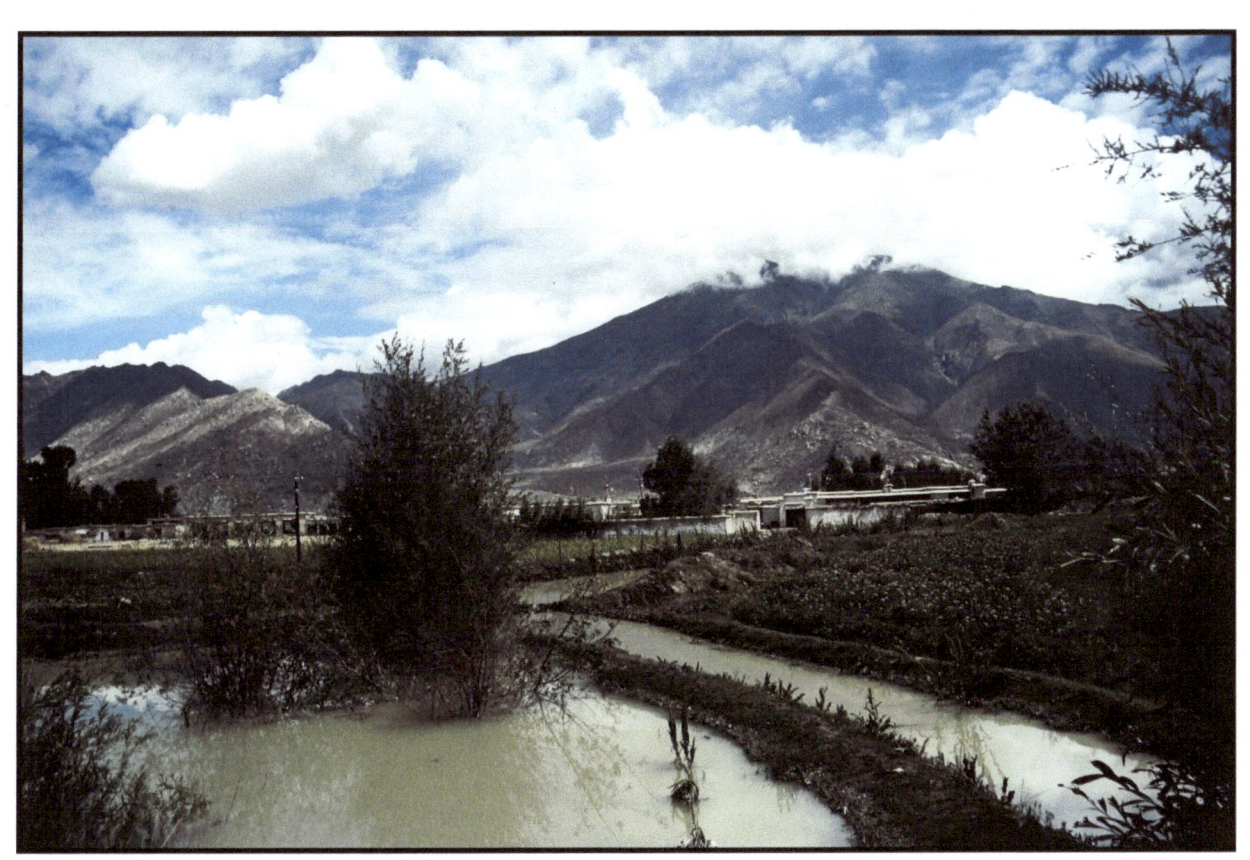

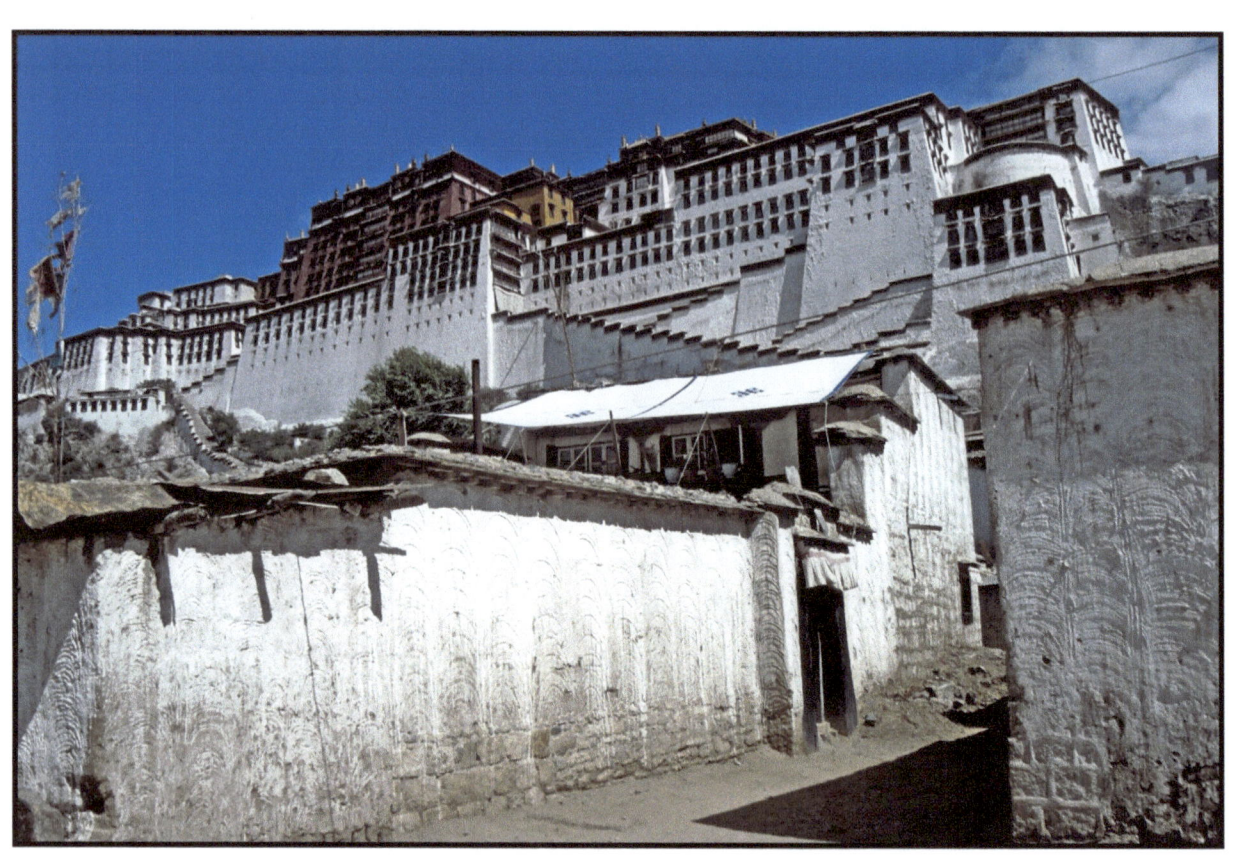

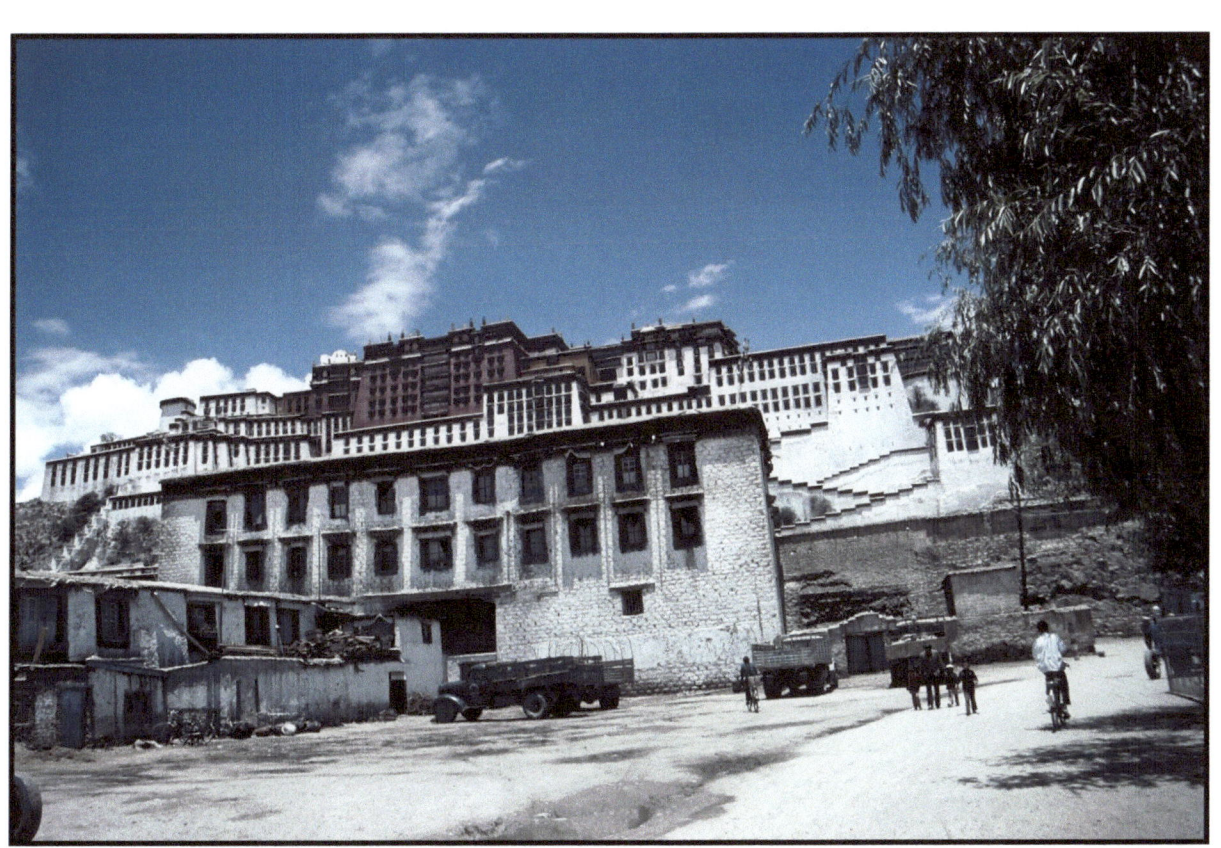

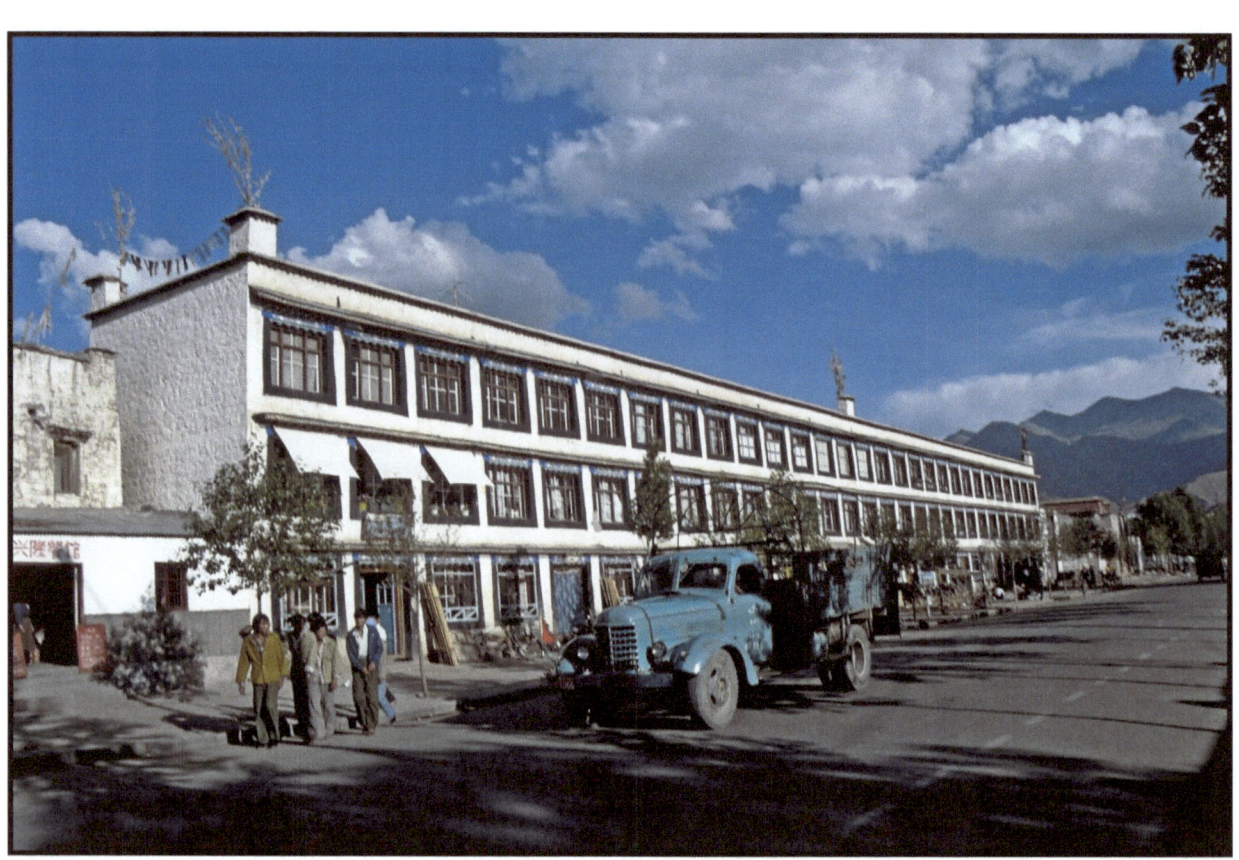

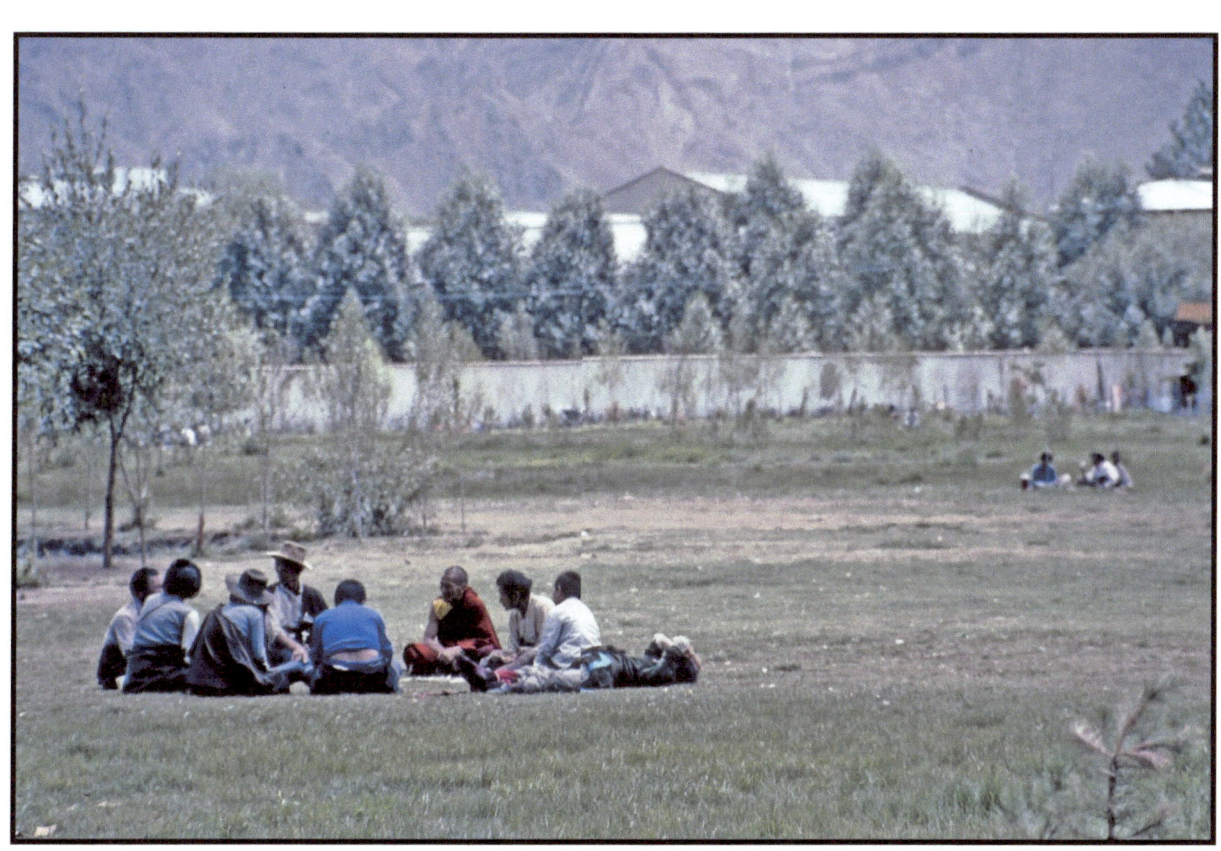

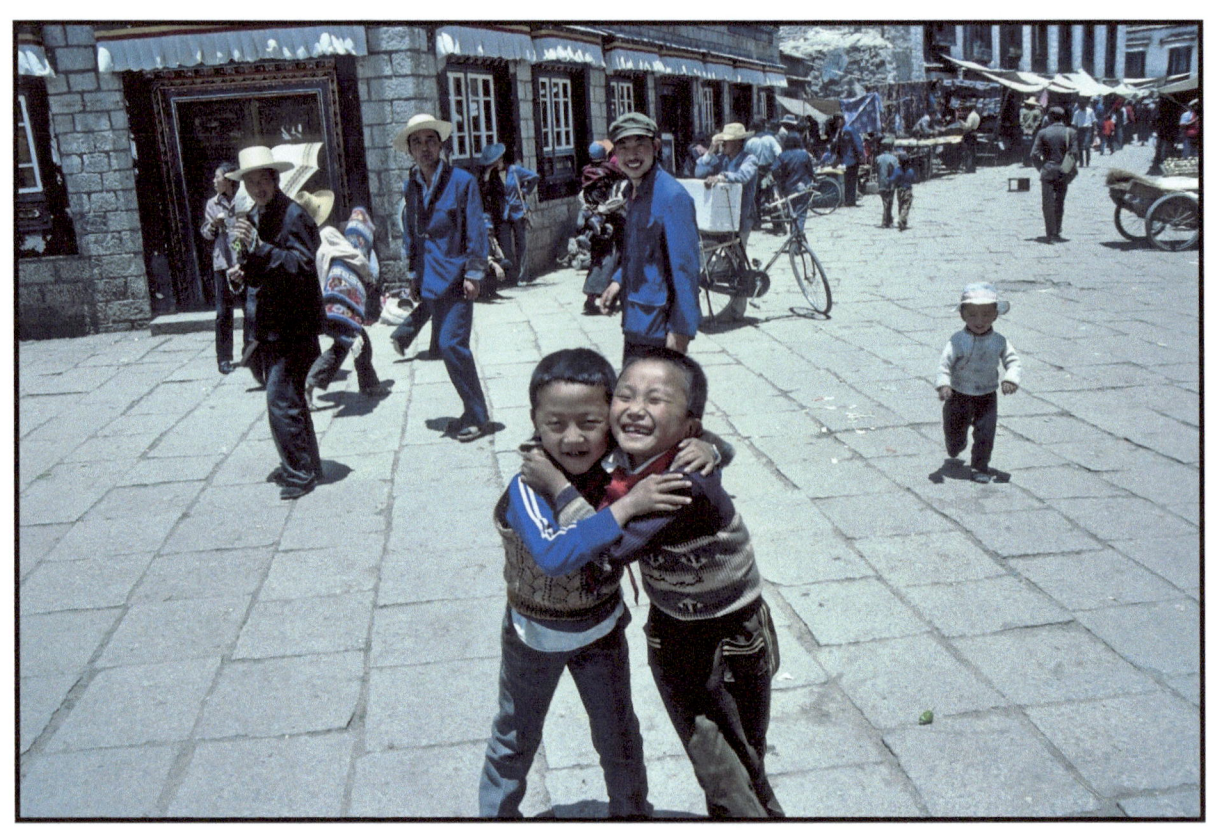

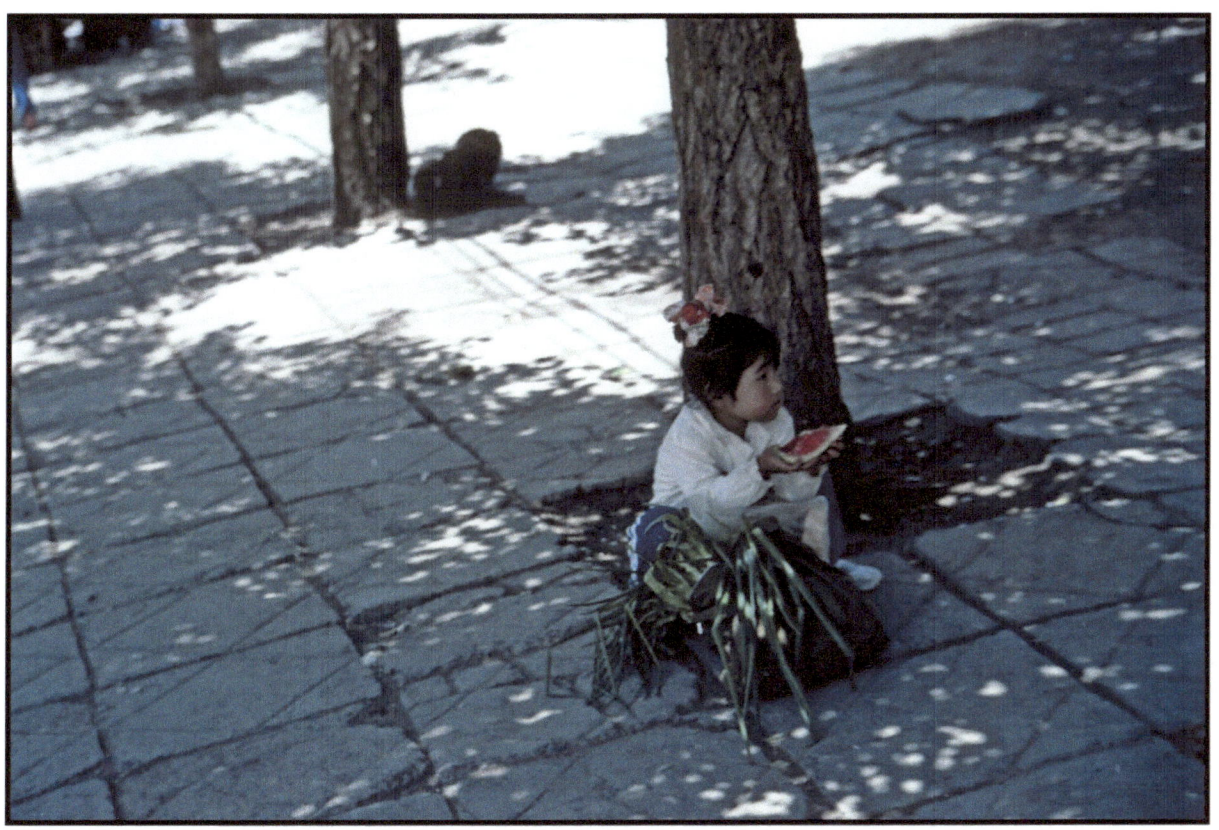

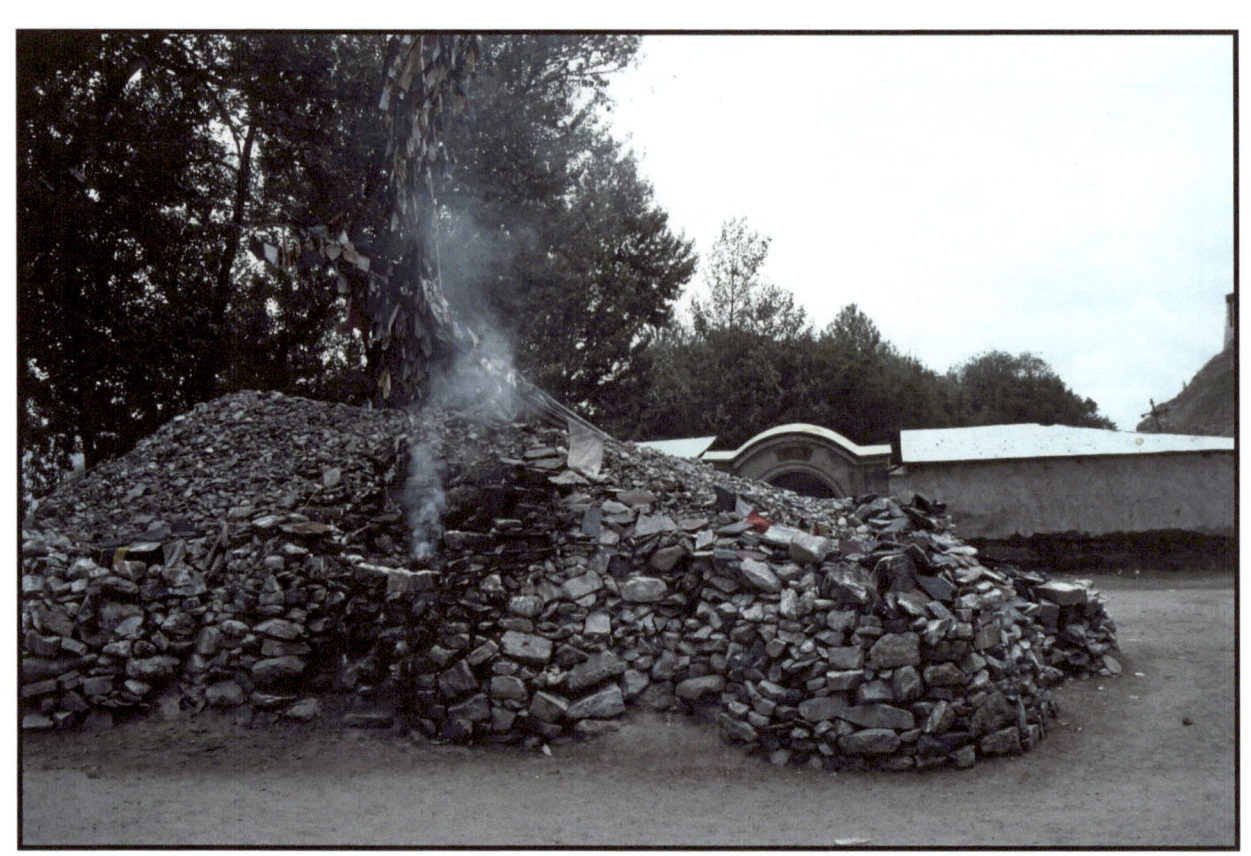

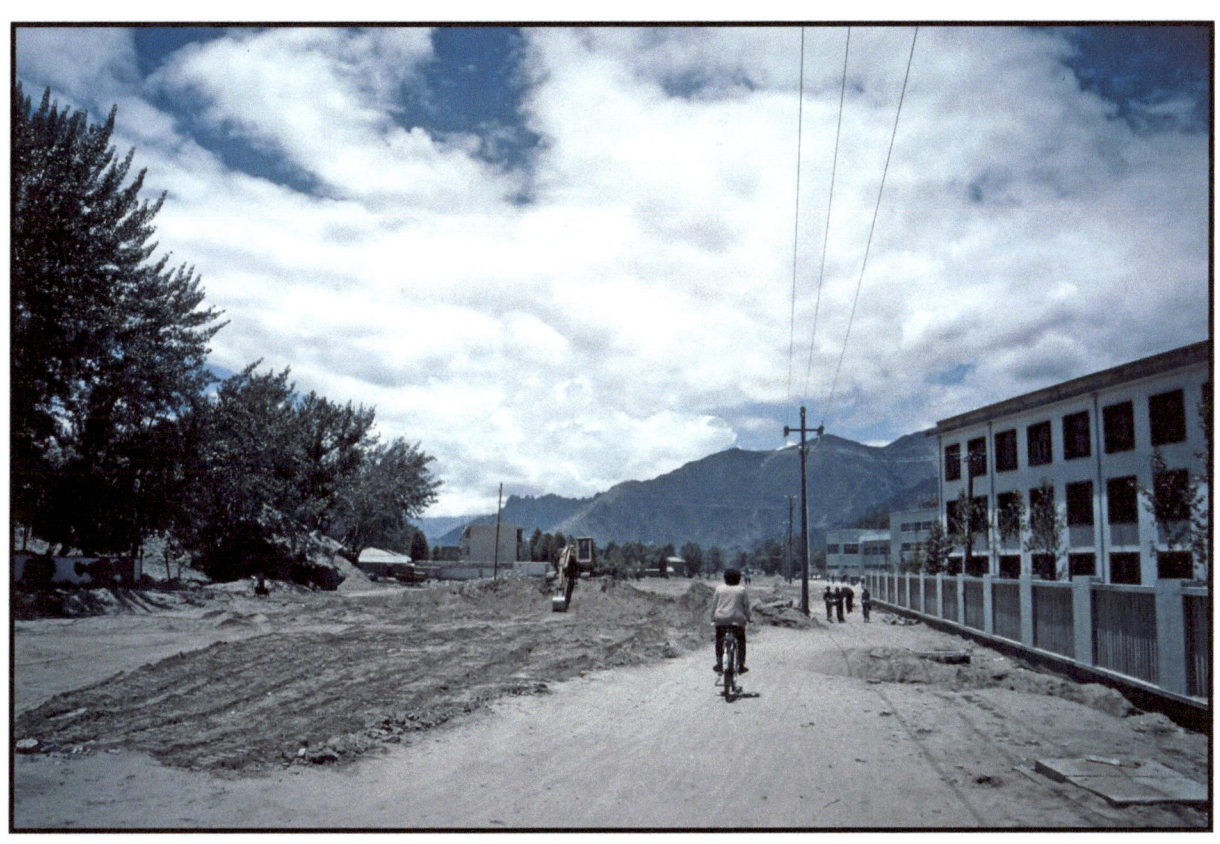

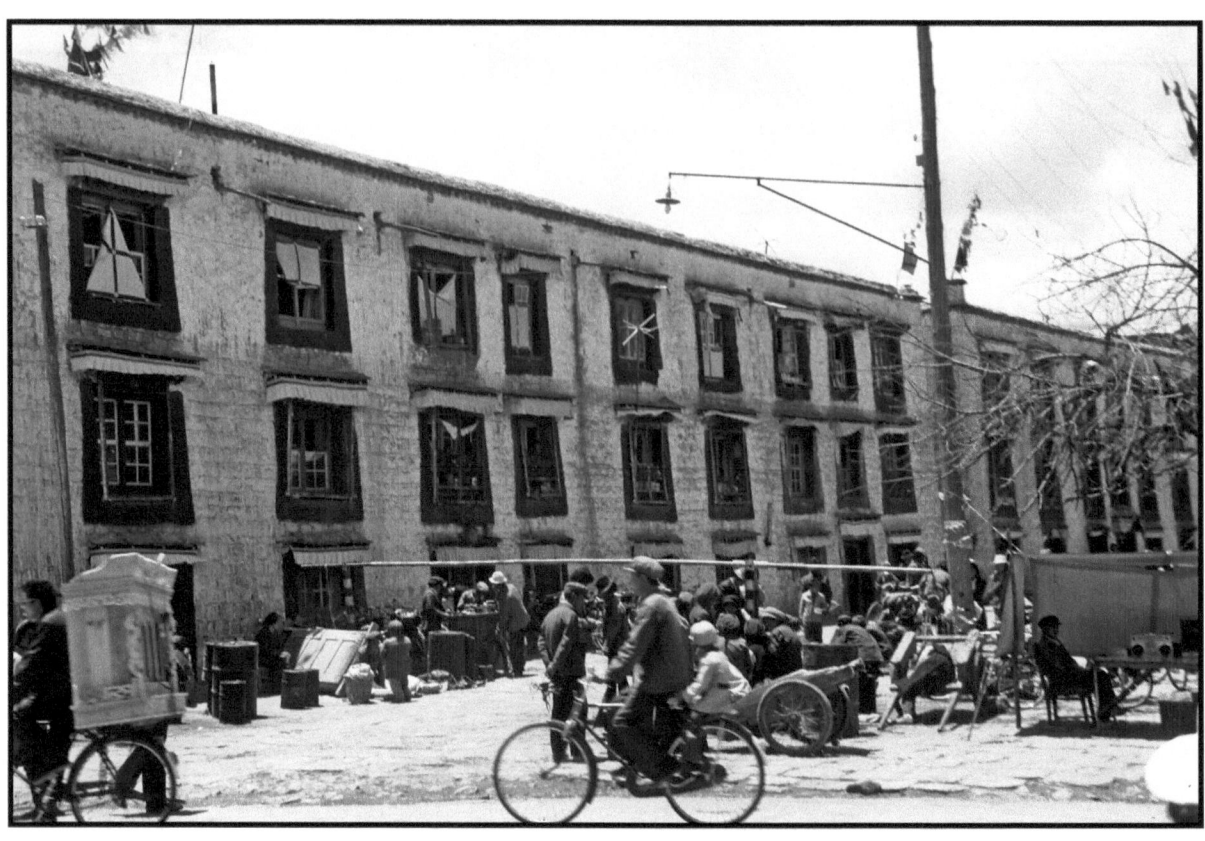

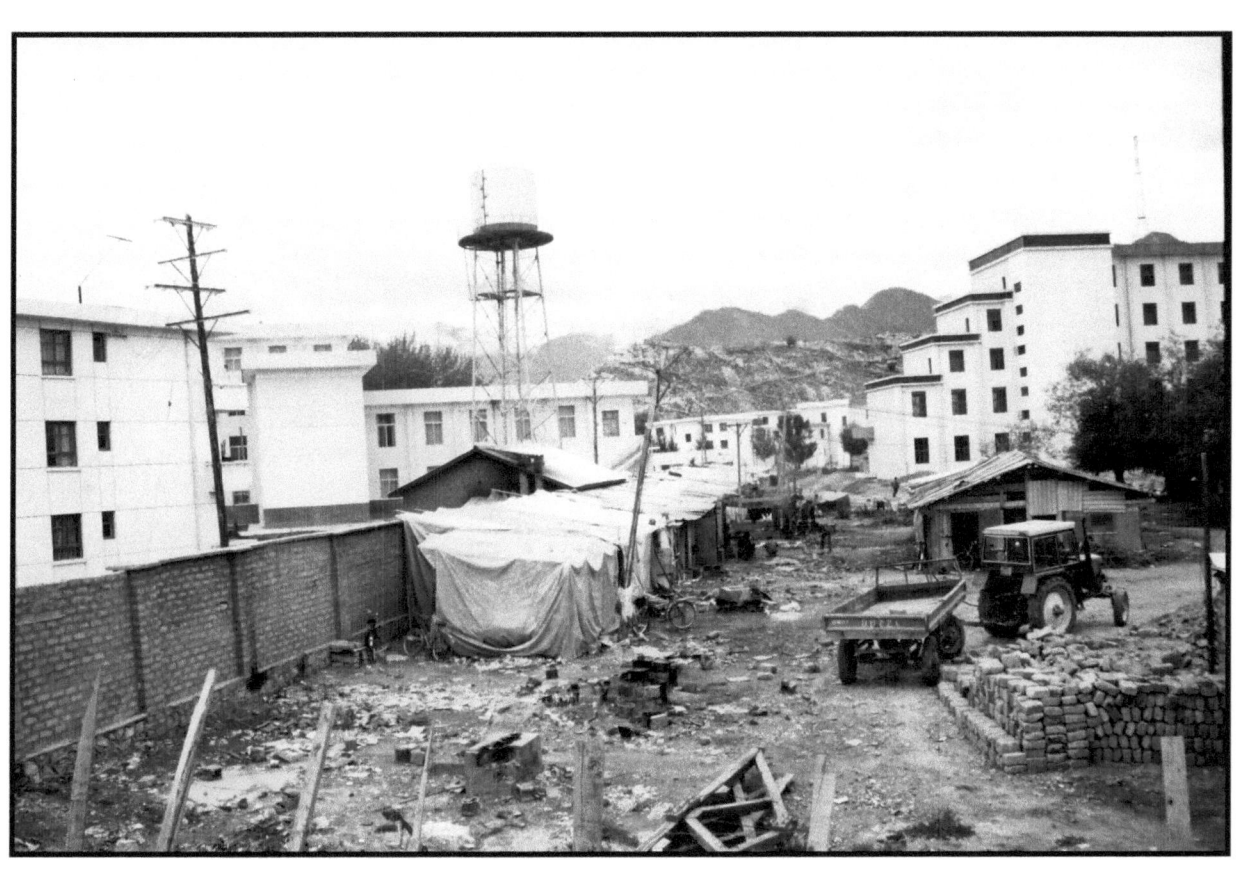

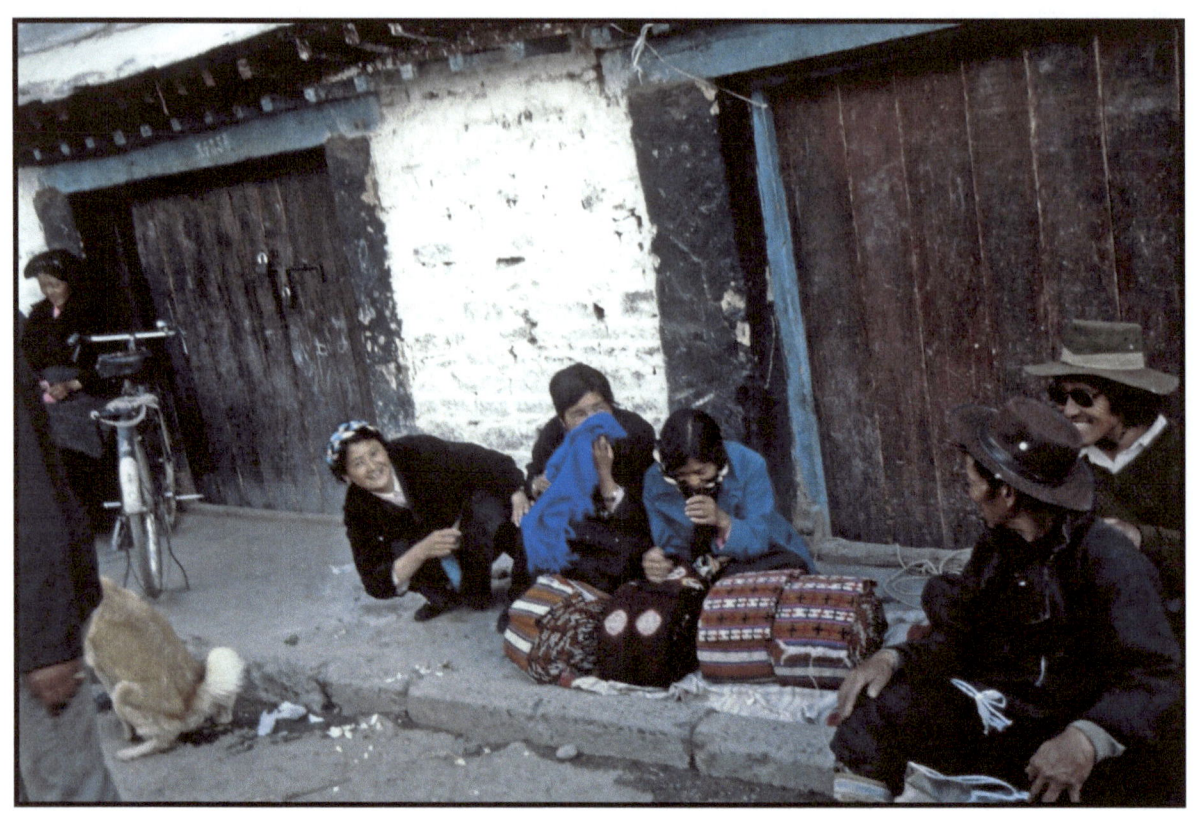

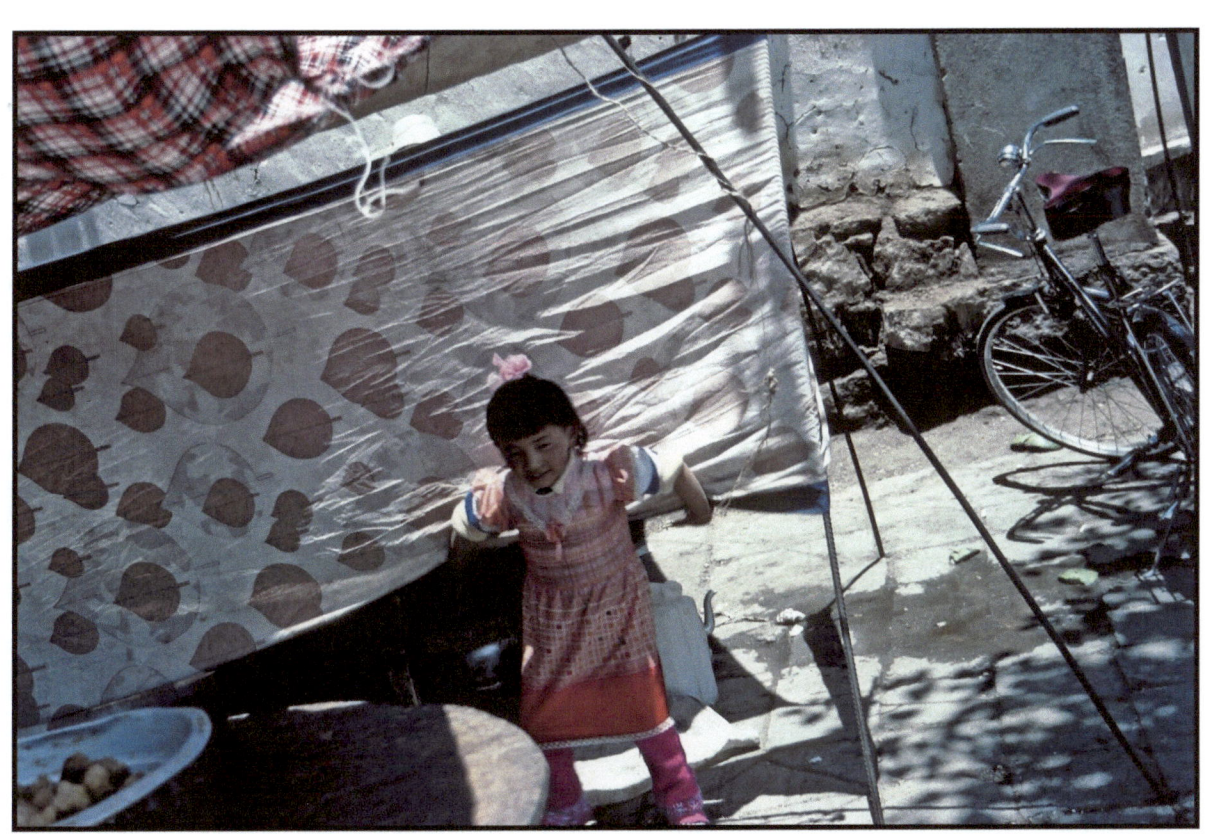

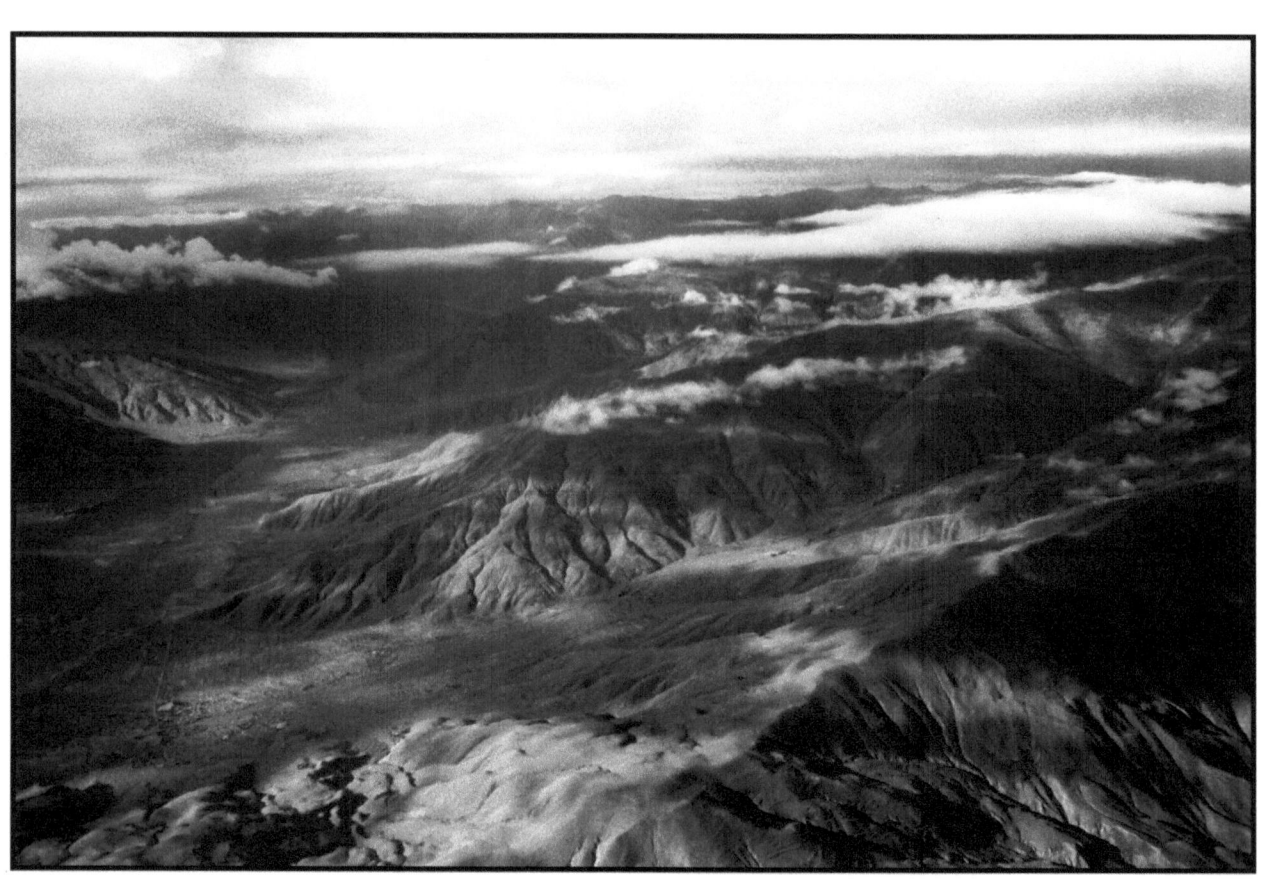

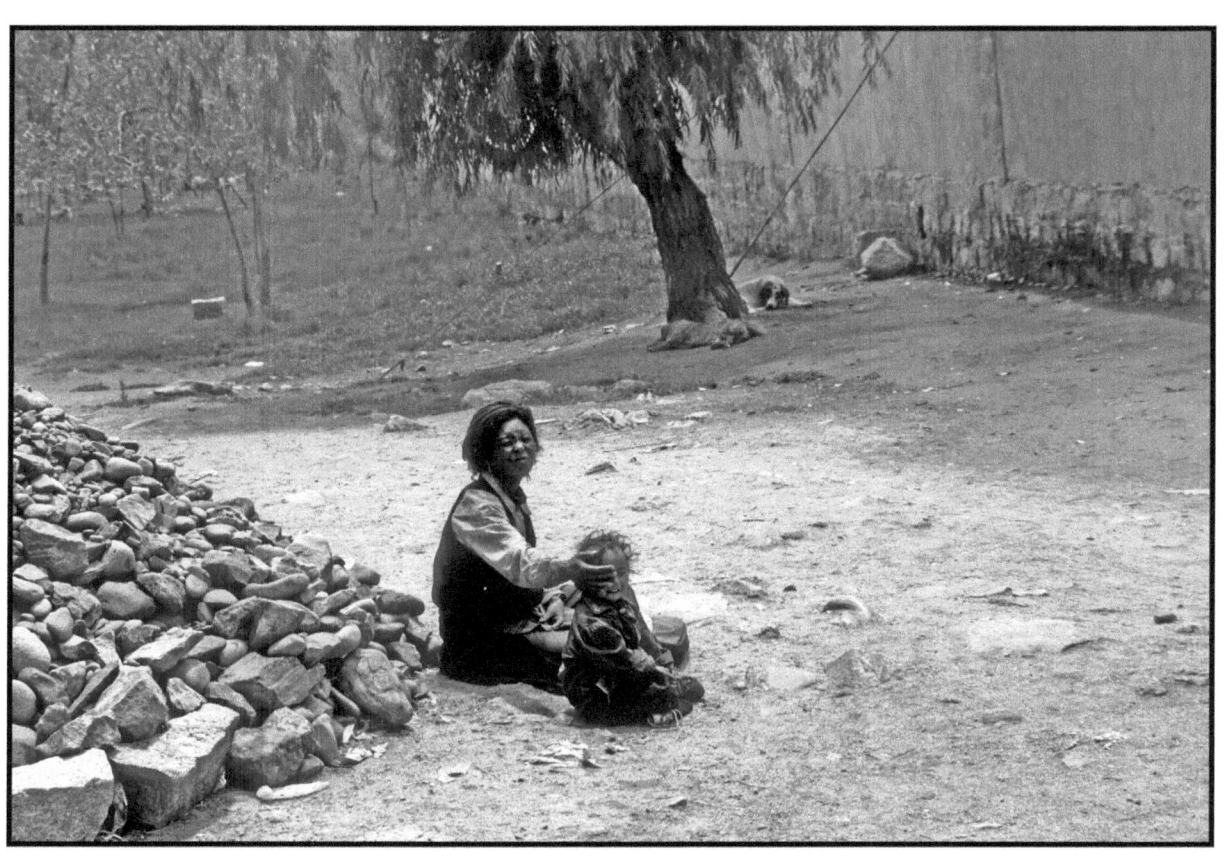